Marlene

The Life of Marlene Dietrich

by Charles Higham

W·W·Norton & Company·Inc·

New York

HOLGATE

First Edition

Library of Congress Cataloging in Publication Data

Higham, Charles, 1931–
    Marlene: the life of Marlene Dietrich.

    1. Dietrich, Marlene, 1904–
    2. Entertainers—Germany—Biography.   I. Title.
PN2658.D5H5   1977   791.43′028′0924   [B]
ISBN 0-393-07515-X   77-24940
1 2 3 4 5 6 7 8 9 0

For Sherry Huber

The Rose, the Lily, the Dove, the Moon
  I've loved them, every one, late and soon.
I love them no more, I only love
  The Beautiful, Graceful, the Pure, who doth
Twine in one Wreath all Beauty, Love's Boon,
  Who Rose is, and Lily, and Dove, and Moon.

—Heinrich Heine
Translation by Charles Higham

Contents

Preface

Hemingway wrote, "If she had nothing but her voice, she could break your heart with it." Cocteau pointed to the duality of her nature when he said, "Your name begins with a caress and ends with the crack of a whip." She is the last of the great diseuses, and is probably the only living woman who would be able to say, as she said once: "Hitler wanted me to be his mistress. I turned him down. Maybe I should have gone to him. I might have saved the lives of six million Jews." (She did, in fact, save the life of her sister, who had been sent to Belsen.) And what other woman could list Erich Maria Remarque, Maurice Chevalier, Jean Gabin, Fritz Lang, Josef von Sternberg, James Stewart, Willi Forst, Douglas Fairbanks, Jr., Mike Todd, Brian Aherne, John Gilbert, John Wayne, and Yul Brynner among the men who loved her?

On December 27, 1976, Marlene turned seventy-five years old. A meaning of *Dietrich* in German is "skeleton key," a key which opens all locks; but Marlene has attempted to lock up most of her secrets, including the date of her birth. Amusingly, reference books contradict each other: *Who's Who in America* omits her birth date, gives her the wrong parents, and misspells the name of her school. The British *Who's Who* is equally inaccurate and and settles on 1904 as a birth date; *Who's Who in France* and the *Oxford Companion to Film* give 1902; *Who's*

Who in Europe, perhaps wisely, under the circumstances, does not list her at all.

Marlene has scarcely been helpful to potential biographers. She has said that she was discovered by the director Josef von Sternberg in the Max Reinhardt drama school and was cast by him in her most famous role, Lola-Lola, the heartless cabaret singer who proves to be the ruination of schoolteacher Emil Jannings in *The Blue Angel.* Actually, she auditioned successfully for the school, reading an excerpt from *Death and the Fool* by Hugo von Hofmannsthal; but she failed her test before Reinhardt, reading Gretchen's prayer in *Faust,* and was not accepted as a student.

Instead, she became a private pupil of Berthold Held, the head of the school. Hers was a classic Cinderella story, of a shy but pretty girl who was transformed by von Sternberg and Hollywood into the supremely glamorous figure who first conquered the world in the 1930s and who did not relinquish her control.

When the Museum of Modern Art gave a retrospective of her work in the 1950s, the historian Richard Griffith put an asterisk alongside the bulk of the German titles and a footnote reading, "Miss Dietrich does not recall having made these films." It is as though she had blotted from her mind the eight years between her lessons with Berthold Held and her appearance in *The Blue Angel,* and with it all memory of herself as the plump, jazzy, gemütlich figure who appeared in German films of the 1920s.

There was a strong moment in the 1929 film *I Kiss Your Hand, Madame* which first signaled to the world the birth of an extraordinary new screen personality. A fat man, who is trying desperately to woo the aloof beauty, says, "I'll do anything for you: anything." She looks suggestively over a large bunch of roses he has bought and briefly, cruelly, kindles his hope. "All right," she says finally. "You can take my dogs for a walk."

That same year, von Sternberg fashioned the image which was to become legendary: the image of a sensual, decadent blonde singing through clouds of cigarette smoke in an overcrowded dive; an amoral temptress in frilly pants, her gartered

legs stretched seductively wide. Following *The Blue Angel* and
her move to Hollywood from Berlin in 1930, she became a
nightclub singer in von Sternberg's *Morocco,* a prostitute in
Shanghai Express, an unfaithful wife in Ernst Lubitsch's *Angel,*
and a jewel thief in Frank Borzage's *Desire.* In *Destry Rides
Again*—the rowdy Western comedy in which she made a come-
back in 1939 after having been labeled box-office poison by
theater exhibitors—she was a saloon moll: a benign reversal of
the Lola-Lola character in *The Blue Angel.* In recent years, she
has appeared onstage as a weary, amused, self-mocking cabaret
entertainer, resplendent in sequins and furs.

She was unlike any screen heroine before her. She was neither clinging ingenue nor heavy vamp; she was, instead, a cool,
assured woman. She was at once desirable and elusive, seemingly soft but actually hard as nails. She symbolized the free
urban woman who chose her own men, earned her own living,
and saw sex not as a consolation but as a challenge. Before long,
Tallulah Bankhead, Claudette Colbert, Carole Lombard, Mary
Astor, and others would play the same kind of woman, but none
of them matched her cool detachment, insolent wit, sexual
frankness, and overtly erotic appeal.

Nor could any of them equal her hypnotic way with a song
—songs like "Falling in Love Again" in the *The Blue Angel,* or
"The Boys in the Back Room" in *Destry Rides Again,* songs
which expressed her personality to perfection. The lyrics were
daring in their eroticism, and she was the most erotic of the
stars. By contrast, Garbo was tender and vulnerable, almost
maternal. Dietrich was never tender. Nor did she parody sex,
as Mae West did. She looked at Gary Cooper or James Stewart
or John Wayne—poor, awkward American types—and, with a
devastating Middle European sureness, accepted their surrender.

She even dared to suggest a bisexual quality on screen which
Kenneth Tynan has described as "sex without gender." In *Morocco* she made an appearance in tie and tails, kissing a woman
full on the lips in one scene, which she improvised; in *Blonde
Venus* she also wore a tuxedo, running a cool eye up and down

a line of chorus girls and chucking one under a breast. Possibly her performances would have seemed too outré were it not for her underlying humor, which announced to the audience: "I don't take myself, or my pictures, too seriously, you know. So you shouldn't either." Audiences picked up on her self-mockery, and they liked her for it. Dietrich's best movies remain alive today largely because we value coolness more than unrestrained passion. She was ahead of her time; she seems as modern now in *Morocco,* made forty-seven years ago, as Faye Dunaway does in *Network.*

Her adored Erich Maria Remarque described her perfectly in his novel *Arch of Triumph:* "The cool, bright face which didn't ask for anything, which simply existed, waiting—it was an empty face, he thought; a face that could change with any wind of expression. One could dream into it anything. It was like a beautiful empty house waiting for carpets and pictures. It had all possibilities—it could become a palace or a brothel. It depended on the one who filled it. How limited by comparison was all that was already completed and labeled—"

He reflects her also in another description of his heroine, the actress Joan Madou: "She lay there, subtle and changeable and exciting because there was nothing left of the woman whom one had known an hour ago; she was everything that enticement and temptation could give without love—and yet all of a sudden he felt something like an aversion to her—a strange resistance mixed with a violent and sudden attraction."

People have been at once drawn to her and afraid of her. She can change very quickly from softness to anger. Her face shifts from expression to expression, and yet remains oddly featureless. Her eyes are challenging: direct, uncompromising. Her hollow cheekbones suggest an ascetic, but her mouth suggests a voluptuary. Her body is taut and strict, but at the same time soft and yielding.

The impression, watching Marlene Dietrich in action, is— incredibly, in view of her screen image—one of North German rectitude; cool intellect, precision, and tact; an iron discipline that brooks no distractions, balanced against an extremely sensitive, self-inquiring, and restlessly dissatisfied personality.

She has no patience with fools, and the slightest fault in her-self or others is immediately seized on. Not a gesture is wasted: the back is pencil-straight, the eyes fix each questioner until the precise moment he or she is finished, the brain refuses to be interrupted, or distracted by others.

For her, clearly, the dedication to the job, to herself, is abso-lute, the will screwed up again and again to the task, despite the pressures of world flights, rushed schedules, the increasingly reduced periods of preparation and, as union charges rise, of rehearsals. Meeting her, one has a uniquely sharp sense of the agony, the rigor of the star's life, the need to maintain a stan-dard of living almost everyone else has been forced to abandon since the 1930s: a world of gowns from expensive fashion houses, of Paris apartments and New York hideaways and Beverly Hills hotels. And above all, in Dietrich's case, there is the problem, for a clever, shrewd woman, of enduring the fatuous routines of stardom.

Marlene is definite—not to say definitive—in her judgments. Her likes and dislikes have an unnerving finality. She lives by codes most of us have not even bothered to learn. I have seen her dislike of indecision, aimlessness, stupidity, self-pity, and sentimentality in anything, especially music. ("April in Paris" is a song she has expressed contempt for because of its line, "What have you done to my heart?".) She has always known what she has done with hers. She has given it not only to the men she has loved, but more importantly, to her daughter Maria and to her four grandsons. If there has been one single motivation in her life which has dominated all others, it has been the drive to help Maria, now in her fifties, and her family. One suspects that every detail of lighting, every touch of makeup, every nuance of performance and precise detail of costume has been insisted on in order that she be an example to them. She has surren-dered her personal fortune to her family, draining herself finan-cially so that her descendants can enjoy a good life.

Behind the masks, Marlene has always been most at ease as what Hemingway called "the Kraut": a Prussian housewife who lives to keep her house spic-and-span, scrubs the front steps of her apartment building, cooks superbly such traditional dishes as pot-au-feu or *Topfenknödeln,* and, when her grandsons were babies, took them for walks in the park disguised as a nurse-maid.

She is also the classic professional, a hard-working trouper who will get down on bended knees and hammer a stage if the surface is irregular. She is a driving taskmistress who can wrangle for hours over an error of lighting or sound in one of her performances. She insists on flawlessness—and can pulverize the flawed.

Her passions are as unrestricted as her disciplines. In the film *Morocco,* which first launched her before an American audience, she was cold and detached and insolent until she discovered that the legionnaire she wanted had carved her name in a table. Believing he loved her, she followed him headlong into the desert. The sequence, made by a man who adored her, tells us that Marlene is a romantic. She went on loving her men after she left them. She has been saddened by their subsequent marriages and has often gone to extraordinary lengths to see them. She told me long ago of her depression at the thought of Erich Maria Remarque marrying Paulette Goddard and of Burt Bacharach marrying Angie Dickinson. Jean Marais describes how she used to stand with him for hours outside Jean Gabin's house in Paris after her romance with Gabin ended, just to catch a glimpse of that great French star.

There has always been a curious ambiguity in Marlene's nature: eyewitnesses constantly remark on her indifference and lack of ambition, and she herself has said, to me, "I never had any ambition." Yet others say that she was ambitious: that, from the earliest days in Berlin she wanted to be a star. I believe there was an ambivalence in her nature, that her indifference and aggression always fought each other.

On the one hand, I think, she wanted to avoid the grueling work of making movies and appearing on the stage: she was cool and detached about film and theater; on the other hand, she had a compulsion to try to make good movies and to be a great star, admired by everyone. Once the legend of Marlene was set in motion by Josef von Sternberg and Paramount Pictures, she became fascinated by it; she watched it grow; she enjoyed it; and finally she was faced with the harrowing burden of living up to it. It was a problem faced by many stars—the problem of sudden and extraordinary fame: the longing on the one hand to hide, to escape, to enjoy a normal life; and, simultaneously, the longing to become respected, the friend of the great. It would be as futile to try to explain the ambivalences of her nature as it would be to resolve them.

She was never quite able to control her Hollywood career. Indeed, no star of the time, except for Katharine Hepburn at RKO Radio Pictures, ever did so. Refusal to act a role (stars were on salary, with a few weeks' vacation a year) could result in immediate suspension and nonpayment of income—which, in view of Marlene's lavish and generous expenditures, would have been a disaster. She had a small hand in choosing to do *Blonde Venus* (1932) and *Desire* (1936). In later years, she begged to do *Witness for the Prosecution* (1958). Otherwise, like a good Prussian, she just took orders, enjoying what her obedience could bring. What she did control utterly (after 1935) was her image: the beauty of her lighting on screen.

It was not until she launched herself as an international solo stage star, singing her songs of love and loss and hatred of war, that she controlled her career. And then her control was absolute. She liked it that way.

Marlene's poetic romanticism is a refrain of this book. There is an extraordinary emphasis on flowers: white roses thrust through the barbed wire to the French prisoners of war in World War I; bouquets of red, white, and blue flowers sent to her beloved French schoolteacher on Bastille Day; gladioli flooding the house of the author Mercedes d'Acosta; more gladioli filling John Gilbert's house and placed on his coffin; a fresh rose sent every day to the Italian director Visconti; white roses sent to the funeral of her friend Hugh Curnow; red roses sent to the funeral of her adored Lili Darvas. When the songwriter Peter Kreuder broke off his friendship with her, he significantly sent her thirteen black carnations.

Like most romantics, she was born to be disappointed: her

standards of behavior, her demands on the loved one, proved impossibly stringent. Her friend Walter Reisch believes that she loved only three men with her whole heart and soul: Igo Sym, the delicate musician and actor who taught her the musical saw in Vienna in the 1920s; Brian Aherne, the handsome leading man of the 1930s and 1940s; and Michael Wilding, the witty British star of the 1940s and 1950s. I would settle instead on Jean Gabin, supreme French star of such classics as *Le Jour se Lève* and *Quai des Brumes,* and Erich Maria Remarque, who, in his novel *Arch of Triumph,* portrayed her better than anyone. These, I believe, were the two men who, in the one case physically and the other intellectually, penetrated her psyche most deeply.

Her magic, the magic which has fascinated us for half a century, cannot be described; it can only be experienced. She is an exciting, challenging, electric presence of our time, a woman who has lived her life fully, who has defied fascism, who has displayed gallantry, audacity, and sheer nerve. What we applaud when we see her perform is not a legend, a star, a nostalgic ghost. We applaud what Dietrich *is:* the personification of glamour, beauty, style, elegance, taste; the last survivor of a vanished civilization, bestowing her grace, without too much seriousness, on our vulgarized society.

Supremely adept in the ways of the world, a consummate actress offscreen, Marlene has assumed and discarded many masks, being able, chameleonlike, to fit into an extraordinary range of situations. It would be easy to say that she was simply a Prussian housewife who got lucky, whose happiest moment is in the kitchen, preparing chicken soup or goulash, or that she is at heart still a girl, starstruck, mooning over the great figures of her time. Yet against this side of her nature one would have to counterpoint another: that of a superlatively well-read, well-informed, open-minded, pacifist enemy of oppression. Her complexities are infinite, which is why, in this book, I have chosen to show her through many eyes.

Her attitudes toward the various forms of entertainment in which she has excelled vary considerably. She dislikes recordings, partly because of the "deadness" of the atmosphere in the recording studios; making these is a job for her, nothing more; but she is, of course, one of the great recording stars, a hardy perennial of the catalogs. Television is most distasteful to her, and she is not at her best in that medium: two specials, one made in Australia, the other in London, are quite inferior. She has loved radio, because of its freedom from the demands of the image.

Most of all, she enjoys her solo stage appearances, on which Burt Bacharach, Joe Davis (her lighting man), and her conductors, Stan Freeman and Bill Blezard, have been strong influences.

Her sound man, Jim Douglas, has for many years executed her subtle technique with the microphone. Her solo stage work is the best thing she has done: she is right at the top, with Sinatra, Crosby, Streisand, Presley, Jagger, and Minnelli. Like these performers, she is her own supreme invention: she has created herself as a work of art.

When Orson Welles was addressing a small audience in the Middle West, he said, "What a pity there are so many of me, and so few of you." In the unlikely event that Marlene's audience were to dwindle comparably, she might very well say the same thing.

Acknowledgments

Writing a biography is rather like joining a club. With each new book, one meets fascinating people, all of whom tend to be linked together emotionally, psychically, or professionally to the person one is writing about. In the case of Marlene Dietrich, one is conscious of the fact that those to whom she has meant most are the gifted European expatriates of New York and Hollywood, especially the Jews. When I wrote my book *Kate: The Life of Katharine Hepburn,* I entered the world of the Broadway theater and of the veteran Hollywood craftsmen of the 1930s and 1940s. Writing *Marlene,* I was fascinated by the former Berliners: their charm, sparkle, and resilience. They made me see events which took place before I was born, as though I myself had witnessed those events. The hard, smart, glittering atmosphere of Berlin in the 1920s, the excitement of the great cafés and restaurants of the Kurfürstendamm, all came alive for me.

The Paris of the prewar years, and the Paris of the late 1940s, also emerged in vivid colors through the descriptions of Marlene's Parisian friends. I had been to Paris in the late 1940s and knew that world, in which she had mingled with the great French stars Jean Gabin and Gérard Philipe, with Cocteau and Hemingway. My mother and I had stayed at the Hôtel Plaza Athénée, opposite Marlene's apartment building, and I remem-

21

ber catching a glimpse of Marlene walking through the Relais (the hotel's coffee shop) with Gabin, apparently involved in an argument. The dripping trees of the Rond-Point; the Pam-Pam, where the American tourists gathered on the Champs Élysées; Maxim's; and above all Fouquet's, where Marlene had liked to sit with Erich Maria Remarque before the war (and where she once met James Joyce)—all were favorite haunts of my adolescence. Without knowing it at the time, I was following in her footsteps, worshiping Gérard Philipe, Louis Jouvet, the Comédie Française, and above all the Barrault company at the Théâtre Marigny, unforgettable in Montherlant's *Malatesta* and Anouilh's *La Repetition.*

I realize now that Marlene has never ceased to be a European, even though she is a naturalized American. She has spent more of her life in Paris than anywhere else. Walking through that Paris in the late 1940s and since, I could understand why: the severity balanced against intense sophistication, the elegance of the great fashion houses and cafés contrasted with Haussmann's somber official buildings, an impression of order and grace, and above all a sense of the fitness of things one associates with Marlene, past and present. Seeing the Arc de Triomphe on July 14, 1949, lit from below and shining against a sudden burst of rain, I felt my heart turn over; and I understood at once, with my Huguenot blood coursing through my veins, what she meant when she so richly described a similar experience in her memoir, *Marlene Dietrich's ABC.*

There were many exciting moments during the writing of this book. I shall not forget walking into the apartment of Max Kohlhaas in Bonn, West Germany, and discovering there complete collections of reviews and articles covering Marlene's Berlin theater career, including reviews by the rival critics, Ihering and Kerr; advertisements; interviews; playbills; programs; and albums full of photographs. Another "moment" was when Richard Kollorsz, designer of the icons in *The Scarlet Empress,* brought from a closet scrapbooks of the period 1930 to 1935, prepared for her by him and lost for over forty years. These included an invaluable autobiographical article by her which appeared in the *Hartungsche Zeitung,* Königsberg, in 1930; and an item of great amusement, a review of *Morocco* in Arabic, published in Mogador, the setting of the film itself.

During the job of coordinating the material in several languages, besides my own researches in Europe, I was helped to conduct my interviews with 170 people of different nationalities; the following were especially kind. Roy Moseley in London was an invaluable contributor to the book and interviewed many, including Marlene's successive impresarios in Britain, her conductors, and members of her band. In Berlin, Christa Maerker found several of Marlene's old friends and colleagues of the German theater of the 1920s, and flew to Switzerland to see Elisabeth Lennartz, who was with Marlene in the chorus line of George Abbott's *Broadway.* In Paris, Gérard Langlois interviewed important figures of the French film, his work translated by the critic Pierre Sauvage, who also interviewed Jean Marais. In Australia, Joel Greenberg interviewed the two surviving members of the Weintraub Syncopators, the energetic dance band which jigged through *The Blue Angel.*

I had the interesting experience of contacting Dr. Ronald Citrine (medical officer at Belsen) in the Bay of Islands, New Zealand. He was summoned to the telephone and announced that it was his first call from the United States since he had moved to New Zealand in 1954. Other people were reached in such far-flung places as Amsterdam, Santa Fe, Wiesbaden, Tucson, Stockholm, Rio, and Helsinki.

Ian and Dorothea Dinmore worked loyally on the job of translating countless thousands of words from over forty German books; Anthony Slide brought a print of Marlene's film *Ship of Lost Men* by plane from New York to Los Angeles, loaned by Paul Killiam so that I could see it.

The late Erich Pommer and the late Josef von Sternberg saw me in 1963. Sam Jaffe, skillful character actor, was a mine of information; and so was his namesake, the former production manager, agent, and producer Sam Jaffe in London. Martin Kosleck, memorable as Goebbels in several films, was a rich source on Marlene's private life in the 1930s. He and his late

friend Hans von Twardowski were as close to Marlene as anyone in those difficult years. Von Sternberg's secretary, Mickey
McGeary, helped a great deal. Walter Reisch, one of Marlene's
few surviving close friends of her struggling years, proved to be
a vivid and entertaining raconteur, recalling the fact that he
was one of Hollywood's most gifted writers in its golden years
and the director of one of my favorite movies, *Men Are Not
Gods.*

The great Carl Zuckmayer wrote me an historic letter which
gave a complete account of the making of the script of *The Blue
Angel.* The memoirs in German of Max Colpet, Peter Kreuder,
Frederick Hollander, Geza von Cziffra, and Hubert von Meyerinck (Peter Kreuder's book formed the basis of the detailed
description of Marlene's departure from Berlin in 1930) were
especially helpful. In English, I drew from the translated recol-
lections of Edith Piaf, Ginette Spanier, and Lily Daché; and in
French, I read those of Marcel Carné, Jean Marais, and Daniel
Gélin.

Mia May, ninety-four-year-old star of the German silent film,
proved an irresistible companion, taking me through the past.
James Card, curator of George Eastman House in Rochester,
New York, was a genial host, screening prints of rare German
films; the staff of the Library of Congress—especially Patrick
Sheean—was also very kind; and I am grateful to Edelbert
Spiess of the Deutsches Institut für Filmkunde, Wiesbaden-
Biebrich for making available to me many valuable items in the
German archives. The authorities at the Viennese archives
were also helpful.

David Bradley showed me the American films again. Joel
McCrea, Cesar Romero, King Vidor, the silent stars Eleanor
Boardman and Leatrice Joy, and Leatrice Joy's daughter, Lea-
trice Fountain, must be given special mention. The screen-
writer Samson Raphaelson was most amusing. Melvyn Douglas,
Broderick Crawford, John Wayne, Raoul Walsh, Fred MacMur-
ray, Danny Thomas, Elsa Lanchester, Mary Hemingway, Jean
Marais, Daniel Gélin, Richard Todd, Alfred Hitchcock, Sir Alec
Guinness, Don Ameche, Mercedes McCambridge, former child

star Dick Moore, Joe Pasternak, Bill Mauldin, and Curtis and Anna-Maria Bernhardt were among those who supplied their memories. I was especially fortunate to talk to several people who knew Marlene as a child, including the photographer and graphologist Elli Marcus and Fritz Lang's friend Lily Latté, who were at school with her. Mahler's nephew, Wolfgang Rosé, was a fellow student of music in Weimar.

Others I should like to mention are Peter Gorian, Mischa Spoliansky, Hedi and Trude Schoop, Gavin Lambert, Ernst Matray, Karl Hartl, Hans Hollander, Hans and Varya Kohn, Alice Bluman, Mrs. Riza Royce von Sternberg, Lee Garmes, S. K. Lauren, Grete Mosheim, Wiard Ihnen, Norma Boleslawski, Denver Lindley, Violla Rubber, Janette Scott, Dolly Haas, and Leonard Gershe. The others, too numerous to mention, are credited in the body of the text. Special thanks are due to the British consulate in Frankfort, which organized an interpreter for me at very short notice during a particularly busy week of international conventions. Peter Lev copied by hand or by Xerox several hundred printed items. Frances Mercer, former musical actress of *Very Warm for May, Something for the Boys,* and Astaire-Rogers's *The Story of Vernon and Irene Castle,* typed the book, and was a witty inspiration throughout.

Los Angeles-London-Paris-
Bonn-Frankfurt-Wiesbaden-
Berlin-San Francisco-Los Angeles,
1975–77.

SPECIAL ACKNOWLEDGMENT

I am most grateful to Max Kohlhaas and the
Deutsches Institute für Filmkunde for supplying
the majority of the photographs in this book.

Marlene

The Life of
Marlene Dietrich

One

An Officer's Daughter

It is appropriate that this twentieth-century legend should have been born at the beginning of the century: December 27, 1901. She came of a distinguished family. Her father, Lieutenant of Police Louis Erich Otto Dietrich, had formerly been a major in the Uhlan Cavalry Regiment. He had served heroically in the Franco-Prussian War of 1870–71 and had been decorated with the Iron Cross, Second Class. In 1883, he had married the beautiful seventeen-year-old Wilhelmina Elisabeth Josephine Felsing, daughter of Conrad Felsing, who had founded the Felsing Watchmakers' and Watch Shop at the fashionable address of 20 Unter den Linden, near the Hotel Adlon. During Marlene's lifetime, the shop was owned and managed by her uncle Willibald Felsing; on her father's side, one uncle was a Rittmeister (cavalry captain), and another became the captain of a zeppelin shot down over the English Channel in 1916.

She was a year younger than her sister Elisabeth, who was destined to become a schoolteacher and to live a life utterly removed from the public eye. Pictures of Marlene as a child reveal her staunchness and her delicacy. Cool, made of snowy lace, each part of her dress is as carefully fashioned as filigree ironwork. She looks spotless and translucent. Her golden hair is alive with light: it is as though she attracted the light, a mysterious magnet, a refractive agent. Her Prussian-blue eyes, soft gray in the black-and-white pictures, are frank and veiled all at once, inviting yet secretive. Her figure is sturdy, with strong shoulders, surprisingly vigorous arms, and a neck of alabaster, in a pose almost like that of a child boxer. Even at the age of five, she looks ready to take on all challengers. She is confident, poised for her attack on life, sprung fully armed from the brow of Minerva.

She was, of course, a Berliner—that is to say, a human being who looked at life without illusions, with a constant critical sense, with the cool cutting edge of a surgeon's knife. A Berliner spares nobody, is without mercy, is seldom tender. Yet we find here a contradiction. Some element in her blood, like a Mediterranean current found mysteriously in the Baltic, warmed and softened her. She was certainly "Berlin" in one side of her brain, but one can see an analogy to her in those Borgia apples which were half-poisoned, half-edible. She could be loving; but she was still a Berliner.

She was born Marie (not Maria, as stated in reference books) Magdalene Dietrich in Schöneberg, under the sign of Capricorn: the sign of determination, of the need to improve, of an antic leaping over obstacles—the sign of the goat. Berlin at the turn of the century was a city sparkling with gaiety and promise. Although it was at the heart of the military state, with brass fanfares announcing the arrival of the Emperor Wilhelm as he rode down the Unter den Linden, Berlin was essentially a citadel of the arts. The galleries and museums were crowded with people for whom culture was daily bread.

Streets were named after composers and writers—can one imagine a Sousa Avenue or a Whitman Street in New York? Three opera houses and a dozen concert halls were emblazoned with announcements of the richest musical life in Europe. Anyone standing on the tower of the Rathaus, or atop the Imperial Palace, or the galleries surrounding the Column of Victory near the Brandenburg Gate, would look down at confidently baroque buildings proudly flanking the avenues and spacious squares of the metropolis. Barbaric monuments indicated a Prussian passion for war. Further off, the exotic birds and beasts of the Zoological Gardens moved through exquisitely pruned bushes among the rich masses of the linden leaves. Further off still, Charlottenburg flourished, with its stained-glass and porcelain factories; and the Grünewald Forest, dotted with blue lakes and white or pink rococo villas among trees, had a fairy-tale charm.

The Berlin streets were jammed day and night with traffic, ranging from the newfangled automobile to a gala display of various forms of horse-drawn carriages, controlled by white-gloved, spike-helmeted policemen carrying sabers, with Union Jacks or the Stars and Stripes stuck in their sleeves as an indication to tourists that they could speak English. Trams clanged and swayed everywhere under the wire-strung lamps which lit the streets from above.

The Stadtbahn (elevated railway) roared over the crowds; the people were skeptical, acid-tongued, bursting with health and energy, from the students with their staffs in their hands and guitars slung on their backs—members of the famous Birds of Passage or Wandervogel movement, which resembled the Boy Scouts and involved the worship of nature and song—to the black-coated businessmen who thrust their way through the people into the huge beer restaurants, the Pschorr-Brau, the Löwenbrau, and Kischinger's, or the marble and bronze luxury automats.

In a few years, movie theaters would proliferate, reaching a culmination in the Kinopalast, with its goddess, Venus, seated over the entrance, light pouring down from twin beams in her eyes, and stained-glass windows radiating colored beams on each side of the proscenium, surmounted by a ceiling glazed with artificial stars and a quarter moon in a black onyx sky.

But the cinema, that shrine or labyrinth, was still to be properly realized, glimpsed only in tiny, flickering pictures which were just beginning to cross the Atlantic. In the early 1900s, the glamor of Berlin life lay in seeing troops march or gallop through the streets. The garrison included twenty-three thousand men, consisting of Foot Guards, Grenadier Guards, Dragoons, Fusiliers, and Cuirassiers, as well as the Uhlan Cavalry, to which Marlene's father had belonged before becoming an officer of the Imperial Police. Berlin had as its staple commodities wool, grain, and liquor; iron foundries, railroad construction factories, munitions factories, and household goods factories helped to make the city of great importance.

Weimar, where Marlene spent part of her adolescence, was the home of Goethe, who lived in the town for fifty-six years until his death in 1832. Schiller also lived there for six years, until his death in 1805. It was an attractive, higgledy-piggledy town, sleepy and backward in everything except culture, with a beautiful location on the River Ilm. We may guess that Marlene was happy in Weimar, since to this day she proclaims, "I was raised with Goethe, who taught me everything I know." When she was young, there were the restaurants Werther, in the Theaterplatz, with its elegant garden, and Jungbrunnen, in the Schillerstrasse; and there were fine cafés: the Sperling, the Tearoom, and the Kaiser Café.

Sundays were extremely strict, and the police swooped down on any shopkeeper who left his blinds up or his doors ajar before two in the afternoon. It was a ritual in Prussian families to pay visits to other members of the family on Sunday afternoons, or to go to the gardens for picnics. The mother of the family would invariably knit or crochet at home when the weather was poor, and the children would read the classic German poems and novels aloud to each other. No doubt it was in these family readings that Marlene developed the delicate phrasing and intonation which were to be of such invaluable help to her as a singer. And, no doubt, when she later became proficient in the violin she played on holy days the music of Bach, performed by tradition within the family on Good Friday Eve.

Prussian homes of the time were traditionally filled with perfect arrangements of freshly cut flowers, and the art of flower arrangement was one of Marlene's greatest skills in later years. Yet even on gala days, despite the floral decorations, the Prussian home was somber and dark, discouraging any sensual feelings.

Partly in order to enable children to gain an appreciation of music, some concerts and operas began early. The doors would open at five-thirty and the performance begin at six. Refreshments were always served in the interval, and mothers took their fancywork with them. Instead of rows of seats, families used individual tables accommodating as many as eight people, where they could sip their hot chocolate or cocoa and eat their smoked meats in an atmosphere free of cigarettes.

Christmases in those days were magical, the streets of Berlin planted for the occasion with trees of every size, ranging from spruces arranged around the churches to baby firs on pedestals outside the shops. Each of the trees was decorated with silver and crystal stars, golden balls, and pendants of imitation emeralds and rubies. On Christmas Night, each house had its specially lit altar, to which the children came with little gifts wrapped in colored paper and tied with bright ribbons. The figure of the Christ Child was placed in a crib made of mahogany and surrounded by the figures of the Wise Men who had come to pay homage.

Marlene's father was one of a police force of four thousand at the time of her birth, later augmented to forty-five hundred. An officer in the Berlin police had to have served at least nine years in the army to be eligible for a position on the force, and the post carried none of the social calumny it carried in America. A police officer was a respected and well-paid member of the community, and as a lieutenant of police, Dietrich would have had under his command two sergeants, two telegraphists, two messengers, twelve policemen, and two detectives with revolvers.

He normally wore a plum-colored uniform, with headgear which resembled the military helmet (*pickelhaube*). With the addition of a brass double seam, it was the equivalent during hot weather of wearing a coal scuttle on the head. He carried a sword with a brass handle, a straight, keenly sharpened blade, and a leather scabbard, half-hidden in plum-colored coattails.

The Prussian upper-middle class was bound to the idea of Church and State. Being an army officer or a police officer was of first importance. Families were strictly organized. The eldest son was expected to run the estate and take care of the family interests. The second son could choose between being a Protestant priest or an officer. Everyone was aware of his position in society. Inferiors were to be considerately treated. Soldiers served at table, but there was always a maid and a cook. The emphasis was on Honor and Duty. Germany was expanding her army and navy, and everyone was expected to buy bonds.

Parental permission had to be given to marry. Every pleasure had to be earned: an outing to the park if your marks in Latin were good, a ride in the snow if you did impeccable needlework. Marlene and her sister were raised like most officers' daughters: they had to earn the right to every pleasure.

Marlene's mother was devoted to the works of Schiller and Goethe, and Marlene responded to the poetry of Heine, with its evocation of the Hartz region. At fifteen, in common with most German schoolgirls, she was introduced to Goethe's *Faust,* with its great scenes of transition from hellish suffering to the celestial clarity of the angel chorus at the end. *Faust* set the tone of her life: the need to make heroic efforts to rise above one's own failings and the purgatory of daily existence, to achieve through discipline and sacrifice and love the sense of well-being of the self-contained. Goethe taught her to have no patience with bloodless ideals and feeble-minded sentiments. She came to understand that goodness must be forceful and tough, as well as healing. Virtue in itself was futile; it must be combined with the ability to teach, to improve oneself and others, to override stupidity and corruption. Moreover, Goethe showed that the will must be paramount. Human weakness must be suppressed. The lover must unhesitatingly seek the loved. To quote *Faust:*

> In the sounding labor of his vast
> Being, is practiced that strength
> Zealous, beneficent, firm!

Marlene's mother was a remarkable woman, very strong and forthright, refusing to brook idiocy from anyone, gifted in cooking, in needlework, and in running a household. She differed from the typical Prussian woman in being capable of tenderness and warmth, but there is no doubt that she raised her children with an iron hand. A stain on a dress was a disaster. Poor marks at school meant punishment. Logic was the rule: if Marlene said anything illogical she had to correct herself. There were cold baths, long walks in the harsh snows, exercises on freezing park playgrounds. This influence undoubtedly gave Marlene the severity which disconcerted her weaker or more casual friends. Her mother made her intolerant of frailty of any kind, of back-sliding, insecurity, uncertainty, and, above all, of disloyalty.

Yet the Prussian upbringing also taught kindness to the weak, when they were truly helpless. The poor and the sick must always be aided. It was only those who could be strong, but faltered, who were not forgiven. Marlene never forgot this.

Marlene's family home was large and airy. According to her friend Walter Reisch, the address in the Kaiserallee, West Berlin, not very far from the apartment building she later lived in, number 54. The house had an attic where, Marlene has written, she liked to hide; an elegantly furnished living room with family photographs; a library; and a spacious garden.

She wrote in the German *Esquire* in 1976 that she remembered her father only as an imposing figure who smelled of leather, whose boots shone brightly, and whose whip cracked regularly across one leg. She grew up mostly in a world of women, she tells us—a world dominated by her beautiful grandmother, who used to ride horseback or drive her carriage past the house windows, and by her more formidable aunts.

Marlene's second language was French—this was typical of her class. She had French governesses; she loved to read about France. A favorite hobby was playing marbles in the Kaiserallee with a friend, Grete Reinwald, who later became a well-known actress. She never forgot her love of marbles, their glass rainbow whorls rolling down the gray sidewalks of Kaiserallee.

During the whole of her life, Marlene almost never referred to her elder sister, Elisabeth, a quiet, grave, intellectual girl. Together, school friends say, she and Marlene used to read Dostoevsky's *White Nights,* the story of a young man's futile pursuit of a pretty girl, and Knut Hamsun's *Hunger,* about a pathetic youth, hungry and lost and unhappy in Christiania, Norway. Marlene became fascinated by the poems of Erich Kästner, author of *Emil and the Detectives,* poems at once elegant and resigned, filled with a bittersweet sense of regret.

The theater fascinated the child. Like so many of her generation, she was drawn to the extraordinary personality of Eleanora Duse, the great Italian actress. Her literature teacher at school was obsessed with Duse, and Marlene haunted the various shops which specialized in theatrical materials, gazing at the many pictures of Duse's hands. She placed a picture of Duse on her mantelpiece and lit a candle beside it. She longed to emulate Duse. Here we can find her earliest interest in becoming a great stage star, as well as the delicate use of her hands, based perhaps unconsciously on Duse's movements in a film Marlene saw—*Cenere,* the only film, it seems, in which Duse appeared.

Marlene says in her *Esquire* article that she was admitted to school one year earlier than other pupils. Since current records show that children were admitted at the age of six, this means she must have been admitted at the age of five, in 1906. She entered the Auguste-Victoria School for Girls, named after the empress of Germany. It was situated on the Nürenbergerstrasse. The principal, an elderly lady, had built the school up from its beginnings in the 1880s, and presided elegantly over her pupils in an exquisite drawing room with a portrait of the empress hanging over the fireplace. There were about thirty resident pupils and about three hundred day pupils, of whom Marlene was one.

The simple furnishings of the classrooms were in contrast with the sumptuous decor of the private quarters. A visitor, Mrs. Minerva Norton, wrote: "The girls sat on plain wooden benches with desks before them on which their notebooks lay open. They used these as those who had been trained to take notes and recite from them. I had been told that the teacher in this class was one of the most excellent in the city. . . .

"I also visited a class in reading for younger girls, about ten or twelve years of age. They were admirably taught, both in reading and memorizing, the latter chiefly of German ballads. I saw no better teaching done in Berlin than that of this class.

"The last visit was to a class in music, taught by a gentleman. It was interesting as affording a view of the methods in this music-loving country, but did not differ materially from what would be considered good instruction and drill on this [American] side of the water. The teacher himself played the piano, the pupils standing in rows on either side."

Marlene was bereaved twice in those years. Her father died in 1911; and her mother married another military man, Eduard von Losch of the Grenadiers, an equally severe and upright Prussian who after service on the French front was killed in World War I on the Russian front. A romantic legend has him uttering with his last breath a request that Marlene devote herself to becoming a concert violinist. Normally, marriage to a dashing young officer from a good family would have been considered far more appropriate, though perhaps a little violin playing would be permitted privately to entertain friends in the evening.

Seven of Marlene's fellow pupils at the Auguste-Victoria School have survived, among them Steffi Sternberg, Margot Stern, Margo Flateau, and Charlotte Abromowsky. One of these classmates is the distinguished photographer and graphologist Elli Marcus. Miss Marcus recalls: "I remember that after the death of Marlene's father, her mother suffered badly from financial problems, and had to take a job as a glorified housekeeper to the comparatively well-to-do von Losch family. She married the young officer Eduard von Losch later.

"Marlene was the shyest girl in our school. She was diffident and nervous, and did not enjoy anything very much. I do not think in any way she was an outstanding pupil. She seemed to have no taste for gymnastics, and she always seemed to find a place in a corner, like a little gray mouse. Even in class she was always at a desk which was way at the back. Nobody had the slightest idea she would amount to anything."

Anna Lehmann (later Hookema), cook to the von Losch family from 1915 to 1919, wrote in the German magazine *Der Spiegel* in 1954: "Marlene was a devoted pupil. I remember Marlene's being confirmed in 1915, in the Lutheran faith. She was religious and dedicated. She always used to get angry with me when I told her she looked young for her age. She longed to look older. I imagine in later years the opposite was true! When she was fifteen, she used to say to me, over and over again, 'Anna, don't I look eighteen?' I well remember her fifteenth birthday in 1916, when I had orders to make a particular kind of cream cake she was crazy about. She loved cakes. There was a butter shortage, and I had to fetch butter from the country specially, it was so hard to obtain. She was adorable."

Marlene recalled in 1931 in a Königsberg newspaper that she still dreamed of the enormous heavy doors of the school, which the little girls had to push themselves through—prison doors. She remembered and would always remember (and she did, in *Esquire*, forty-five years later) pushing her back against a door to make it budge, until at last she could free herself, force open a tiny crack, and squeeze through. She wrote: "Then I could run out into the freedom and sunlight of the street! Across the way was a magical shop with candies and cakes, a fairyland." Trade directories of the time show that the name of the shop was Luise Voigt's. Elli Marcus says: "I never forgot that candy store either. It was the very center of our existences—the place we could escape to." With enormous jars filled with rainbow-colored bonbons, Fraulein Voigt's shop was the end of the rainbow for Marlene and her fellow pupils.

Marlene discussed her early adolescence in the German *Esquire*. She indirectly confirmed the statements made by Elli Marcus that she was small, nervous, underprivileged; her tearful loneliness, she says, was eased by a kind French teacher, Marguerite Bréguand. It is interesting that Mlle. Bréguand used to make annotations in red in the margins of Marlene's homework essays; Marlene in later years used to send me reviews of her shows marked in red ink. Mlle. Bréguand was forced to leave the school when World War I broke out because Germany was at war with France. Marlene recorded that she actually fainted when she first noticed Mlle. Bréguand's absence from the school assembly in 1914.

Anna Lehmann Hookema was right when she said that Marlene wanted to be older than she was, because this is a recurrent theme of the article in *Esquire*. Marlene recalled spending most of the war knitting clothes for the soldiers or singing patriotic songs. But she felt a deep loyalty to France because of Mlle. Bréguand, and because French was her second language and she had both French and German antecedents. She hated the fact that Germany was at war with France, and she wrote that while at summer school on Bastille Day she ran up to some French prisoners of war in a nearby camp and pressed white roses into their hands across the barbed wire.

She described in *Esquire* how she spent her evenings at the piano with her mother, earning the pleasure of playing Chopin études by grinding away at Bach or Handel. Her mother would look day after day for letters from her husband at the front or from relatives, and would watch notices on the Town Hall giving lists of the dead and wounded. The war brought food shortages, no milk, very little meat or cheese, and variations of dishes made out of turnips. Yet the von Losch household was a happy one.

Marlene was outstanding in literary studies, able to recite poems with taste and artistry, and head of her class in music. She led the school orchestra on the violin at sixteen, and in 1917, on the fiftieth anniversary of the death of Maximilan of Austria in Mexico, executed by the orders of the patriot Benito Juarez, she appeared in an event, described by a fellow pupil in the *Berlin News Illustrated:* "Prior to [the emperor's execution] a military band fulfilled his last wish: it played 'La Paloma'. The tune about the white pigeon became the requiem for an empire. Yradier's revolutionary 'Habanera' did not appear again until our century, as the song of sailors, as a tango, a living revival of Spanish folklore. Our students recreated 'La Paloma' with Fraulein Dietrich . . . as violinist. She performed admirably."

Photographs show her dressed as a man, in broad-brimmed hat, velvet breeches, and silk shirt, playing her instrument while a quartet of girls in traditional Spanish costume bang tambourines over their heads.

Her schoolmate Lily Latté remembers: "Marlene fascinated us all. I remember many of us came by ordinary means of transportation, mostly on foot. She always arrived in her own little carriage, like a fairy princess."

Marlene graduated from the Auguste-Victoria School in 1918. She seems to gleam in the graduation photograph, superior to the schoolgirls who surround her. Already she is "Dietrich": the heavy-lidded eyes, the broad, almost Slavic nose, the strong line of the mouth, the sturdy shoulders. Her lips carry the faint suggestion of a smile, but her expression is sad and reflective in repose. She looks downward and inward, introspective, mysterious, and remote. Her arm is linked with that of a dark, melancholy girl seated next to her, in a characteristic gesture of affection and protection.

Toward the end of her school days, Marlene became fascinated by Henny Porten, one of the greatest German stars of the period. Many of Porten's movies were romantic dramas in which the star was an innocent girl who, despite overwhelming odds, managed to capture the man of her choice. Marlene clearly identified with the celluloid Cinderella stories in which Miss Porten appeared. In her own words, Marlene regarded Porten as "the finest of womanhood, the epitome of the actor's art."

Porten's grace and style impressed her to the point of tears. Leaving a movie theater where a Porten vehicle, *The Wandering Light*, was running, she powdered her face in the theater lobby so that her sentiment-hating mother would not know she had been crying. When she got home, she dismissed the film's plot as "forget-me-nots dipped in milk," but she did say that Porten was wonderful.

There was a shop near the Auguste-Victoria School which sold picture postcards of the stars. Marlene bought *Pfennig* postcards of Henny Porten, painting them with tempera. She took them with her to the Matthiaskirchstrasse, near St. Matthew's Church, where Henny Porten lived, not far from Marlene's grandmother.

Marlene would hide behind an advertising pillar outside the

house, gazing up longingly at Henny Porten's windows. When
Fraulein Porten came out, Marlene would rush up to her and
press the postcards she had specially painted into her hand.
Porten would thank her as she stepped into her automobile.

Marlene used to save her pocket money to buy cream cakes
from Luise Voigt's shop and send them, carefully wrapped, to
her idol, when the great star appeared at premieres of new
films. She also sent her a Gobelin-embroidered pillow. As a
special treat, Marlene's mother took her and her sister Elisabeth to the premiere of a film starring Henny Porten. The
family's expensive seats were next to Porten's own. One scene
in the film made Marlene rise from her seat with a cry: on the
screen, Henny Porten was pictured sinking into a chair which
contained the pillow Marlene had sent her. Annoyed by Marlene's repeated exclamations, people turned around and asked
her to be quiet.

On Henny Porten's thirtieth birthday, in 1918, Marlene stood
outside the star's door and played Braga's "Engellied" ("Angel
Serenade") on her violin. Porten appeared and invited her in
for breakfast; but Marlene was too excited and terrified to say
anything, and finally sat without eating, on the edge of a chair,
watching her idol. Later, overcome by her feelings, Marlene
fled with the words "I have to go back to school."

Shortly afterward, when winter came, Marlene wrote that
she and several of her school friends went to the Mittenwald
skiing region for the winter holidays. Each morning, they would
examine the list of arrivals in the local resorts, posted on a
bulletin board in the hotel lobby.

One morning Marlene noticed that Porten had arrived with
her entourage at the nearby town of Garmisch. She slipped
down a ladder from her window and, like a figure in a fairy tale,
walked through the snow with her violin under her arm to the
railroad station and steamed off on the morning train to Garmisch.

A fair-haired, pretty girl in the snow, Marlene stood outside
Henny Porten's hotel and played the violin plaintively under
her window. This time, Henny Porten slammed the window

shut. Heartbroken, Marlene crept back to her hotel.

Later, when Marlene became established as a star, she came to know Henny Porten well. She wrote in the Königsberg newspaper *Hartungsche Zeitung*, "I still felt, in meeting her, the feeling of being in an elevator, going down very fast—the feeling one has when one meets a person in every way superior."

Because of the riots and revolution which disrupted Berlin just after the war, Marlene traveled to Weimar in 1919 to study violin at the Konservatorium. The Hochschule (College) of Music in Berlin, so often listed as her alma mater, in fact has no record of her being a student there. Her tutor at the Konservatorium was Professor Paul Elgers, who had been a well-known professional violinist in Berlin for several years. Wolfgang Rosé, nephew of the composer Gustav Mahler, studied piano at the Konservatorium. He recollects: "I will never forget the sensation Marlene caused when she arrived to study the violin with Elgers. Her beauty astonished us all, and the young men were lining up to take her out. But she was not at all 'flighty.' She was very modest and shy, and seemed almost unaware of her loveliness. She was not by any means an outstanding pupil, and I very much doubt if she would have enjoyed a career as a violinist. Of course, if she had continued to study with the passionate diligence that she displayed, she *might* have made it to the concert stage. But I think she was discouraged, and after eleven months she returned to Berlin."

According to her brief memoir, *Marlene Dietrich's ABC*, she pulled a ligament in the third finger of her left hand while playing a Bach sonata which involved stretching during the fingering. The hand had to be put in a cast. After the cast was removed, the muscles were weakened. A doctor told her she might falter in her first concert because of the injury, and she was so embittered by this announcement that she disliked Bach's music forever afterward, gave up the violin, and attempted the stage instead.

This decision seriously unsettled both the Dietrich and von

Losch families, with their profound disdain for the stage. Marlene's relationship with them was strained for years to come. But, with a characteristic touch of steel, she pressed on toward a career.

Two

Jazz Baby

Berlin in the years after the First World War was harsh and cheerless, a place somber with defeat. Crowds pressed through the dirty streets, pushing aside the slow, the old, and the lame. People were cynical and heartless, their humor acrid and mocking. Carl Zuckmayer wrote in his autobiography, *Second Wind:* "Despite all this, there was already in the air that incomparable feeling of intensity, the breath of a passionate upward surge which was to make Berlin within a few short years the most interesting, the most exciting metropolis in Europe."

Amid the beggars on the street corners, the raffish war profiteers in their orange or lilac sack suits, the transvestites with their heavy lip rouge, sitting with skirts pulled up above hairy thighs in the sidewalk cafés, there was a spirit of creativity abroad. At the Romanische Café or the Schwanneke Artists' Club near the Kurfürstendamm, with its windows coated in mother-of-pearl, its air filled with cigarette smoke, young playwrights and poets and novelists dreamed of new successes. If one was lucky enough to have a play produced—at the State Theater, directed by Ludwig Berger, was the persistent hope —then everyone in the literary clique gathered at Uncle Tom's Cabin, a restaurant with a beer garden under lime trees, drank hot coffee from midnight to dawn, and leafed through piles of newspapers looking for the reviews.

Marlene's visits to Schwanneke's were to come later, when she obtained more work in the theater. For the time being, she had to face the foul, slushy cold of Berlin in winter, the unheated trams, the shoddy shops and peeling billboards of a devastated capital. Though theoretically under contract to the Reinhardt theaters, she at first did little. Much of the time she sat in drafty cafés eating cheap food and looking through the want ads. Yet she was tough: she stayed healthy, she kept going. Her blonde hair curled in a bun behind her neck, her cheeks fresh and pink, she was already a sturdy beauty.

One day, she walked into a restaurant on the Kurfürstendamm, and asked a pretty blonde girl who was sitting there if she might sit with her. The girl nodded. After a while, the girl introduced herself as Gerda Huber, a struggling journalist.

Marlene began devouring a large pork chop soaked in greasy gravy. Gerda Huber was astonished by her appetite. Marlene said, "I've got to eat as much as I can now, because I don't know when I'm going to eat again."

"I'm in the same boat," Gerda Huber replied. "I have no savings."

"I'm looking for work," Marlene told her. "I'm well educated, I'm well read, but there isn't a job to be had."

Taking pity on her new acquaintance, Gerda Huber invited her to be her roommate at the small pension she lived in. "You know my dream?" Marlene said as they walked through the falling snow from the café. "I want to marry, buy a little farm, and keep chickens."

Gerda Huber said later: "Marlene preferred to spend long hours indoors and cared little for dancing or amusement. She became the pet of the landlady, Trude, because she was always buzzing about in the kitchen helping to prepare the meat and puddings, and because she kept her room in perfect order and could sew very well."

In an article in *Film Pictorial* of September 30, 1933, Gerda, who was at that time living as Marlene's house guest in Hollywood, wrote, presumably authentically, about Marlene's devotion to cats, her passionate adoption of Puck, her landlady's fat marmalade cat, her superstitions ("I'm sure cats bring me luck"), her addiction to reading, her love of singing—she would sometimes sing current songs well into the night—and her fondness for children:

"Once, when I had to go to the office of my newspaper, about one of my articles, she [Marlene] made an appointment to meet me in the Park. When I joined her I found her flushed and overheated . . . presiding over a tribe of ragamuffins even more disreputable-looking than herself. I lectured her. She began to laugh and put her arm through mine. Ten minutes after my lecture, she was buying roast chestnuts at a fruit stall. . . ."

Gerda Huber also wrote of Dietrich's passion for the theater. Marlene judged plays on the basis of realism, and if something was phony she would say: "It's not natural. It's not human. It isn't *life!*" Her shrewd assessment of quality was obvious even then. She laughed at the posturings of movie vamps and thought most motion pictures worthless—sentimental, false, affected. In 1931, she put this feeling in an article in the London *Saturday Review.* Yet the odd contradiction in her character asserted itself. Shrewd about life and art, she could still be superstitious. She spent many hours with the landlady, who read tarot cards or a crystal ball or tea leaves, predicting a great future for Marlene.

She had invented the name "Marlene" as a telescoping of Marie Magdalene. Hoping even at that stage for success in England or America, Marlene somehow found sufficient money to take English lessons from an eccentric old Englishwoman named Elsie Grace, who lived with her equally bizarre sister in a cold-water walk-up flat. With her dyed black hair, hook nose, and hunchback, Elsie Grace looked like a witch in a fairy tale, but each night as she came home she would say: "Oh, dear me. Something terrible happened today. I met a handsome young man as I was letting myself in at the front door. He screwed me right through my pants." Even as she looked shocked, Elsie smiled. She repeated the story over and over again, forgetting that she had told it before and that it was pure fiction.

Elsie made her living not only giving English lessons but

doing illustrations for magazines. She would take a head from one magazine picture, a nose from another, ears from a third, and a body from a fourth, tracing each in turn until she had a composite illustration she could sell. Martin Kosleck, the well-known character actor, says: "Years later, I discovered that Marlene and I had both been taught by Elsie Grace. Elsie had a crazy method of teaching. She would make us repeat English nursery rhymes hundreds of time over. I said to Marlene in Hollywood, 'Do you recall Elsie making you say, "The cow jumped over the moon" for 180 repetitions?' Marlene roared with laughter."

Marlene earned her living selling gloves on commission, appearing in cheap cabarets, and, according to Gerda Huber, playing the violin in a pit orchestra accompanying silent films. She replaced an actress in a play called *The Great Baritone.* She was afraid of failure; once she saw an old actress who lived in the same lodging house appear as an ingenue in a play, and when she observed the woman's aging face and body in a grotesque masquerade of youth and health, she was filled with despair. "Maybe that's what will happen to me," she told Gerda Huber.

She took a small role in a society drama, struggling miserably through several long speeches. One line, "Would you light this cigarette for me, *mein Herr?*" proved too difficult for her, and she stumbled over it. Later, in the film *Morocco,* she more expertly spoke a very similar line, introduced by her as a private joke. She just missed getting a part in *The Fight for Oneself* with William Dieterle and Olga Tchechowa.

Marlene danced in the chorus with Guido Thielscher's Revue and with Rudolf Nelson's Girls. Although she sang and danced rather inexpertly in these shows both in Berlin and on tour, audiences responded to her animal sexuality, superb body, and plumply pretty face. Not taking herself seriously, longing for more prominence, she performed without thinking or feeling. She was successful in spite of herself.

The best way for an actress to be launched into a serious career in those days was through the Max Reinhardt drama school. Under the direction of one of Max Reinhardt's earliest associates, the physically imposing but undistinguished Berthold Held, the school was located above the Kammerspiele Theater, in the Schumannstrasse. From it had emerged many of the distinguished young actors of the day, but its discipline was very severe.

Late in 1921, Marlene arrived for a reading test. With a book under her arm, Hoffmannsthal's *Der Tor und der Tod* (*Death and the Fool*), her hair in a long braid around her head, she stood nervously at the entrance. A man with an enormous beard emerged. He snapped, "What do you want?" She told him that she wanted to give a reading. Asked who had recommended her, she was forced to admit that nobody had. The man looked at her intently and took pity on her. He said, "Pretend that you came from Herr Arthur Kahane." Kahane was an associate of Reinhardt's.

She went up into the hall of the building, where the formidable head of the drama school, the tall, sharp-featured Berthold Held, was standing with his associate Albert Heine. She read a speech from *Der Tor und der Tod,* and this was warmly received. But later she had to do a test piece for Reinhardt, the prayer of Gretchen to the Holy Virgin in *Faust.* Although she cried real tears, Reinhardt, cold and indifferent, sitting in the orchestra with a coat draped over his shoulders, was unimpressed. She was not accepted.

But Berthold Held was sympathetic and took her on as a private pupil. She trained at his house with only one other actress, Grete Mosheim, who later emerged as a leading figure of the Berlin stage.

Grete Mosheim recalls, "I'm afraid Marlene and I did not think too much of Held. I do not like to be unkind to a dead man, and please don't make me *seem* unkind, but he was rather a fool, really. He had been an old associate of Reinhardt's from the early days, but he didn't know much about anything. We used to laugh at him a little behind his back, and we'd spend far more time taking long walks or attending Swedish gymnastics classes than taking any notice of this old, pompous man.

"I loved Marlene and have remained friendly with her all my life. I always used to notice that, whereas I would wear socks and flat shoes, she wore the most exquisite hose and the finest high-heeled shoes. I don't know how she afforded it. But she could knock your eye out at seven o'clock in the morning.

"We didn't stay the prescribed two years with Held. We left after just under one year, having learned nothing. But working with him entitled us to appear in the Reinhardt theaters."

Marlene would soon emerge as a Reinhardt actress.

In 1922, Marlene appeared in her first important film, *Der Kleine Napoleon*, as a maid. Fritz Maurischaat, who knew her then, says: "Marlene conducted a rather charming flirtation with the director of the film, Georg Jacoby. I think Jacoby was in love with her, but I'm not sure. At all events, his interest was obvious for everyone to see."

A few months later, a handsome young Sudeten German named Rudolph Sieber who was working as production assistant and casting director for Joe May, husband of the great star Mia May and one of the finest directors of the period, ran into Marlene at the Romanische Café. She came into the studio for a reading with Grete Mosheim, and Sieber was in charge of the audition. This was for a film starring Emil Jannings and called *Tragedy of Love*. Grete Mosheim did not get the part.

Marlene would be able, if she won the role, to dominate two scenes, as the voluptuous girl friend of the prosecutor in a murder trial whose antic behavior in the spectators' gallery seriously distracts the judge.

Fritz Maurischaat, then of the Mayfilm Company, will never forget Marlene coming in for the reading. More than half a century later, her image is still fresh in his mind. In his house in Wiesbaden he consulted his diary and recalled: "She came to us, this Marlene, applying for the job. Every day, the long lines of struggling young actresses were there. Most of them were turned away.

"It was my job to interview these girls. One morning, a line formed which went all the way down the corridor and down the stairs. In this line was a tiny, fragile creature, dressed in a loose wrap almost as intimate as a negligee. Despite this revealing garment, she could easily have been overlooked, since most of the girls were doing their best to attract attention by throwing their breasts or legs at me, and she was shy and modest.

"But she had with her a puppy on a leash, and none of the other girls did. That drew attention to her. I remember she had fashioned a necklace of horsehair round the dog's neck, a fashion in those days. The dog did not follow her obediently, but pulled furiously in the opposite direction, obviously wanting to seek out a lamppost. Everyone looked at it nervously in case it should raise its leg. Fortunately, it didn't. Seeing how the dog affected everyone, Marlene picked it up and held it in her arms. She came to my desk. As she did so, there was something about her movements that made me say to myself, under my breath, 'My *God!* How attractive she is!' "

Maurischaat and Joe May both agreed with Sieber that Marlene would be excellent in the picture. Inquiring around the Kurfürstendamm, they quickly learned that she was a well-established local theatrical "character."

Mia May, Joe May's widow and the star of *Tragedy of Love,* is ninety-four years old and living in Hollywood. She says: "I'll never forget the impression Marlene made on all of us. I don't recall the dog but I do recall that she was very amusing and diverting and attractive and original. She was irresistible to men. She used to go everywhere with a monocle and a boa, or sometimes five red fox furs. On other occasions, she wore wolf skins, the kind you spread on beds. People used to follow her through the streets of Berlin; they would laugh at her, but she fascinated them; she made them talk.

"She went around with a group of young actresses. At first, they all wore monocles except her; then it was the other way around. I knew she was attracted to Rudi Sieber from the first. He was about twenty-five, a dear friend of mine, athletic, blond, muscular, beautiful—a splendid Aryan type. He was my husband's general factotum, doing everything that needed to be done. Whenever she looked at him, I could read her eyes. They were saying, 'You're going to be the father of my child.' "

Sieber not only helped Marlene obtain her job; he advised her on the best way to arrange her hair and the ideal clothes to wear in the picture. He was a charmer: modest, considerate, and in love with Marlene from the first.

Tragedy of Love, skillfully directed by May, still exists in a print at George Eastman House, Rochester, New York. It fascinates because it shows both a young Emil Jannings on the verge of a great career and Marlene in a different mood from the one we are familiar with. Sexy, full of energy and charm, she already possessed the style and temperament of a star. In her first scene, she is on the telephone, screaming at her lover in this silent film, accusing him of failing to secure her a seat at a murder trial. In the second scene, she flirts with his assistant, who gives her a pass to the trial, thereby insuring the immediate transfer of her affections. She is splendid in the trial itself: conscious of her allure; jazzily drawing attention to herself by jigging up and down; peering through her monocle at the judge, who is visibly unsettled by her erotic appeal; scowling at her former lover or vamping her imminent one; giggling and sensual all at once.

She laughed at herself at a preview, telling Maurischaat, "I look like a potato with hair!" But the critics singled her out, observing that she was lively and attractive, and she was signed to a contract with the Reinhardt theaters at the time.

Her career had begun. But, it was not a good time for it. Nineteen twenty-three was the year of the great inflation. Erich Maria Remarque, her intimate, summed it up in his novel *The Black Obelisk:* "The day is blue and beautiful. Over the city the sky hangs like a giant silken tent. The cool of morning still lingers in the crowns of trees. Birds are twittering as though nothing existed but early summer, their nests, and their young. It doesn't matter to them that the dollar, like an ugly spongy toadstool, has puffed itself up to 50,000 marks. Nor that the morning paper contains the notices of three suicides."

A building could be bought for twenty-two dollars, which would have been thousands of billions of marks. A loaf of bread cost ten million marks, a theater ticket a hundred million. Rentals ran into billions a month. When an American student made up a coat of mark bills for a gag, a crowd rushed at him and stripped him. There was a feeling of craziness in the air, a craziness mirrored in the harsh jazz of the period, the acid lyrics, the brutal caricatures of the famous magazine *Simplicissimus* and the satirical revues. There seemed to be more prosperity in the air, but when a pair of black shoes could be bought for 850 million marks, no one felt completely sane. Felix Jackson has described the time in an as yet unpublished biography of Kurt Weill: "The boys in their big suits walk by, coats down to their ankles, dirty sandals on their feet. And the girls in see-through blouses and black stockings, their skirts shoved up high to display their offerings. A whiff of sweet perfume and sweat. And then the pimps with their caps aslant, their scarves draped around their necks. Keeping their glacial eyes on their strolling wares."

It was into this atmosphere of inflation and decadence that the twenty-two-year-old Marlene was plunged. It was a far cry from the life of a policeman's daughter; yet, with her zest for living and her earthy good humor, we cannot doubt that she flung herself headlong into the new Berlin. Her career as a stage actress began to flourish along with her romantic relationship with Sieber.

She was working almost constantly in the theater during the 1920s. She made her debut in legitimate theater in 1922, as a society woman (Mrs. Shenstone) in *The Circle,* by Somerset Maugham, at Max Reinhardt's Kammerspiele. She appeared in *The Taming of the Shrew* as Widow, sister of Elisabeth Bergner's Katharina, at Reinhardt's converted circus arena, the Grosses Schauspielhaus, and later on tour; Bergner admired Marlene, and influenced her style. Marlene also appeared that year as Hippolyta in *A Midsummer Night's Dream;* the cast included Hilde Hildebrandt. Later in the twenties, Marlene would be in Rehfisch's society comedy *Duell am Lido,* and in Sternheim's *Die Schule von Uznach,* both at the Staatstheater.

In 1923 and 1924 she was in three plays: Björnson's *When the New Vine Blossoms,* Molière's *The Imaginary Invalid,* and Wedekind's *Spring's Awakening. When the New Vine Blossoms* was based on Bjornson's idyllic life at Aulestad, his country retreat, as described for his daughter Bergliot in a series of beautiful letters written to her in Paris. The play showed the effect of the ripening of their young daughters on sexually parched and sterile parents, who for the last time feel vicariously the stirrings of passion as the spring begins in the vineyard and the lovely young girls feel the first pressure of erotic feelings. Marlene, as the most beautiful of the daughters, portrayed with extraordinary sensuality and delicacy the burgeoning of young love, singing expertly in several choral scenes led by the accomplished Erika Meingast. The critic W. Spael wrote of the play: "Björnsterne Björnson was far advanced in his eighties when he wrote this charming comedy. He has magically created the spring of life from his eternally young poet's heart. The young girls, hardly grown out of their short dresses, flutter across the stage like bright blooms, alive with joy. . . ."

Other critics wrote enthusiastically about the setting of the two-story family home: the flowers outside the windows, the giggling girls with their faces pressed to the windows when the stuffy young provost kisses one of the sisters for the first time. Although Herman Vallentin and Lucie Hoflich got the lion's share of attention as the parents, Marlene was singled out, along with Hilde Hildebrandt, who played the eldest daughter. On the verge of marriage to Rudi, happy, trembling with anticipation of motherhood, she was the incarnation of Björnson's ideal of youthful hope, love, and desire.

A different side of her personality emerged in the role of a maid in *The Imaginary Invalid*. Ernst Matray, the choreographer and dancer, witnessed the performance. He recalls, "She used to outline her nipples with pencil before she went on to the stage. A fireman, placed behind the canvas on each side of the stage because of the many candles, would peep out through a hole. She didn't know he was there, and she went up against the canvas so that her nipples went into his eyes. He almost fainted!"

Of her three performances of the period, it seems that her most remarkable was in *Spring's Awakening*. This play, one of the finest of Wedekind's career, had been written in 1891 and had become a standard of Reinhardt's repertoire. His formal direction had been laid down, and was followed by his subordinates. It was almost certainly the first play to offer masturbation and homosexual embraces on the stage. Marlene played the smallish but nevertheless significant part of Ilse, a painter's model and prostitute, who, giving the details of her useless and miserable life in the beds of many men, drives a heroic youthful student to despair and to an early suicide.

Critics remarked on her delivery of Wedekind's speeches, in which she evoked the hopelessness of a career which consisted only of lust. It is all the more sad that she did not recreate Gertrud Eysoldt's Lulu, Wedekind's famous destroyer of men, in his *Pandora's Box,* on either stage or screen. But her Ilse, sulky, erotic, brutally pessimistic, was certainly a warm-up for her Lola-Lola in *The Blue Angel.*

Willy Fritsch was a memorable Melchior Gabor in the play. He said later: "At one performance, I noticed Marlene was lacking in concentration. I was to find out why.

"After the final curtain, I approached her. 'Marlene, what's the matter?' I asked her. 'Is something wrong?'

" 'Yes, terribly,' " she sighed. 'Willy, you'll have to help me. I've lost a ring somewhere among the scenery.' "

"We crawled around on the floor for a good half hour until the beginning of the evening performance, and just before the curtain went up, we found the ring lodged in a crack of the floor.

" 'Thank God!' Marlene said. 'It's my engagement ring!' "

Marlene and Rudi were married at the Kaiser Wilhelm Gedächtniskirche in Berlin on May 17, 1924. Rudi was Roman Catholic and Marlene Lutheran. The marriage was conducted according to the ritual of the Lutheran faith because, by the rules of the time, the Catholic church would not permit a Catholic service when the bride was a Protestant. The wedding was like a comic scene from an old German film. The guests arrived late at the ceremony; Rudi was in such a hurry he put on a borrowed bowler hat which didn't fit and which he carried awkwardly in his hand after it fell off several times on his way to the church; Marlene's dress also failed to fit, since it had been incorrectly made.

The young couple moved into a comfortable and fashionable apartment house, 54 Kaiserallee. The apartment was on the top floor, the cheapest of the four floors because it was a walk-up. Another tenant was Leni Riefenstahl, later a favorite of Hitler and director of *Triumph of the Will,* the Berlin Olympic Games films, and other Nazi propaganda films.

The apartment was decorated with icons, many of them filling the wall behind the double bed in the young couple's bedroom. The furniture was baroque and painted white. Marlene and Rudi knew many White Russian émigrés, refugees from the Revolution, who sold icons cheaply and who swarmed through Berlin serving as waiters, gigolos, kept women, professional dancing partners, nightclub hosts or hostesses—any jobs they could get. She loved the Russian people for the rest of her life, their food, literature, and music; and when she first went to Russia in the 1960s, she told them so.

Shortly after her marriage (in January 1925) a daughter was born. At first she was known as Heidede. She was a very pretty child. She had blonde hair, a lovely complexion, and extraordinarily intelligent, acute eyes. Marlene always used to joke that she had eaten apples during her pregnancy to insure the child's good health. Marlene became softer, warmer, happier—but plumper—after Heidede was born.

Marlene adored Heidede. As she took her for walks in the little park in her baby carriage, or sang gentle songs to her, movies and the stage seemed futile and ridiculous. She obtained a release from her theater contract and devoted almost two years to being a mother. It was probably the happiest time of her life.

The young couple had a struggle to exist. Rudi did not earn a large salary working as a production manager for various companies after he left Mayfilms. It was economic necessity rather than ambition that made Marlene look for work again.

In 1925, Marlene appeared with Garbo in Pabst's classic *The*

Joyless Street. She played the small role of a poverty-stricken girl waiting endlessly in line outside a butcher shop in the depths of the 1919 depression in Vienna. Garbo is near her in the line, and when she collapses with hunger, Marlene assists her. In a later scene, angered by the butcher's callousness, Marlene murders him and runs out, pursued by his angry dog. Her acting was vibrant, passionate, and committed.

She managed to obtain a significant role in Arthur Robison's movie *Manon Lescaut,* starring Lya de Putti. In this picture, Marlene appeared memorably in two scenes. She descends furiously on her rival, Manon, when the latter is reduced to the poorhouse, mocking her cruelly. Later, in a cell to which Manon has managed to lure her, she struggles with da Putti in a fight which forecasts her famous bout with Una Merkel in *Destry Rides Again.*

Presumably to help raise Heidede, Marlene worked overtime in movies in 1926. Alexander Korda, the Hungarian director who was later to be the eccentric genius of the British film industry in the 1930s and 1940s, selected her for the role of a coquette in *A Modern Du Barry.* In this picture, Marlene was a jazz-mad, electrically excitable girl, flirting with everybody in sight, in an ermine wrap. In another Korda picture, *Madame Doesn't Want Children,* she appeared as a joke for two minutes in a party scene, in her well-known current persona of Charlestoning, Black-Bottoming 1920s jazz baby. In *Heads Up, Charly!* she was a dizzy French society girl, flirtatiously batting her eyes under a cloche hat.

In all of these pictures, Marlene acted with irresistible brio, virtually reproducing on screen her own life as the charmer whom the Kurfürstendamm fashionable set would run into at Schwanneke's or Mutzbauer's. There was not a hint of the bored, world-weary sophisticate we are familiar with from the 1930s movies. She was closer in spirit in these pictures to the earthy enchantress of *Destry Rides Again* and *The Spoilers* in the 1940s.

She was at her most characteristic as the singing, dancing mistress of ceremonies in Erik Charell's revue *From Mouth to*

Mouth, at Max Reinhardt's Grosses Schauspielhaus—a typically provocative title for a typically exotic example of Charell kitsch. Charell, later to become famous as the creator of *White Horse Inn,* was a swarthy, handsome, fierce-tempered, and flamboyant homosexual who insisted on arriving at the theater for morning rehearsals dressed in the tall silk hat, white tie, and tails he had slept in the night before. He directed the show with frequent petulant screams of rage, which the cast greatly appreciated.

The story of *From Mouth to Mouth* was, of course, quite inane. Five children, falling asleep in the Garden of Desire, dream of the Creation, in which God descends from a pink cloud dressed in a cotton beard; of an Indian war dance; of a magic castle from which a knight rescues an imprisoned beauty; of Casanova's amorous adventures (why the infants are dreaming of these was not explained); of dancing dolls; and of flights of birds. The show lasted four hours and was divided into eighteen scenes, largely set (with total incongruity) to the music of Offenbach.

At first, Erika Glassner was cast as the mistress of ceremonies. But she fell ill, and Marlene, in true show business tradition, took over at a moment's notice. She wore a bizarre costume with a headdress like a lampshade, yards and yards of tulle, a necklace of red roses, and a train of yellow silk. What she thought of this garment can only be conjectured. She had to dance, in sequined shoes which cut her ankles, all the way down a long ramp which led into the audience.

The specialty of the show was a star appearance by the notorious lesbian entertainer Claire Waldoff. She was known as the "bus headlamp" because of her red hair, or as "the big mouth" *(Schnauze).* Short and muscular, crackling with energy and vitality, she was the daughter of a coal miner and looked it. She had trained to be a doctor, but her family's poverty had prevented her from completing her studies. She was like a Heinrich Zille caricature; she made her reputation quickly, befriended by Zille himself, who was known as "Paintbrush Henry." She sang a famous earthy Pflanzer ballad about him, which Marlene was to recall nostalgically in her record *Marlene Dietrich's Berlin* (Capitol T–10443) some thirty-five years later.

Waldoff had been the sensation of the Linden-Cabaret, with her other great hit, "Willem, Don't Talk So Much!" She was referring directly to the Kaiser Wilhelm II, and the official censor, von Glasenapp, cross-examined her about the lyrics. When he did so, Waldoff put her hands on her hips and flung back her head with a raucous laugh. "I mean any old Willem!" she yelled. Her song "Hermann" later got her into trouble with Göring, and she narrowly escaped arrest.

Waldoff was unquestionably the most powerful personality in Marlene's life at the time. Her coarse, throaty, arrogant voice can still be appreciated on disc, and one can see clearly how it influenced Marlene's singing style. Marlene removed the coarseness in her own interpretations of Waldoff songs, and indeed when she recreated the Zille song she had the lyrics reworked (by Max Colpet) in less vulgar language. But the depth of the voice, the phrasing, the sheer attack, were adopted by her often in later years.

Alexa von Proembsky, who played the Japanese girl in an Oriental fantasy scene of *From Mouth to Mouth*, recalls: "Marlene and I and Claire Waldoff used to go with Marlene's husband to the El Dorado, after the show. It was a famous nightclub for transvestites, on the Martin Lutherstrasse."

It is possible Marlene first thought of her famous performance in male attire when she saw Waldoff on the stage, or it may have been from seeing the extraordinary Margo Lion in various revues. Tall and skinny, made up of bizarre angles like the hero of *The Cabinet of Dr. Caligari,* Margo Lion wore black lipstick and black nail polish, and her face was powdered dead white. She had a high, thin voice and a poisonous wit. A genius of popular song, she was undoubtedly an influence as strong as Waldoff on the young Marlene. She was married to the equally brilliant Marcellus Schiffer, an effeminate lyricist whose intricate rhymes and savage plays on words resembled the work of a malign Ogden Nash. Together, they made an extraordinary team. They were seen everywhere, he with his plump powdered face and she with her thin powdered one, looking like a pair of effervescent ghosts.

Marlene was a hit in *From Mouth to Mouth.* She made a movie in 1926, *The Imaginary Baron,* wearing a monocle once more and flirting outrageously as Sophie, daughter of the immensely rich but uncouth Baron von Kimmel. The high point of the picture was a tramp ball in which Sophie hires a tramp to pose as a baron and all the guests at the castle dress up as mendicants in rags.

By early 1927, Marlene had become known in Berlin. The city was going through an American phase. Among other hits, *Rose Marie, The Constant Wife, The Royal Family, The Road to Rome, Burlesque,* and *The Trial of Mary Dugan* were all running to packed houses in German translations. It was typical that *From Mouth to Mouth* should be at the Grosses Schauspielhaus, because Reinhardt, who had created this colosseum of the theatrical art, had failed to make money with his Shakespeare seasons there.

The American critic Joseph Wood Krutch wrote of the era: "The very things which seemed to us the most banal are doubtless those which, superficially at least, are the most characteristically American. They are therefore those which seem the most piquantly interesting to Berliners. 'Broadwayish' may be a term which implies certain derogation in America, but it implies a compliment here. It is the neatly mechanical structure, the hard smartness of the language, and the representations of unfamiliar and violent happenings in the popular American drama which appeals most to Germany. Bootleggers and bandits are romantic figures, the modern equivalents of redskins and cowboys. And the Berliners who used to suppose that Cooper's novels gave a pretty accurate picture of life in New York City now suppose that we expect to have a battle between highjackers nearly every evening in Times Square."

Berlin in 1927 was in most ways even more exciting than New York. Recovered from the inflation and depression, it had a crude, raw thrust, a vulgar, sophisticated drive no other world capital could match. Its laughter was defiant, its humor cutting.

In the theater world sexual partners were exchanged; nobody restricted himself to any sexual preference—despite rigid laws and blackmail threats. Homosexuality and lesbianism were perfectly in order, and those who refused to sleep with their own sex were laughed at in smart circles. Women went ice-skating naked, and only a short time afterward Josephine Baker would dance dressed only in bananas. At one nightclub, popular with visiting farmers, women could call each other on table telephones. The only rule was that if a man beckoned a pretty girl, she must prove when she came to his table that she really had breasts. Often, the unwary male could find himself caressing the leg of a well-known athlete dressed in convincing drag.

The dance floor of the famous Femina nightclub was jammed all night long with couples glued together, sweat drenching their bodies in the smoky heat, groping each other, vibrating to the hot jazz of a Negro band. The band members wore pink straw hats and bit on cheap cigars. One night, the band leader emptied a basket of white mice onto the dance floor, and many of the girls leaped onto the tables, only to resume dancing hectically with each other on top of them.

Black taxis striped in gold, multicolored motor buses, and squeaking trams filled the Berlin streets. Mounted police galloped by in their pearl-gray coats, their scabbards jangling. Cafés were sheltered by privet hedges under gay awnings and were alive from morning to midnight with the sounds of violins. In many restaurants the walls were covered with silk, and bunches of flowers sprang from vases along the wall. Money was spent prodigally, and most revelers stayed up until dawn, when the alleys were heaped with pyramids of empty champagne bottles. People hysterically indulged themselves, whether in the handsome beer gardens under glittering canopies of leaves, in the watery byways of the Wannsee, or in the more outré, Aubrey Beardsleyan boîtes and the dance palaces with rainbow lights spinning in the ceilings. Many pleasure houses combined, on different floors, cafés, restaurants, bars, and dance halls, where there were great murals of traditional scenes of German history or evocations of the German countryside, the Lorelei of the Rhine, the mountains of the south, the Hamburg water-front, or the palaces and castles of the very rich.

It seems only appropriate that in the hectic "American" period of the Berlin theater, the greatest hit should be the play *Broadway* itself. Written by George Abbott and Philip Dunning (their last names were accidentally reversed in the advertisements and billboards), *Broadway* had opened in 1926 to acclaim at the Broadhurst Theatre in New York and at the Strand Theatre in London earlier that year. Marlene was cast in the minor role of Ruby, but even this was an honor: practically every good young actress in Berlin who could sing or dance wanted to be in the cast.

The play dealt with the activities of bootleggers, jazz musicians, and chorus girls in the raffish setting of Nick Verdis's Paradise Club on Times Square. As commentators on the action, five girls, Mazie, Grace, Ruby, Pearl, and Ann, fought and made slangy, bitter remarks throughout. The big scene was when Pearl, with the words, "Turn around, rat—I don't want to give it to you, like you gave it to him—in the back!" shoots the man who killed her lover. She adds the words: "I'm giving you more chance than you gave him—I'm looking at you—and the last thing you'll see before you go straight to hell is Joe Edwards' woman, who swore to hell she'd get you!"

The production was perfect for Berlin, the procession of criminals, pimps, prostitutes, and low-grade dancers providing a spectacle of coruscating excitement, an abstraction of the American underworld. Germans loved strong-meat melodramatic confrontations, and here, in the words of Joseph Wood Krutch, was "sinister villain matched against simple-minded hero . . . killing done by revengeful woman . . . the man of the law who slips away when he realizes that justice, though irregular, has been done. . . ."

The chorus line of girls was uniformly praised by the Berlin critics when it opened in 1927. Alfred Kerr wrote in the *Berliner Tageblatt:* "And the dancing girls? Each of them is a contemporary symbol, a summing up of an era. . . . [They are led by] Harald Paulsen, who does a Chaplinesque routine . . . it's won-

derful how he jumps; how he glides; how his joints move; how
he expresses compassion; how he pretends he is poor . . . one
of the few men in the theater and film worth knowing. Just
great." Kerr praised Rosa Valetti ("heavenly . . . she gives an
unforgettable rendition of an exhausted singer"); and he mentioned each of the chorus girls by name: "Yes, all of these girls
should be named one by one, Ruth Albu, Marlene Dietrich,
Elisabeth Lennartz, Clara Guyl, Marianne Kupfer. . . ."

Elisabeth Lennartz, who played Grace, says: "Marlene at the
time was delightful and happy. After the show she and I used
to sit together talking for hours, with the actors Willi Forst, Paul
Nikolaus, and others at Schwanneke's. She never wore a bra or
panties. That was modern and daring then. She had the best
legs of all of us girls.

"We were drilled for weeks in tap dancing; it was grueling.
The director, Eugen Robert, was a hard taskmaster. Marlene
didn't seem fazed, she was zippy and outgoing. Everything
came to her easily. She didn't strain herself too much. She didn't
even give me the feeling she wanted to be superlative in everything. She was modest, and happily married. With forty or fifty
theaters needing pretty girls, she had no fear of not getting
work.

"I don't think she bothered to read notices. Most of us *hung*
on notices—we knew that if Kerr [Alfred Kerr] liked a play, his
rival, Ihering, would hate it. Around midnight on the first night
we all rushed out to buy the papers, but Marlene just went
home to her husband and baby.

"I remember halfway through the run of the show she fell
and broke her arm. Well, she still had to play the chorus line!
So she wrapped the arm very elegantly in a chiffon shawl, and
kept going. She was, she told me, in terrible, terrible pain, all
the time, and she never complained once. Off-duty she wore
her famous fox furs, and you never saw her arm.

"She kept in hard training. Literally. Each morning she and
I went to see a very famous man, Sabri Mahia, a Turk, who
trained professional boxers. He had a very successful boxing
school in Berlin. We would punch a bag and jump rope and do

the footwork and everything. Mahi, as we called him, would measure us each morning and keep saying, 'You're just an *inch* too fat!' Marlene used to take her little daughter Heidede to him because the child's legs were just slightly bowed. Sabri was wonderful with the child. He knew exactly what exercises to do. Marlene adored him because he cured Heidede.

"He was crazy—manic, frantic, but he was fantastic—he knew exactly what to do with a body, what it needed. Sometimes, I could have killed him, he drove me so hard. But after, I was grateful. Some people used to say: 'This Marlene and this Lennartz, they're insane! They take boxing lessons! Why don't they take a walk instead?' "

In a contrasting reminiscence, the Hollywood writer Felix Jackson says: "I was the assistant to Viktor Barnowsky, who produced *Broadway*. Marlene made an impression on everyone. She showed off her figure without underwear, I also remember. She gave me a picture of her daughter and said to me, 'I shall be a very big star, very soon!' I didn't believe a word of it. I said, 'Yes, sure," and thought, 'They're all like that, those young girls. She'll get over it.' Well, she didn't!

"She quickly became a famous beauty in Berlin; she made the most one could of being a woman; she was always generous, the most helpful person in the world to anyone in need. She lived her life freely."

The Berlin actress Käthe Haack remembers her at the time: "I'll never forget Marlene in *Broadway*. She played one scene on her own, lying downstage. She was very, very sexy, and she bicycled her legs in the air, slowly, in front of the audience. The legs were so breathtaking everyone was talking about this terrific woman. Berlin in those days was the most exciting city in the world. At parties and festivities everybody talked about this woman. Her name was already a trademark for sex.

"But nobody really thought that she would ever be a big movie star. I remember one night I was at a restaurant on the Marburgerstrasse and Gunther Rittau, the famous cameraman, was at the next table. Somebody was saying that a girl was needed for a picture. Maybe Dietrich would be good? And

Rittau said, 'No, her nose is unphotographable. It's a duck's nose.' And later he did her photography in *The Blue Angel!*

"I met her frequently at balls. I remember a wonderful ball at the lovely house of Professor Robert, who owned the *Tribune* newspaper and also the Schlosspark Theater. Everyone was there—Max Reinhardt, Ferenc Molnár, Peter Lorre, Conrad Veidt, Carola Neher—and yet, and yet—one woman stood out: Dietrich. We were all in a great crowd and suddenly she emerged, took Carola Neher's hand—Carola was a great beauty; she died later in Russia—and they danced a tango. It was unforgettable—the crowd parted—we watched amazed.

"We had another great party. Everyone from the crown prince of Germany to big stars like Henny Porten and Asta Nielsen. There was a famous dressmaker, Mrs. Becker. All the young aspiring actresses would wear her latest creations and next day she'd have free advertisements in all the papers. When I was at this party they whispered: Marlene is changing in the ladies' room. She had ordered a dress with seven silver foxes at the back, and it had been finished at the last minute. She walked out after all the other girls appeared—and 'stole the show.' "

After a three-month run, *Broadway* went on tour, opening in Vienna early in June. Willi Forst took over as the romantic leading man. He had made his name on the Berlin musical stage, and had become notable for his lilting voice and charming, insouciant wit. Tall and good-looking, with an apparently bland but shrewdly sophisticated face, he was very attractive to women and had established a considerable reputation as a boulevardier.

Marlene took over the important part of Pearl, the girl who shot her lover's murderer. She evidently acted the part with skill, temperament, and attack, earning good notices from the Austrian critics. She seems to have carried off the murder scene with frightening intensity, eyes dead and staring in a powdered white face, body muscled and tense. Dancing, chain-smoking, wisecracking in a Berlin argot which skillfully echoed sub-Broadway slang, she was a fascination. Forst proved encouraging, helping her with timing and emphasis, and instructing her in the modulation of her movements and voice. They became close friends and, most people who knew them agree, probably more than that.

They were seen at parties and balls, restaurants, and night clubs together, she plump, jazzy, and gemütlich, he dashing and debonair. They were the objects of gossip everywhere. *Broadway*'s tremendous local success was at least partly due to the widespread discussion of their presumed "romance."

She and Forst lived in separate suites at the elegant Krantz-Ambassador Hotel, only a short walk from the famous Vienna Opera House. They were the persistent talk of the society crowd in the Krantz-Ambassador's red plush dining room. They liked the same things, music and literature and dancing and good champagne. They were not seen at the Sacher, Bristol, and Imperial Hotels, avoiding the fashionable set and preferring smaller restaurants.

Because of their success in *Broadway,* Forst and Marlene were approached to appear in an Austrian film, *Café Electric.* Produced by Karl Hartl for Sascha Films, Vienna, and directed by Gustav Ucicky, it was the story of a dance-hall hostess who falls in love with a professional pickpocket. Forst was hired without more than a brief reading. However, Marlene, in view of her comparative unimportance, had to make a screen test. In the coffee shop of the century-old Hotel Sacher, the distinguished Karl Hartl recalled: "Marlene was quite a glamour girl in 1927. She came in for the test in a red costume and cloche hat, which was probably the best she could afford, given the fact that she was earning very little and that she was most certainly quite poor. She managed to give style to clothes that were not of the finest quality. Her taste, her selection of colors, made up for, and to some extent concealed, the cheap materials she wore.

"I took a look at her legs as she walked into my office, and, I must say, they lived up to the buildup! She arrived coolly, sat down, and we talked over the role. She showed some modified enthusiasm, but I got the impression that her heart was not really in pictures; she felt that she didn't photograph well and that she should devote herself exclusively to the stage. Her solo test was a little awkward, so we did another one with Forst, of a love scene. Because of their romance, that wasn't exactly difficult for her to do. She was excellent. But I don't think she was too happy with the test, and we didn't make up our minds about her at once."

Willi Forst was horrified when he discovered that Hartl and Ucicky were uncertain about using Marlene in the picture. Forst told a reporter in 1965 at his house in Switzerland: "I told them, no Marlene, no Forst! She was wonderful, and would be perfect as the dance hall hostess. She danced superbly, and she had just the right quality of gaiety and charm."

Confronted with Forst's ultimatum, Hartl and Ucicky had little alternative but to cast Marlene. She shrugged and proceeded into rehearsals, acting in the movie in the daytime and in *Broadway* at night. The film, released in 1927, is interesting to see today. In the opening sequences, Marlene is at her most energetic: dancing the Charleston with Forst, quarreling with him when she discovers he is a thief, leading him on, or romancing him, and ruling her smoke-filled, seedy dance hall with subtle authority. Dark-haired for the role, her lips painted in the bee-stung style of the period, heavy in black satin dresses, Marlene was more sensual than ever. Ucicky directed the movie with a crude, unflagging pace which did not disguise the essential thinness of the subject matter.

The shooting progressed amiably, Marlene's energy seemingly inexhaustible as she rushed from theater to studio and back again, filming at all hours of the night. A very strange occurrence during the production is recalled by Karl Hartl: "The head of Sascha Films was a man named Count Sascha Kolowrat. He was quite young at the time, about forty-one years of age. He was married to the famous and beautiful Princess Troubetskoy. He was enormously fat, over three hundred and fifty pounds. Of all people, he fell in love with Marlene in the middle of the picture. He was a fan of legs. He found her irresistible. That was not unusual; so did most men. She did not respond: not just because of his weight, but because she was totally involved with Forst. Now this Count Kolowrat was shocked into a deep depression when Marlene turned him down. In his sadness, he was stricken with cancer. That huge man shriveled from three hundred and fifty pounds to seventy pounds in a six-month period.

"He went to a private nursing home in Semmering, near Vienna. When the picture was finished shooting we brought it to him, following his last operation, and ran it for him in his room. He said after the screening, with tears brimming his eyes, 'I have only one wish left. To see Marlene, and to see her legs, just once more before I die.' Marlene was still working in *Broadway*. I went backstage at a matinee and told her what Count Kolowrat had said. She looked at me very straight in the eye, and nodded without a word. Next day, the necessary arrangements were made. I had a chauffeur drive her in a studio car through the Vienna Woods to Semmering. She went up to the nursing home and asked for his room. She walked in there, and he was lying desperately ill, and in very great pain. She pulled up her skirt and showed him her legs. She said a few sweet words to him and then left. It was *exquisite* of her. He called me that night and said: 'Thank you. Now I can die happily. Thank you.' He passed away only three weeks later. Isn't that a lovely story?"

An actor in *Café Electric* named Igo Sym, who specialized in playing the musical saw, taught Marlene to perform expertly on this strange instrument. The saw was a piece of metal similar to a carpenter's saw with no teeth, and was played with a heavily rosined violin bow. The saw was held on the knee, and the more it was bent the higher-pitched sound it gave. It offered a kind of wailing vibrato and could never manage an allegro or fast passage in music. It was ideal only for slow numbers, such as "Dark Eyes" or "Smoke Gets in Your Eyes."

Marlene became fascinated by Igo Sym. He was a Bavarian of striking good looks who played the piano most skillfully, providing variations in an Austrian style of the works of Chopin. Despite his handsome appearance, he was excessively shy, nervous, and unsure of himself. He was probably bisexual. Marlene was extraordinarily considerate of his temperament and helped him in every way she could to overcome his handicaps. Seeing his great talent, and loving music as only she could, she entered into a platonic relationship with him of great beauty and tenderness, almost as though she were living in the pages of a novella by Stefan Zweig. Her friend Walter Reisch used to watch her, her fair hair loose, enraptured by the music he played.

Back home, Rudi took care of Heidede with the aid of a cleaning woman. He was continually depressed and used to speak of his sadness to his friends Joe and Mia May.

Marlene and Willi Forst returned to Berlin together in June 1928 and were greeted by Rudi and Heidede. She appeared in the film *Princess Olala* in 1928 as another cocotte, an expert in the art of kissing. She gave a sparkling performance, and despite mixed reviews for this movie and for *Café Electric* her personal reputation in Europe was greatly enhanced. It was a rich season in Berlin. Through Willi Forst, Marlene was introduced to a smartly intelligent circle of friends who met each day for lunch at a special table at Mutzbauer's: the actors Hans von Twardowski and Hubert von Meyerinck, known as "Hubsi"; the young journalist Billy Wilder, later the director of *Lost Weekend* and *Some Like it Hot;* Erich Maria Remarque, soon to become world famous as the author of *All Quiet on the Western Front.* The great air ace Ernst Udet often dropped by the table. The director Geza von Cziffra wrote in his memoirs: "If I want to portray the Marlene of those days I must state: she was anything but a sex bomb. Not even a little sex bomb. She was like a free and easy boy, and with her buddylike comradeship she stifled every possible emotion of most of her would-be dates."

According to von Cziffra, Marlene greatly attracted Remarque and Udet, but remained "involved" only with Forst. Von Cziffra garishly describes Marlene's spending her evenings hobnobbing with gorgeous transvestites in ball gowns and high heels and crimson lipstick, or dropping by the Ring Club, of which she was not a member; it was an organization which permitted membership only to those who had served at least three years in jail. According to von Schiffra, she was seen frequently at the Silhouette, the White Rose, Germanic Power, and Always Faithful, exotic and notorious night spots of the era. She was also seen at the bar of the Hotel Eden with the great comedian Max Pallenberg; his wife, the singer Fritzi Massary; and the novelists Leonhard Frank and Heinrich Mann.

Fritzi Massary, who died several years ago, told me during an interview at her Los Angeles house in 1965:

"Marlene was easily able to hold her own with our circle. She had the greatest capacity a person can have: she could laugh at herself. I know she always told me that I had a great influence on her style, though I think Waldoff and Lion influenced her more deeply.

"She had a good grasp of politics. She knew that within a few years Germany would be a fascist state. I think even then she was thinking of working in England or America so that her child would not have to grow up in a totalitarian system.

"Most of us at the time were giddy; we drank too much, and sniffed cocaine, though of course I didn't because of my performing. But she was serious, despite her self-mockery and her irony.

"She was filled with pity and understanding of the fleetingness of life. That gave a poetry, a feeling of energy and the heart's seasons, which made her supreme as a performer."

It must seem paradoxical, even in the 1970s, that Marlene was able to sustain her marriage and her relationship with her little daughter Heidede despite her journey to Vienna, her apparent affair with Forst, and her frequent nightclubbing and performing. The fact is that she had become an emancipated woman, living with freedom and by her own rules.

She took Heidede for little excursions in the Schöneberger Volkspark or to the Zoological Gardens, and bought her toys and dolls, more than she could afford; but she also was seen everywhere with Forst. In Berlin in the late 1920s, nobody saw anything extraordinary in this.

In late 1927, Marlene learned that Marcellus Schiffer, husband of Margo Lion, had written a new revue, *It's in the Air,* with music by the sparkling Mischa Spoliansky. Schiffer was now at the peak of his fame. He had published a notorious book of immoral fairy tales in which every little child was turned into a wicked monster, every dear old granny became a witch, and every wicked stepmother became a nunlike picture of virtue. He shocked Berlin with a picture of Sisters of Mercy going to heaven with crosses thrust between their legs. He and his wife gave parties at which everybody was expected to bring the most hideously tasteless gift they could find. Thus, after one of these soirees, their apartment was full of plaster of Paris sculptures of pairs of lips, painted teakwood goblets, toilet seats, shoes filled with cement, and a coat made out of cats' tails.

Delighted with Marlene, Schiffer and Lion cast her in *It's in the Air* immediately. The show went into rehearsal in the early spring of 1928. The story took place in an elegant Berlin department store, a kind of satirical microcosm of Germany itself. In the hurry and distraction of shopping, a young mother and father lose their twin children, a boy and girl. The lost children are raised in secrecy by the store clerks. We see them at every phase of life. Finally, very old and infirm, the parents come to the store and inquire about their lost twins. Meanwhile, the children have married and have become parents themselves. When the old parents see their grandchildren, they believe that they are their own children. They had not realized that after twenty-five years their offspring would have grown up, because everything else—politics, art, domestic problems, social problems—is still the same.

The cast, headed by Oskar Karlweiss (later spelled Oscar Karlweis), Lion, and Marlene, played all the occupants of the store, including animals in the lost-and-found department, thieves, floorwalkers, telephone operators, supervisors, and managers. One of the most popular songs of the show was sung by Marlene with Hubert von Meyerinck. It was about kleptomaniacs, who sneak through the shop looking for things they can steal in order to excite themselves sexually. Marlene wore a green silk dress, tightly fitting and provocative, a little black hat, and red fox furs around her shoulders. She sported shoulder-length black gloves and diamond bracelets on each wrist. Von Meyerinck wore an elegant black suit with a white waistcoat, white gloves, and a white silk hat. The ditty included lyrics like:

> We steal as birds do
> In spite of the fact
> We are rich!
>
> We do it for sexual
> Kicks!

The title song of *It's in the Air,* sung by Marlene with von Meyerinck, Oskar Karlweiss, and Margo Lion, was delivered at breakneck speed by the principals in order to suggest that they themselves were carried into the air. The lyrics also contained engagingly spiteful observations about contemporary Berlin. But the song which put Marlene on top of the heap was her stunning duet with Margo Lion, "My Best Girl Friend," which ran:

> When the best friend
> Meets the best friend
> And goes to buy lingerie,
> They both go quite astray!
> They wander through town
> And talk nonsense!

The song continues with a rallentando in which the two girls indicate that although they are the best of friends, they are also more comfortable when they are not together. This cynical twist was typical of Schiffer's wit, and the lesbian implication is obvious. The idea is that these two girls are very close but that when they meet a rivalry invariably develops. The subtle implication that they are buying underwear not only to impress but perhaps to seduce each other is woven into the number.

It's in the Air was an immediate smash hit. Spoliansky's ironical music and Schiffer's devastating libretto knocked the audi-

ence cold. "My Best Girl Friend" brought the normally jaded
Berliners to their feet for a standing ovation that lasted twenty
minutes, and five encores had to be given before they would sit
down. Overnight, Marlene and Margo Lion were the toasts of
Berlin. Alfred Kerr wrote: "The songs are shrill and sharp, spinning, mockingly suave. Lion is charmingly unreasonable and
spiteful and Marlene Dietrich, more gentle in her satire, is
equally effective." This observation, from the dean of German
theater critics, pushed Marlene over the edge to fame. One
evening to celebrate, she, Walter Reisch and other friends went
to the dress rehearsal of *Die Dreigroschenoper (The Three-
penny Opera)*, Kurt Weill's and Bertolt Brecht's masterpiece
based on John Gay's *The Beggar's Opera*. They listened, en-
tranced, to song after song. Reisch recalls: "But only one song
made Marlene say, 'That's going to be a world hit.' It was the
organ grinder's song.

"We all thought she was crazy. It was a show with so many
numbers that seemed far more extraordinary. It took many
years, but Marlene was proven right. That organ grinder's song
became 'Mack the Knife.' "

After the run of *It's in the Air* ended, Marlene went into two
Bernard Shaw plays, both staged at the Komödie Theater in
1928. In *Misalliance*, retitled *Parents and Children* (after the
name of Shaw's preface to the play), she played Hypatia, the
liberated daughter of a middle-class family who shocks her el-
ders by frankly dwelling on the physical beauty of the men she
is interested in, and who chases a pilot who has crashed near her
house.

She was knowingly cast: it was an immensely shrewd idea to
have this Free Woman of the twenties play the part. "She is
arrogant as Shaw wanted her to be," wrote Ihering, while Kerr
wrote, "When she sits downstage and shows her legs, one for-
gets the whole middle-class social theme. Her legs are certainly
better than any of the mediocre cast, to say the least."

In waistcoat, man's shirt, striped tie, and pleated skirt (the
play, first produced in 1910, was updated to the 1920s) Marlene
exerted a distinctly ambivalent appeal. The photographs of the

production show her at her most elegantly cool and composed, and one is prepared to believe that she responded warmly to the direction of Heinz Hilpert.

During the run of the play, Marlene formed a close friendship with another actress in the cast, Lili Darvas, whom she admired for her intelligence and polished technique, and who was an example to her in the playing of light comedy. Marlene, unlike most performers, never hesitated to gain knowledge from others, or unselfishly to praise them. Some years ago the late Lili Darvas said: "Marlene already had extraordinary equipment when I worked with her. She had the rarest capacity of all, the capacity to be completely still on the stage and yet to command the complete attention of an audience. Another actress might work hysterically, rearranging objects on mantelpieces, straightening curtains, or sliding her hands up and down her body. Marlene would simply sit downstage smoking a cigarette very slowly and sexily, and people forgot the rest of us were around. She had such natural poise, there was so much melody in her voice, she had such an economy of gesture, that she became as absorbing to the viewer as a Modigliani. For years afterwards, I admired and marveled at this girl. She had the one essential star quality: she could be magnificent doing nothing."

In the same short 1928 season, Marlene was an amusing Eve in *Back to Methuselah*. In a flesh-colored garment which covered her from head to toe, Marlene appeared to be nude, a ravishing sylph in a baroque version of the Garden of Eden. Once again she had excellent reviews and brought an unexpected quality to the role, a suggestion of the eternal feminine. According to contemporary reviewers, she managed to suggest the precise quality of eroticism which brought about man's downfall from grace. One has reason to believe that she lit fires in the hearts of all her male watchers, and Willi Forst has written that he was extraordinarily proud of her in the role.

In 1929, Marlene appeared in a film directed by Robert Land, who had made *Princess Olala*. The title was *I Kiss Your Hand, Madame*. In some versions, songs were dubbed onto this silent movie to cash in on the newfangled vogue for talkies; these were sung by Marlene and by Richard Tauber, who dubbed for the leading man, Harry Liedtke. The movie is today in the collection of George Eastman House. In it, Marlene plays a ruthless Parisienne who uses men with contempt. She is at her best, temperamental, passionate, and cynical.

Here in embryo is the callous Lola-Lola of *The Blue Angel,* humiliating her suitor. Throughout the movie, Marlene is very much in command, whether powdering her nose viciously in an enormous close-up or smoothing her skirt over her thighs as her lover approaches, deliberately exciting him and yet, when he kisses her, coyly thrusting him away. The woman in the film, given the oddly masculine name of Laurence Gerard, has a distinctly bisexual look. No doubt it was this movie which made her future mentor and director Josef von Sternberg say of her performance, "She looked like a man in drag."

No sooner had she finished this picture than Marlene rushed into another, *The Woman One Longs For,* directed by the talented Kurt (later Curtis) Bernhardt. Set partly on a train, this was the story of a glamorous woman who plays one man against another until finally she gets her comeuppance by being shot dead in the last reel. Bernhardt says: "In 1959, the UFA studios in Berlin asked me to please attend a luncheon because they had invited Marlene, and I was the only one left from the old days. I did. I kept way in the background, but she saw me coming in; she rushed toward me and kissed me and kissed me; she whispered into my ear, 'The woman one does *not* long for.'

"When I hired her, I had seen her in *Misalliance.* In the fancy version of hers, she was an innocent little girl in acting school when the great director from America came and took her and put her in the lead in *The Blue Angel!* Absurd! Marlene propaganda!

"She looked gorgeous in *Misalliance.* Ravishing! I asked my boss if he would let me use her in the lead. He said, 'Who is Marlene Dietrich?' I told him to see her in the show. I don't know whether he did or not, but at all events he wanted someone who was a big name. He turned me down. Finally he gave way to my insistence and hired her. Her costar, Fritz Kortner, was very, very big. Ugliness itself, but a fine actor. She was talented, too.

"She had a quirk which I found out about only when we started working. She was so conscious of her face, and that her nose had a tilt upwards at the end, that she refused to do profile shots. She kept her face in the direction of the spotlight which was behind the camera, so that when she had to talk to somebody who was to the right or the left of her she would simply peep at him out of the corner of her eye, she would never face him! It drove Kortner crazy! For a thousand rubles she wouldn't move her bloody face! I got pretty impatient with her!

"We shot most of the picture on the Blue Train, which we took over—it was the great train that went to Paris. We started off in the Bahnhof Station in Berlin and went out a few miles.

"Marlene looked fantastic. But she was a pain in the neck as an actress. Kortner, who wanted—excuse me—to lay her, defended her. It came to a kind of tension between him and me, which was completely unnecessary, and all because of Madame! Maybe she hit the chalk marks for von Sternberg, but not for me! She was quite insubordinate!

"I once visited Marlene and her husband during the shooting. Across from their apartment was a tiny little park. She took me for a walk with little Heidede. She bent down to the child, pressed her against her heart, and kissed her. And the child said something which, roughly translated, would be, 'Let go of me, you old goat!' "

Marlene obtained an almost continuous stream of work in the early months of 1929. In *The Ship of Lost Men* she played an American millionairess aviatrix, in leather suit and goggles, who crashes near a ship filled with pirates, contrabandists, and rum runners. At first, she is mistaken for a man, but when the crew realizes she is a woman, she narrowly escapes gang rape. Oddly enough, an almost identical real-life episode was to occur during her tour of the fronts in World War II.

The film was pictorially handsome, directed by the great Maurice Tourneur, but Marlene was wasted as an ingenue; the chief interest of her performance is that she played almost throughout in male attire. The English actor Robin Irvine appeared with Marlene in *The Ship of Lost Men*. He remembered her later in her dressing room, playing a waltz by Waldteufel on her musical saw. She was wearing a black tailor-made man's suit, collar and tie, and brogues. She went everywhere with a portable gramophone on which she never stopped playing Irving Berlin's "Always," and "La fille aux cheveux d'or," by Debussy. She was also obsessed with Ravel.

Irvine recalled that her love of music dominated her life. She liked sentimental music and invited him home to the Kaiserallee, where she played French works of the turn of the century. They went dancing together when Rudi was working at night, in the various ballrooms of the city.

Irvine recalled that, always superstitious, Marlene carried a good luck charm with her everywhere: a Negro doll (or golliwog) she had been given as a child. This, and a Japanese doll, she even used as props in her films, beginning with *I Kiss Your Hand, Madame* and *The Blue Angel*.

In 1929, she made the film *Nights of Love* with Willi Forst, a jumble of nonsense memorable for one thing: the Brazilian version contained a sequence in which Forst and Marlene appeared to be masturbating each other under a table. Needless to say, Brazilian actors' hands were substituted for the sequence. When Marlene heard about this from her friend, the writer Walter Reisch, she laughed so violently that she fell over.

Marlene's major setback of the period was losing the part of Lulu in G. W. Pabst's film version of *Pandora's Box*, by Wedekind. She would have been fascinating as this ruthless charmer who destroys men's lives. She gave a very good audition, but Pabst, about to hire her, happened to see a movie entitled *A Girl in Every Port*, with Louise Brooks, a former Ziegfeld girl. At once he dropped Marlene and hired Miss Brooks.

Three

Birth of a Blue Angel

In the summer of 1929, Marlene's friend and admirer, the effervescent Mischa Spoliansky, recommended her for the role of Mabel, the cynical, money-mad American heiress to thirty million dollars, in *Zwei Krawatten (Two Bow Ties)*, a satirical "revue in nine pictures," to open at the Berliner Theater in September. Spoliansky had composed the radiant score, with book and lyrics by the Expressionist playwright Georg Kaiser. The plot was an antic conceit: at a grand ball, Jean, a black-tied waiter loaded down with a tray covered in champagne glasses, has an unexpected stroke of luck.

A gangster, fleeing the police, pays him a thousand marks, a tombola (lottery) ticket, and a ticket to the ball to exchange bow ties with him to facilitate the gangster's getaway. The tombola ticket wins Jean a free, first-class trip on a luxury liner to America. Mabel, who is booked on the same steamer, toasts him at the ball, and a romance begins.

Aboard the liner, they carry on an elaborate flirtation, surreptitiously watched by his fiancée, Trude. Mabel invites Jean to Chicago to meet her rich aunt, Mrs. Robinson. After a party for a senator in Chicago, the couple announce their engagement in Miami. The ending is bittersweet. Jean decides to return to Trude, only to find she has fallen heir to ten million dollars more than Mabel.

With its cosmopolitan charm, its snatches of American dialogue, its acidulous lyrics and lilting, hummable score, *Two Bow
Ties* was a joy, and Marlene responded at once to the material.
Kaiser and Spoliansky had most expertly tailored the part for
her. Her conflicting moods of ironical humor and world-weariness, her shifting feelings of excitement and coldness were
adroitly captured in the writing.

She had several good opportunities in the show. Kaiser's lyrics
for her to sing were harshly materialistic: "Wonderful /
fabulous / the way he makes his career! / He makes money, he
makes money! / I am bewitched by money / And one who has
it / If I look at his bank account / My knees grow weak!" She
delivered this cynical Kaiser lyric with the utmost skill. She was,
say the critics, equally expert in her duet with the romantic
Trude ("TRUDE: The love of my heart loves me! MABEL [heart-
lessly]: She speaks of *Love!* / Of love she speaks / She speaks of
Love! / Of Love! Love! Love!")

Two Bow Ties opened at the Berliner Theater on September
15, 1929. Its cool attack on American millionaires and the capi-
talist system unwittingly foretold the stock market crash only a
few weeks later, and World War II. Marlene was joined by Hans
Albers (handsome and dashing as Jean) and by Rosa Valetti (as
Mrs. Robinson), a dumpy, frowsy, inspired actress who sported
a pet parrot and to whom Marlene had become close when they
appeared together in *Broadway.*

From her first entrance at the ball, calling out, in English,
"Where is the man who won the grand prize?" Marlene made
a sensation. For once the rival critics Ihering and Kerr agreed:
she and her fellow performers were admirable. Berlin talked
about the scene in which Marlene coldly leaned against the
ship's rail or walked with Albers past her hidden rival, a ma-
chine-made wind catching her long red skirt and whipping it
tightly around her legs as she greeted Albers with an air of
indifference which only half-concealed her sexual interest.

During the first weeks of the run of *Two Bow Ties* the Fates
were at the spinning wheel. The first protagonist in the drama
who would, as fortune tellers say, change her life, was Emil

Jannings, perhaps the leading star of Germany at the time, then at his peak following his great success in *The Last Command.*

Built like a stoker, with brutal shoulders and a corpulent but still powerful body, Jannings was a miserable human being. His favorite possession was a parrot called Mauritz Stiller, given him by Garbo. Uncultured, and semiliterate, he liked to stuff himself with heavy German food. While eating, he referred to himself in the third person, making remarks like: "Emil does not like this big sausage. Emil is crazy about the cheese dumplings." He was strictly in pictures for the money. He kept all of his capital, about a quarter of a million dollars, in a large iron box under his bed. During a recent visit to Hollywood, his secretary, Hans Hollander, had taken the box and deposited it in the nearest bank. Jannings asked to see the bank. It looked like a hot dog joint. Jannings said to his secretary: "You must be out of your mind! The *building* isn't worth two hundred and fifty thousand dollars!" He immediately collected the box and returned it to its place under his bed.

Jannings, who needed to fear competition from no one, was convinced that everyone in a picture was trying to steal his scenes. If he didn't like the way a sequence was being directed, he would clown so outrageously that it had to be completely reshot.

The other person who was about to affect Marlene's life was the great Austrian-American director Josef "von" Sternberg. Von Sternberg—he had added the "von" himself—was also at the pinnacle of his career, having directed Jannings in *The Last Command;* he had also made the first major gangster picture, *Underworld,* and the highly praised *The Docks of New York.* Von Sternberg boasted a shock of dark hair, broodingly somber brown eyes, and a drooping black mustache. He had pale skin and a small, fragile body that was nevertheless beautifully formed. His hands were his most striking feature: white and almost translucent, with manicured fingernails, they were the hands of a decadent poet. He leaned on a cane or a knobbed stick, and affected poison-green coats with an air of conscious and chilly pessimism. He asserted power over others by staring at them coldly, under heavy, snakelike lids, his mouth a contemptuous thin line and his expression one of having just discovered, inside a Fabergé eggcup, a particularly large and rotten egg.

There were endless legends about him. Annoyed with a Mae Murray picture he was making, he turned the camera upward and took pictures of the cobwebbed ceiling before walking off the set. He used to stand in the Hollywood Hills looking at the lights below and crying, "My Hollywood!" When visitors arrived he would appear to be casually reading the poems of Hafiz in the original Persian, a language with which he was not familiar. When he went to a restaurant there had to be six large black grapes on the table or he would not sit down.

If he was not a genius, it was not for want of trying. If people had not believed in him, he would most certainly have invented people who did. Under his pose of cold and grandiose self-sufficiency, von Sternberg was a sensitive and passionate sentimentalist whose love letters to his wife, the actress Riza Royce, still make incandescent reading.

He had arrived in Berlin three weeks before *Two Bow Ties* opened, accompanied by his wife. Shortly afterward, the couple moved into the apartment of the producer-director Erwin Piscator, where they unearthed a hypodermic needle from one of the armchairs.

Erich Pommer of UFA (the largest German studio) had invited von Sternberg to come to Berlin to make a version of Heinrich Mann's novel *Professor Unrat*. He had done so at the urgent request of Karl Volmoeller, author of *The Miracle*, who was the go-between arranging deals with Hollywood. Since von Sternberg had worked with Jannings before, it was felt he would be ideal to direct the temperamental star in this story of a professor of English in a German provincial seaport town who falls in love disastrously with a singer, Rosa Frölich.

The dramatist Carl Zuckmayer wrote to me in 1976: "Without von Sternberg the film would never have been what it was to become. Karl Volmoeller wrote not a line. He was given a credit by UFA because he was our contact man with Hollywood, and it was he who inspired von Sternberg to come to Berlin and convinced UFA that von Sternberg was the only masterful director for our film.

"Volmoeller took part in our sessions with Pommer, Jannings, von Sternberg, and I, and acted as a kind of interpreter, since none of us spoke correct English at the time and von Sternberg did not like to remember his German descent. Before von Sternberg arrived in Europe, I had written a basic dialogue treatment which laid the groundwork of the shooting and contained the construction and all-important situations of the film, including most of the dialogue.

"Some of these I could take from Heinrich Mann's novel. The end of the film, in which the professor is shown utterly defeated, and returns, a broken man, to his old schoolroom, was von Sternberg's own invention, but I introduced the character of Lola-Lola's lover Mazeppa to give a chance in movies to my old friend Hans Albers.

"The other author, Robert Liebmann, did very little. He only wrote a part of the lyrics to Frederick Hollander's songs. These songs, of course, were not contained in my original script."

The von Sternbergs had gone to Switzerland, where they met Karl Volmoeller, who traveled with them across the border into Germany. They discussed an idea for Jannings, the circus story to follow *Professor Unrat,* and both expressed relief that a Pommer idea to do the life of Rasputin for Jannings had been dropped for a variety of reasons.

Volmoeller and Zuckmayer both wanted Marlene to play Lola-Lola, but Erich Pommer, head of UFA, in bed with a broken ankle, screamed "Not that whore!" and refused to consider the idea. As a result, a talent hunt began, accompanied by the usual ballyhoo, for girls to play Rosa Fröhlich, whose name was changed to Lola-Lola, a corruption of Lulu, the villainess of Wedekind's *Pandora's Box.* Von Sternberg turned this small-time trollop into a vicious macho symbol of woman as predator, the last role in the world Marlene, a liberated woman who admired women, would want to play. Von Sternberg wanted Brigitte Helm, but she was busy with another picture and then had an appendectomy. His wife suggested Phyllis Haver, but she had married a millionaire and retired from the screen. Erich Pommer wanted the famous Berlin actress, Trude Hesterberg. Frederick Hollander, who had been engaged to write the lyrics and score, wanted Lucie Mannheim, and with Hollander at the piano she gave an expert but quite unsuitable audition for von Sternberg.

After six weeks, there was still no leading lady. According to Walter Reisch, one evening Marlene, who had no interest whatsoever in applying for the role, met von Sternberg at a party at Max Reinhardt's castle. She created a stir playing Toselli's *Serenade* on the musical saw she had been given in Vienna, her skirt drawn up. Von Sternberg was aroused, but despite his strong sexual interest, he did not consider Marlene a prospect for Lola-Lola. He had seen a picture of her submitted by the manager Max Pick, and had passed it over with the words, "Her bottom's OK, but don't we need a face as well?"

Two nights after the Reinhardt party, he went with his wife, Mrs. Erich Pommer, Karl Volmoeller, and a close friend—a Viennese champagne bottler named Johnny Sojka—to see Hans Albers in *Two Bow Ties;* Albers had been tentatively chalked in for the part of the juvenile lead in *Professor Unrat,* as Zuckmayer had wished. Von Sternberg also wanted to see Rosa Valetti as Mrs. Robinson, feeling she might be ideal for another part in the picture. Ironically, Jannings and his friend Luis Adlon, owner of the Adlon Hotel, said to von Sternberg over drinks before he left for the theater: "Since you're going to look at Albers and Valetti anyway, why not look at the girl Dietrich as well? She's an erotic earthquake, an elemental."

Both Marlene and Hans Albers had been told that the von Sternbergs and Karl Volmoeller would be in the audience that night. Arriving late, seated in the front row, von Sternberg looked so rapturously at Marlene's insolently self-assured, leggy pose at the ship's rail that the jealous Hans Albers told the stage manager in the interval, "I could have pissed on his head."

Von Sternberg knew at once that he had his Lola-Lola. The role of Mabel was the essence of Berlin, sexual and cynical all at once, satiated with worldly pleasures. But there was another quality as well: a quality of tenderness and warmth, a womanliness alongside the veiled masculinity of the direct stare. This quality of sex without gender proved intoxicating to the young director.

According to Riza von Sternberg, her husband accompanied her backstage and asked Marlene to see him the following day. He also saw Albers and Valetti, and hired them at once. A casting director telephoned Marlene in the morning at her apartment in the Kaiserallee suggesting that she come in for an interview, and Willi Forst urged her to go ahead.

Everyone agrees that she was quite unenthusiastic about reading for a part which most young actresses in Berlin would have given almost anything to obtain. Still convinced that movies were inferior to the stage, and not at all keen about playing a whore and a cheap nightclub singer, she probably also remembered Jannings's obnoxiousness when she had made *Tragedy of Love.* She had seen von Sternberg's films, and though she had liked his direction of Jannings in *The Last Command* and George Bancroft in *Underworld,* she had not liked his handling of the exotic actress Evelyn Brent in these pictures.

The well-known Berlin actor's manager, Alice Bluman, will never forget Marlene's arrival at UFA. She ran into her as she entered the main office door on a cold, gray afternoon. "Marlene was wearing black furs—I think they were astrakhans—a tall, Russian-style hat, and a muff. She was in high boots and opaque stockings.

"She was very flustered, more than uneasy. She said, 'They want me to play this prostitute, Blümchen.' That was her affectionate term for me. 'The von Losch family never wanted me to do movies in the first place. Now I'm going to be a tart; assuming they want me, what will my family say? It will horrify my mother!'

"I could see she was genuine, not just being coy. She really didn't want to do the cocotte. And anyway, everyone thought, Trude Hesterberg would get the part."

At von Sternberg's office Pommer and Jannings watched her

walk up and down and dismissed her. Jannings, who now regretted having recommended that von Sternberg consider her, said: "She's different offstage. She won't photograph. She veils her eyes. Cows do that—when they're giving birth."

The two men walked out. Von Sternberg said, "I want you to test for Lola-Lola."

She hung her head. "Nobody can photograph me. I'm terrible in pictures. They say I don't open my eyes."

Despite her reluctance, Willi Forst persuaded her to proceed with a test. Without warning, somebody pushed her with the flat of his hand onto the sound stage. She sang a German song by Peter Kreuder which went, "Why cry when you leave someone? / There's someone else waiting at the next corner," and, she says, an American song, "You're the Cream in My Coffee."

Von Sternberg was standing there, wearing a floppy hat, a green velvet jacket, and white ducks, and carrying a long cane. The composer Frederick Hollander was at the piano. She sweated as she stumbled through the songs, and Hollander, a beginner, was so nervous his fingers missed several notes. Von Sternberg watched her with seeming impassivity, like a sulky Persian cat. Finally he put his hand up to end the performance.

On the verge of tears, Marlene stumbled down a ramp into the orchestra pit. She was convinced she had failed. She did not care, since she hadn't wanted the part in the first place, but she hated to be humiliated. Hollander recalls what followed. Von Sternberg walked after her and muttered something to her. She didn't hear what he said, so he repeated it louder: "You're good!" She replied, "I can stand many things in life, Herr von Sternberg. But don't kid me, don't lie to me! Why don't you tell the truth? I'm no good, am I? I've had so many years of disappointment. . . ." Von Sternberg embraced her reassuringly. "You'll hear from us, Fraulein Dietrich," he said.

Next day, von Sternberg ran the tests of Lucie Mannheim and Marlene for Pommer and the other UFA executives. They all agreed that Mannheim was the best. Von Sternberg sardonically pretended to agree, then told them they were "crazy."

Finally, Pommer settled the matter by telling von Sternberg that he had the right to cast whom he chose and that the studio would honor that right. When Jannings' wife, the actress Gussi Holl, told Jannings to cast Marlene, the matter was settled.

First von Sternberg, then Pommer's assistant telephoned Marlene to let her know she had been chosen. She received the news without much excitement. Indeed, she said later, she felt considerable unease. She would have to act in the film and continue in *Two Bow Ties* at night. With a daughter only just over four years old, this was a serious problem for a mother. She was afraid she would be neglecting the child at a formative stage. Moreover, she undoubtedly must have sensed von Sternberg's sexual interest in her, an interest she could not by any means reciprocate.

There are numerous conflicting accounts of her friends' celebration of her victory after the performance of *Two Bow Ties* that night. Frederick Hollander described in his memoirs rushing into what he called "the homosexual nightclub" Silhouette to tell her she had won the role. He wrote: "Some people say she fainted. Actually, she ordered champagne all around. After she heard the news, everything became a silhouette." Later that evening, she walked into the bar of the Eden Hotel and told a group of friends: "You've always said I can't act. Now you'll know you're wrong." Whereupon the group is supposed to have replied in chorus, "You *still* can't act!"

Perhaps the one element in this entire project Marlene genuinely warmed to was the music. It was soon placed in the safe hands of Hollander, an inspired gnome whose songs she was to carry with her for the rest of her career. He wrote many of them while on the toilet, the music manuscript paper fastened with brass tacks to a message board in front of him. Absent-minded, he tended to wear one black shoe and one brown shoe, one blue sock and one white sock, and forgot to eat when he was in the grip of a musical idea.

News of Marlene's selection brought a horde of reporters to her door, but even at that early stage she proved resistant to interviews. She despised journalists and in later years had little reason to change her mind. She spent many afternoons in Pommer's office, while Hollander played and sang the songs he had composed for the picture. He began by bawling out the lyric

> Ich bin die fesche Lola
> Der Liebling der Saison . . .
>
> I am the lovely Lola
> The darling of the hour . . .

Each time a new song came along, von Sternberg, Volmoeller, Zuckmayer, Pommer, and even Marlene whooped with joy. They all insisted that the picture needed a love song. Hollander pointed out that a woman who could not love, who was a cold, heartless prostitute, could not sing a love song. Instead, he locked himself in his toilet and came up with another song. This was the ravishing "From head to toe / I'm made for love / For that's my world, and nothing else at all . . ." (In English it became "Falling in love again / Never wanted to," which was ridiculously contrary to Lola-Lola's character.)

After he heard the song for the first time, Jannings turned to Marlene and said: "If you sing that, my girl, I'll be finished! Nobody will ever see *me* on the screen!"

Day after day, Hollander poured out his acrid music while a visitor from America, Buster Keaton, sat beside him, watching his small hands flitter like white mice across the keys.

To perform the music, the Weintraub Syncopators, a jazz band which performed all over Berlin, were engaged. They had made a hit playing in *Charley's Aunt* with Curt Bois, and had issued several successful recordings. The youngest member of the band, Horst Graff, spent many evenings teaching Rudi the saxophone while Marlene was acting in *Two Bow Ties*.

Shooting began on *Die Blaue Engel (The Blue Angel)*, the new title of *Professor Unrat*, on November 4, 1929. Marlene, tired after late-night shows and a succession of nightclubs, had to arrive at the studio exceptionally early to get into makeup. Von Sternberg changed her hair, dying it a brassy blonde, and drew a silver line down the middle of her nose with a small, wax-stiffened brush in order to reduce its width and give the impression of straightness. The silver line became her trademark for years. He made her look at the camera, not in the fixed way she had done before, but with a glance of bold contempt.

Von Sternberg made the extraordinary demand that the entire film be shot in chronological order. Pommer, autocratic and dictatorial, screamed with rage at this announcement, since it would mean that sets used in one part of the picture would have to be retained, occupying much-needed studio space until von Sternberg was ready to use them again. Worse, von Sternberg decided to shoot the German version on Mondays, the English version on Tuesdays, and so on through the week. This method was unheard of even in those very early days of talkies, and involved considerable problems for the technicians.

Not only did Marlene feel the role of Lola-Lola was demeaning of women, she found working on the picture an ordeal. Technique at the time was primitive: the cameras were enormous blimps, the size of four telephone booths, in which the operators often fainted from lack of air. Because radiators hissed and spat and the noise would be recorded on the sensitive film, they had to be turned off, and the cold was cruel. Marlene had to play most of her scenes in the thinnest clothes and in tights, and only her willpower prevented her from showing her discomfiture.

Von Sternberg, in love with his star already, seemed to be obsessed, drugged, all through the shooting. She admired him. Her infallible instinct for talent made her see his striking command of the medium, his aesthetic sensibility and his superior knowledge of every aspect of lighting. At night she would watch the rushes, seated on the floor with her arm on his knee, like a courtier or a page, fascinated and repelled by the image she presented on the screen.

Everyone who knew them at the time confirms that from the beginning there was tension in their relationship. Von Sternberg, besides a romantic obsession with women which his then wife Riza still confirms, undoubtedly looked down at women from some macho position. In all of his pictures up to that time, women had been villains or romantic fools. Yet now for the first time he was confronted by a woman with an intellect, a woman with a will as strong as his own, with a fully developed sense of order and beauty, who could be his equal. In an attempt to make her act, he forced her to rehearse or to repeat scenes over and over again. She claimed she didn't know what she was doing, but she made Lola-Lola, the brutal, humiliating whore who destroys the professor and makes him crow like a cock, disturbingly real.

She never ceased, she told me, to hate the part of Lola-Lola. But she was fascinated by von Sternberg's artistry: she knew at once that she was part of a perverse and extraordinary work of art made by a remarkable artist. This made her serve the purpose of art by adding her own brush strokes. She remained liberated even when she was a captive in an artifact.

Their relationship was never soft and sentimental. It was a fierce, argumentative confrontation of male virility and female energy. They collided, and sparks flew. They discussed, they tangled, they sought each other's deepest feelings out. In all of this, Riza von Sternberg and Rudi Sieber suffered.

Fritz Maurischaat remembers: "I was in a little place near Berlin at the time when I wandered into an orchard of pear and apple trees. There was a heavy scent in the air, and it was a golden afternoon. Suddenly, I saw Rudolph Sieber lying under the trees. He looked very sad. 'Hello,' I said. 'What's the matter with you?' There were tears in his eyes when he said, 'Marlene is constantly with von Sternberg. Today they're watching *The Three Musketeers* at the Grosses Schauspielhaus. They have left me all alone. Oh, God, how I ache for her!' "

Making the English version proved to be an especially harrowing experience for Marlene. Having never studied English in great depth at school, and having as background only the feeble teaching efforts of Elsie Grace and her absurd nursery rhymes, Marlene used a coach. She desperately wanted to please von Sternberg.

Singing "Falling in Love Again," she stumbled. When she came to the line, "Men cluster to me / Like moths around a flame," she could not say the word "moths." It kept coming out as "moss." Von Sternberg took her through the song 235 times over two days of shooting, until the Weintraub Syncopators, accompanying her, were as ready to collapse as she was. Finally, von Sternberg threw up his hands in despair. "All right!" he said to Horst Graff of the Syncopators. "When she comes to the word 'moths' I want you to shout, 'Bring me a beer, bring me a beer!' from the crowd."

Graff obeyed. As a result, nobody heard Marlene mispronounce the word. Thirty-six years later in Australia, where the Weintraub Syncopators had settled just before World War II, Marlene was giving a concert. Just as she reached the word "moths" in the song, Graff shouted out, "Bring me a beer, bring me a beer!" She didn't hear him.

Emil Jannings, seeing the picture stolen from him by an actress who appeared not to be acting at all, was hysterical throughout the shooting. According to Peter Kreuder, he kept rushing into von Sternberg's office, moaning, holding his head, and complaining about that "nincompoop idiot fool I'm working with!" He would tell anyone who would listen, "How dare this creature play opposite me, the great Emil Jannings!" until someone was rude enough to point out that he had recommended her in the first place. According to Peter Kreuder, he got his big chance in the scene in which Professor Unrat, humiliated by Lola-Lola, attacks her violently. He rushed off the stage, seized her, and flung her against a couch. She tried to pry his fingers from her neck. It was useless. Before anyone realized what was happening, he started to strangle her—and he wasn't just acting. Suddenly von Sternberg snapped to attention and dragged Jannings loose. Hans Albers struck Jannings across the face. Jannings burst into tears and ran from the set. Marlene, whose genuine terror is recorded indelibly on the screen, was rushed to her dressing room and revived. She carried the marks on her neck for weeks afterward. Jannings narrowly escaped being charged with attempted murder.

During the shooting of the picture, it became known in Berlin that a great star was being born. Von Sternberg was determined to secure a Hollywood contract for Marlene. He bombarded his old boss at Paramount, Adolph Zukor, and Zukor's second-in-command, Jesse L. Lasky, with telegrams and letters demanding that they sign up this new and exotic beauty. Meanwhile, the producer Joe Pasternak, who was later to make the Deanna Durbin and Mario Lanza films, was asked by Universal to watch Marlene working. "She was the sexiest woman I had ever seen," Pasternak says. "She moved like a cat. She was glamor personified. When she bestrode a stool and opened her legs, showing frilly pants, it was an almost brutal invitation. The moment I saw her do the scene, I knew every red-blooded man in the world would want to answer that invitation.

"I knew she would be world-famous, I knew she would have the one essential ingredient of international stardom: millions of guys would want to make love to her. Finally, my director on the picture I was doing, Bill Dieterle, said: 'You're spending more time on von Sternberg's set than you are on your own. Why? Aren't you more interested in working with *me?*'

" 'Yes,' I said, 'but you're not a woman in tights.' "

Pasternak and Universal were beaten by Paramount. Lasky, hearing that his old colleague Sidney Kent was going to Berlin, asked him to cable an immediate report on Marlene from the rushes. SHE'S SENSATIONAL, Kent cabled; HIRE HER, Lasky cabled back. WAIT A MINUTE, Zukor cabled Kent, and took the next ship to Germany to check out the merchandise.

Tiny and foxlike in a tall fur cap, Zukor bowed, sweeping his cap almost to the floor, as he entered Marlene's dressing room for their first meeting. Surrounded by a cloud of perfume, looking at her legs, he felt slightly dizzy. Within five minutes, he had offered her a contract. She was not impressed, dreading the idea of leaving her daughter, but she accepted to please von Sternberg.

Von Sternberg left for America on the last day of shooting, not even waiting to supervise the dubbing, mixing, and scoring of the picture. He told the musical arranger Peter Kreuder to be sure to do one thing: he must leave some black frames of film after Marlene's "I am switched on to love / From head to toe."

The idea was that only darkness would be seen by the movie audience for almost a minute, thus cueing them in to applaud. But when the audience saw Marlene sing the song, perched on a barrel, her legs spread wide in those frilly pants, a tall silk hat perched rakishly on her blonde curls, they did not need to be cued. Black screen or no black screen, they would have applauded hysterically anyway.

Von Sternberg arranged in advance for fifty selected actors to be placed in the Gloriapalast Theater audience for the premiere. He told Kreuder (whose memoirs are the source of the following passages): "I don't know whether the audience would dare take the risk of applauding. Certainly, they'd be nervous to cheer after the song. The fifty actors can take care of that. When they leap to their feet and yell, everyone around them will follow them like sheep." Once again, this device, clever as it was, proved unnecessary. The rest of the audience was on its feet before the fifty planted actors could stand.

There were three performances in Berlin on the day of the premiere, and after the second and third of these, the principals were to make appearances after the movie was shown. The stars foregathered in a special dressing room for sandwiches and champagne before going onstage. Kreuder reported in his memoirs that Jannings was brooding in a corner while Marlene and the others sat looking at the audience through the glass windows of the room, listening to snatches of dialogue and music as they floated up from the auditorium. When Kreuder came in during the middle of the second screening, Jannings leaped up threateningly and loomed over him with the air of a wounded rhinoceros. "I understand," Jannings said to Kreuder, "that you inserted fifteen meters of black film after Dietrich's big song. Is that correct?" "Yes," Kreuder nervously replied. Jannings continued, "You will immediately go up to the projection room, take the reel of film and a pair of scissors, and excise those feet!" Kreuder recalled: "I was aware of the reason for his fury. The fifteen meters of black film signified the birth of a world star. The star's name was *not* Emil Jannings."

"I added the fifteen meters on the instructions of the direc-

tor," Kreuder screamed at Jannings. "You are neither the director nor the musical director!" Jannings saw red: "Don't give me
such rubbish, or you'll get something from me you'll never
forget!" Kreuder stood his ground. Jannings hit Kreuder such a
powerful blow that the composer fell bleeding to the ground.
Then Kreuder picked himself up off the floor and stumbled out
of the artists' room. He did not cut out the black film.

When *The Blue Angel* came to an end, the audience stood
and roared its approval. It was an electric moment as the stars
took their bows. One can only speculate on Marlene's feelings
as, after eleven years of struggle, she knew she had achieved
her goal. No one was calling Jannings's name—or Albers's. They
called, not "Dietrich," but "Marlene! Marlene!" In ninety minutes Marlene had been launched internationally. Within two
weeks she was a household word in Europe, and within six
months her fame was known from coast to coast in America.

Despite her excitement, the third performance proved somewhat nerve-racking for Marlene. She had to catch the eleven
o'clock train for Bremerhaven in order to board the luxury liner
Bremen for New York. She was committed to taking her final
bows. Peter Kreuder recalls that he left the theater while she
was onstage to check that everything was in order. But he
hadn't realized that a mob of enthusiastic Berliners was outside
the Gloriapalast. Kreuder says that the audiences for the first
and second screenings had not left, but crowded every inch of
the lobby and the sidewalks outside. There were traffic jams for
miles around. Police were strung across the crowd, struggling
futilely to hold the people back. Fortunately, the UFA bosses
did not rely on a limousine to make its way through, but instead
provided Marlene with a large truck. The back of the truck was
lashed down with ropes. Her thirty-six pieces of luggage were
already stored in it.

Kreuder also says that as the applause was heard from the
theater following the last performance, the crowd outside
roared with all the force of a hurricane. A line of Prussian police,
their spiked helmets askew, formed a narrow alleyway in the
mob for Marlene and Willi Forst to rush to the back of the truck.

As she sprinted down the alley ahead of Willi, dressed in her magnificent white evening costume and ermine wrap, the crowd went berserk. A group of UFA officials literally flung Marlene and Forst into the truck. Sounding a klaxon horn, the truck thrust its way inch by inch through the crowd. On board the truck, Kreuder says he played the upright piano while the group drank champagne and tossed the glasses out into the street. At last they made their getaway. Marlene and Forst Charlestoned as the truck made a jolting, swaying progress through the dark streets of Berlin. At the Lehrter Station, porters whisked Marlene's luggage off the truck, and she jumped expertly to the ground. Left alone in the truck, Kreuder, very drunk, burst into tears.

Marlene, with Willi Forst and the actor Franz (later Francis) Lederer, who met her at the station, ran to the train. She leaned from the window as it drew out, holding a bouquet of roses and lilacs, and smiling triumphantly. She was on her way at last.

Four

To Hollywood

Marlene left Germany in 1930 without Rudi and Heidede, evidently not wanting to take such a small child from her home. She left at the right moment. Even while she had been making *The Blue Angel,* her country had grown black and swollen with decay. During the filming, the streets not far from UFA at Neubabelsberg had been filled with rioters and demonstrators, carrying garish placards which announced their dissatisfaction with mass unemployment. Sometimes, explosions had shaken the sound equipment, forcing scenes to be rerecorded. Hitler was already a poisonous influence in Berlin, screaming at rallies with a voice which conveyed the frustration most Germans felt in that sinister winter. The crazy extravagance, the hedonism of the late 1920s had evaporated in the depression. Hitler turned against the bankers along the Tiergartenstrasse, and the Jewish industrialists whom he blamed for Germany's plight.

Only six months after Marlene sailed on the *Bremen,* the newly elected Nazi members of the Reichstag would assemble in the Hotel Kaiserhof to declare allegiance to Hitler, the former postcard painter.

Marlene's departure for America was not only politic but symbolic. She was to become a symbol of a free Germany in exile, an inspiration for German expatriates whom she would devote herself to reestablishing across the Atlantic. To this day, the survivors worship her. When in later years Hitler offered her not only the chance to go back, with her own choice of film vehicles, but the chance to be his mistress as well, she raised her proud Prussian head high and refused.

Although none of her forebears were Jewish, Marlene felt an intense sympathy for the Jewish people which was to emerge most strongly in her tour of Israel in the early 1960s. She has written that her favorite book is *Job,* by Joseph Roth, which had been published in Germany the week she sailed. It is the story of the Jew Mendel Singer, whose child is horribly crippled, and over whom the unhappy man cries to God in his misery. At last, God sends a miracle which cures the creature. Marlene was soon to learn that the Jewish race would be aided not by a miracle, but by the efforts of millions like her who yearned for justice and peace.

The *Bremen* cannot have been very inspiring. Sleek and impersonal, the vessel featured a fountain in the middle of the dance floor which shot up and down, lit with colored lights which changed from pink to mauve to purple as a silly little orchestra jigged away at "Yes Sir, That's My Baby" or "Yes! We Have No Bananas." It is nice to imagine Marlene, blonde hair caught in the fairy lights, swaying in a tango in white satin, or strolling the deck while passengers walked by with their dogs, perhaps few of them recognizing her, in those weeks before *The Blue Angel* made her the leading female star of the world.

The Blue Angel was to prove prophetic, because in the insolent, cruel Lola-Lola, the schoolboys pruriently blowing up the feathered skirt of the picture postcard of her, the teacher ruined and reduced to playing a clown in her seedy vaudeville show, it was possible to see what Nazism already was, and would be. This is a film permeated with evil, a mixture of the director's own wickedness and his foreseeing of wickedness to come. It is a film in which the Devil wins: at the finale, the professor dies defeated, while Lola-Lola sings on triumphantly, her legs spread wide. Even the professor is cruel, torturing the schoolboys very much as von Sternberg tortured Marlene, making them repeat the word "the" hundreds of times in an English lesson.

One of the bosses of UFA almost stopped the film's release,

seeing himself in the character of the professor; and it is ironical that, given his supreme professional opportunity by Germany, von Sternberg should condemn that country by implication in his greatest work.

It is ironical, too, that Marlene, who obtained her career as a world star by strolling lazily on a fake ship's deck against a cardboard sky in *Two Bow Ties,* should now be making the same journey on a real ship on a real Atlantic as a reward for that very performance.

Gerda Huber revealed in the pages of a fan magazine that Marlene would never have gone to Hollywood if UFA had held her to a contract. But UFA had not held her: the studio executives did not feel she was worth keeping.

Leaving Heidede must have been an agonizing wrench for Marlene. When she reached America, she sent both letters and recordings of herself, talking to her child, giving her all the news, each record expertly packed by Marlene, wrapped tight against breakage more deftly than any store clerk could have done it.

Published while Marlene was crossing the Atlantic, the reviews for *The Blue Angel,* and for Marlene's performance in it, were ecstatic. The *Berliner Reichsfilmblatt,* a leading German movie magazine, said: "One is almost stunned by Miss Dietrich's performance. Her ability to take over scenes effortlessly but with simple and total command is something we have until now never experienced."

The newspaper *Berliner Börsenkourier* announced: "The Sensation: Marlene Dietrich! She sings and plays almost without effort, phlegmatically. But this knowing phlegmaticism excites. She does not 'act' common: she is."

Later, the greatest historian of German film, Siegfried Kracauer, wrote: "Dietrich's Lola-Lola was a new incarnation of sex. This petty-bourgeois Berlin tart, with her provocative legs and easy manners, showed an impassivity which incited one to grope for the secret behind her callous egotism and cool insolence."

She arrived in New York on April 9, 1930. Paramount executives came aboard the press launch with the reporters, and had her perch on the luggage, skirt pulled up to show her legs. She had complete contempt for this approach. She had hoped she would be greeted as a serious actress. She was rushed headlong to the Ritz-Carlton for a press conference at which she was buzzed pitilessly about leaving her baby and her husband, and asked about her diet. Paramount had worked hard to make her known as the New Thing from Germany, but nobody had seen *The Blue Angel* yet, and she wound up on page 36 of the *New York Times.*

Moreover, she ran slap into anti-German feelings. Most Germans had fled the United States if they were in movies, because the talkies presented an accent problem. Yet, here she was, arriving when most of her compatriots had gone. Moreover, anti-German feeling lingered on, twelve years after World War I. Lasky and Zukor were made to feel they had lost their minds in importing her.

In late April, when she arrived by train in Hollywood, Marlene was given another press luncheon, at the Ambassador. She disliked Hollywood at once. She wrote letters filled with misery to Gerda Huber in Berlin, complaining about the sterile social life, the dull evenings, and the arid, palm-lined streets.

Worst of all was the shock of discovering that von Sternberg had decided to cast her in the leading role of a version of a novel she had packed into his luggage for his amusement on the transatlantic voyage, when he left Berlin. This was *Amy Jolly, the Woman of Marrakesh,* an autobiographical work by a Berlin journalist named Benno Vigny who had once served with the Foreign Legion. Von Sternberg wanted her to play the role of a floozy with whom a legionnaire falls in love. It was just the kind of part Marlene wanted to avoid after *The Blue Angel.*

It was typical of von Sternberg's perversity that he should want to reduce Marlene to histrionic as well as professional prostitution. He had written and dictated the script with the aid of Jules Furthman, who owed the studio bosses so much money in gambling debts they had to keep him on the payroll in order to recoup. Von Sternberg and Furthman changed the story so that the legionnaire became a coldly indifferent seducer of women and the cabaret singer, Amy, a wholehearted romantic who abandons her prospective husband to follow the soldier into the desert wearing high heels. This neurotic nonsense seemed to Marlene a waste of her time and talents, but because of her admiration for the director, she reluctantly accepted his demand that she proceed.

The parallel with her own life is clear: like Amy Jolly, she had sung for years to lecherous men whom she despised; she had left Europe for the desert—the desert of California, and of California culture; she had taken off in the high fashion of the day; and she was going to be a female camp follower, like the packwomen who huddled together in the last scene of the film, behind the camels and the costar donkeys, while the fake studio wind blew up. There was much gossip about a romance between Marlene and her costar, Gary Cooper. It is easy to see von Sternberg flattering himself in the role of the kind and considerate man she gives up—Menjou is even made up to look like him—and casting Cooper as the icy and indifferent legionnaire who coolly accepts Amy Jolly's devotion. Amy Jolly's character was acutely based on Marlene's: her extraordinary mixture of romanticism and fatalism, her seeming callousness only a mask for absorption in the ideal of love.

Marlene never saw a script. She was told by her Professor Higgins that he would "supply her with pages from day to day." Meanwhile, the studio machine ground into action. She had to lose thirty pounds; her ankles were massaged free of fat; her eyebrows were plucked and imitation eyebrows painted high on her forehead; her cheekbones were deeply shadowed; her pale face was rendered even paler with powder; her hair was sprinkled with gold dust. When Tallulah Bankhead was told of this in New York, she said: "I'm going to go one better. I'm going to sprinkle gold dust on my *pubic* hair."

Marlene insisted on wearing slacks around Hollywood. She told Blake McVeigh, the publicity man assigned to her, that she had liked dressing in trousers in Berlin, and she certainly wasn't going to change. McVeigh was shocked. He told her: "Slacks are

unknown in this country. Men consider them masculine and
unattractive. It's quite impossible." "OK," Marlene shrugged.
"Then I won't have any publicity pictures taken!"

McVeigh was desperate. He had to satisfy his bosses. He had
no alternative but to take a gamble. "All right. We'll try it," he
said. "But if they don't like the photographs, it's curtains for
me."

The studio chiefs were as dismayed by the slacks as McVeigh
knew they would be. One night, Marlene deliberately arrived
at a party wearing a yachting cap, a navy blue blazer, and white
bell-bottom trousers. She created a sensation. Immediately,
every woman in Hollywood rushed to copy her. Paramount
changed its collective mind overnight. The studio issued hundreds of pictures of Marlene in her new garb, with a daring
slogan, "The Woman Even Women Can Adore."

Marlene became friendly with the head of the hairdressing
department, Nellie Manley, and her makeup woman, Dotty
Ponedel. According to a statement made by Nellie Manley to
the actress Anna Lee, she had her wisdom teeth removed to
allow her cheeks to sink in more effectively, painted a white line
along her lower eyelids, and, eschewing underwear, put surgi-
cal tape under her breasts to hold them high.

To von Sternberg's annoyance, Marlene enjoyed the company of Maurice Chevalier and went dancing with him at the
Coconut Grove. When Paramount took pictures of them together, von Sternberg did his utmost to have them withdrawn
and destroyed—then two of them turned up in *Photoplay.*

His letters and telegrams to his wife Riza, who was in New
York, written in those first weeks of Marlene's arrival in Hollywood, make extraordinary reading. It is clear from them that
von Sternberg desperately wanted to reunite with Riza but was
unable to control his need for Marlene. When Riza insisted that
he come to New York to discuss possible divorce proceedings,
he sent her a telegram pleading with her to move into the
vacated apartment next door.

In response to this telegram, Riza von Sternberg came out to
Hollywood and, instead of taking the apartment next door,

moved in with him. She says, "Marlene, on Jo's insistence, moved into the apartment opposite. Each night, Dietrich's maid would come running over to us and tell us Dietrich was crying, miserable, and lonely, and wanted to go back to her husband and daughter in Germany. Jo would go over to try to calm her down. He was terrified she would go back to Berlin before the picture started. *The Blue Angel* still hadn't been released, and many people at the studio thought he had made a mistake in taking a gamble with her. He knew his career was on the chopping block. He *had* to make a Hollywood star of her; he was on his mettle to do so. On the surface, he was haughty and arrogant, utterly self-assured; underneath, I could see he was frightened, hopelessly insecure, afraid she might fail.

"Night after night he crossed the corridor; he would stay one, three, five hours pleading with her, and come back finally wrung out like a dishrag. Well, at last I had had enough, and I said to him: 'This is insane. I can't sleep nights. Why don't you just marry her? Maybe that will make her happy.' And he said, 'I'd as soon share a telephone booth with a frightened cobra.' "

For the next year, von Sternberg was to struggle with his feelings for both women. A typical letter written to Riza when she returned to New York in the summer of 1930 scarcely suggests the icy autocrat the world knew. He said that he had been weeping for days and had never felt more desolate in his life. Wouldn't Riza, he begged, come back to him?

The fan magazines were filled with gimmicky stories about Marlene, either written by, or based on the purple prose of the various press agents. For example, Leonard Hall in his article in *Photoplay*, "The Perils of Marlene," wrote: "I'd far rather look at Marlene Dietrich's legs than at the Taj Mahal by moonlight, or even at a fat lady slipping on a banana peel." Dubbing her the "Potsdam Peacherino," Hall warned "Herr Doktor von Sternberg" that "just as pigs are pigs, legs are only legs be they ever so magnificent." Many fan writers complained that they could not see "Marlene's limbs from the trees, as it were."

Interviews with her were invariably inane, the reporters mistaking her barely concealed impatience with their stupidity for the restless sexual allure of a temperamental great star. After they left her dressing room, she did not restrict her amusement to her critics. She often laughed among friends about herself on the screen, while von Sternberg was absent, saying, typically, "Look at me! I turn my eyes this way and then that way, and that's my performance!"

A newspaper writer, Burn Parton, was assigned to her. He recalls: "Our problem was, in the press department, that the stars required us to provide obvious flattery in our releases, but the press simply wouldn't use anything so blatant. We tried to provide *subtle* flattery, which simply didn't please either party. I remember that Marlene was always furious when the material we provided actually got into print.

"We had to do a dual biography of von Sternberg and Marlene. It ran for five pages. I handed it to von Sternberg. He took out a red pencil and ran a line through every single page except the first paragraph, which began, 'Von Sternberg is the greatest director in the world.' I was forced to release that one paragraph to the press! It wound up in five hundred waste baskets. Every morning he'd ask me, 'Why wasn't that article on the front page of every newspaper?' I didn't have the guts to tell him."

The Paramount production manager, Sam Jaffe, says: "I can still remember, after forty-six years, von Sternberg introducing Marlene around the studio. It was obvious that he was infatuated with her or in love with her. Only his deep feeling for her made it possible for him to present her as he did. In my opinion, no director in the world could have done for her what he did for her, always presenting her through gauze, with smoke, making her very mysterious. The settings were unique. I recently turned on television, I didn't know what was on, I pushed the button and I immediately said, before I knew what I was seeing, 'Oh, that's a von Sternberg picture.' He had a clear trademark. The reason he did every scene over and over again was not to humiliate her, but to insure she was perfectly glamorous. In my opinion, he was completely responsible for the Dietrich the world knows.

"I don't think anyone else could have presented her in quite
that extraordinary fashion. They would have wanted her to be
an actress. They would have tried to have gotten performances,
whereas von Sternberg simply arranged for her to move exquisitely; she would turn and say one or two words and puff at a
cigarette and look out of a window, and he would say to her,
'Look down, look up, look aside, look this way,'—it was like
someone controlling a puppet. She was 'put together,' every
shot of her like a piece of a jigsaw puzzle, and the result was
marvelous.

"He taught her presentation above all else. It was the way she
timed herself, delivered herself, which counted more than any
small acting ability she may have had. She has never forgotten
this. Her presentation still exceeds her talent.

"Nobody at Paramount was permitted to have direct contact
with her. We all had to discuss everything with von Sternberg.
Our wishes had to be conveyed to her through him. Von Sternberg knew what she needed, and he fought for her. I never
knew of a relationship as intense as this in pictures. I don't think
she 'loved' him. But she had great respect for him. A very high
regard. She was devoted to him. I don't think she was physically
attracted to him at all. He was not an attractive man. He was
small, he wasn't glamorous, he was eccentric, he wore oversized
Chinese jackets, he didn't turn women on. I think he expected
too much of Marlene emotionally, just as he was making her a
big star.

"I never actually saw them—him and Marlene—in a confrontation on the set. Whenever they had discussions, they tried to
be sure no one else was present. If they had an argument, which
they always conducted in German, the set was cleared."

Morocco, the new title for *Amy Jolly,* began shooting in high
summer of 1930. Despite her contempt for her role, Marlene
continued to learn from her mentor. She told the critic and
historian Richard Griffith years later: "Von Sternberg wanted to
create *camera* vehicles, and that was the meaning and purpose
of his pictorialism. He taught me that the image of a screen
character is built not alone from her acting and appearance but

out of everything that is cumulatively visible in a film. He taught me about camera angles, lighting, costumes, makeup, timing, matching scenes, cutting, and editing. He gave me the opportunity for the most creative experience I ever had."

Marlene made many suggestions for the film, trying to bring to life the impossible situations and characters. She told the director and critic Curtis Harrington in the 1950s: "I felt it might be interesting to have Amy Jolly, during a singing routine, kiss a female member of the audience on the lips. Von Sternberg said, 'The studio might censor it.' 'OK,' I replied, 'then we'll have Amy take a rose from the woman, carry it across the room, and give it to the legionnaire. That way, they'll have to let the kiss stay in. Otherwise, people will say, 'Where did the rose come from?' "

The cameraman for *Morocco*, the great Lee Garmes, has never forgotten a detail of the shooting: "I made tests of Dietrich. She spoke very little English. She had to speak her lines phonetically. She wasn't the beauty Harlow was, but she had a perfect body, wonderful legs, and the hair was lovely. She was a very good actress. She was a little bit nervous. She was full of little butterflies. She wasn't sure of herself, she had to be guided in everything.

"Joe knew how to handle her; he was very considerate of her, he was in love with her, and he did everything he could to help her. She was extremely mechanical. I would say to her, 'You start here and you stop here,' I'd say it a hundred times and she'd do it to perfection each time. Meticulous, methodical, but in a 'natural' way; it didn't look contrived or forced on the screen. She was smart enough to know how to do it so it looked relaxed.

"Von Sternberg never made her 'act' through a whole scene. In a room, he would show the audience the left wall, the back wall, and the right wall, and from then on he would show nothing but close-ups. He never took three pages of dialogue from just one angle; the actors would speak one line of dialogue to go with each wall. This was lucky for Dietrich: she had only to speak one line or two at a time. If she'd had to learn a whole page she would have been in real trouble. She'd have run out of breath.

"He'd take the scene over and over. There was a time when she had to speak just two words, 'I will' or 'I won't,' something like that. He made her do it a hundred and forty times. He wanted to get a certain 'intonation' in the voice. The sound man, Harry Mills, came to Joe and said: 'The needle isn't moving. Her voice isn't registering. I'd appreciate it very much if you'd ask her to talk up just a little bit.' Joe went to her and said in German, 'Marlene, you're talking too loud.' My assistant was a German, he overheard it and he came to me and said, 'The sound man wants her to go higher and von Sternberg is telling her to go lower.' I went to Harry and said, 'Do you know what they're doing?' He said, 'The son of a bitch!' Well, the outcome was that when the picture was released, Harry Mills won the sound track Academy Award!

"We had fun with Gary Cooper as the legionnaire. It was very stuffy on the set that hot summer of 1930 and we were all yawning a lot. At lunch, I yawned a little, and Gary, who often yawned, started to yawn. This went on for three or four hours during the shooting. It was about three-thirty in the afternoon, very hot, and Joe said: 'Look, Mr. Cooper and Mr. Garmes, we have a yawning competition on today. Are you so bored with what's going on?' Coop said nothing. I said, 'No, it's kinda stuffy in here, and it makes me do an awful lot of yawning.' Cooper said, yawning, 'I do a lot of yaaaaaaawning too!' We both yawned a couple more times. Joe said: 'I want to tell you something. I'm getting tired of your yawning. The next time anybody yawns we're going to quit work for the day!' Well, we *all* yawned at once—Marlene included—and, thank God, we *did* stop work! Joe never looked so furious in his life!"

Lee Garmes adds: "The first scene, of Dietrich arriving in the fog and meeting Adolphe Menjou on deck, was shot on the biggest stage at Paramount. We had to cover the set with canvas and put fog machines in—it was as hot as hell! Marlene took it very courageously. I lit her with a side light, I shot all day Monday, and until noon on Tuesday without a break. . . . I don't know how we got through. After lunch on Tuesday, we looked at the rushes! Well, I said to myself: 'My God, Lee Garmes, this is impossible! There's another Greta Garbo up there on the screen! You'd better go back to your regular lighting, which you've always had!'

"I never told von Sternberg, but I at once altered the lighting. Ever since I began my career in 1916, Rembrandt has been my favorite artist. I've always used his technique of north light—of having my main source of light on a set always coming from the north. Rembrandt used to have a great window in his studio ceiling or at the end of the room which always caught that particular light. I lit Dietrich with that technique. It suited her cheekbones.

"A lot of the scenes with her were shot at night, then lit to give an impression it was high noon. The effect was very strange and beautiful. Her close-ups were done against a white wall.

"We worked through every goddamned Saturday night. We'd start around nine, then work to one, one-thirty in the morning each day. There were no unions in those days.

"We didn't have producers at that time, we had what we called 'supervisors.' A tough guy named Hector Turnbull was our supervisor. One time we came in from the ranch to see the rushes at six-thirty or seven. He picked us up at the gate. He said, 'Look, you guys are taking too long. Jo, you're going to go over budget. We make fifty-two pictures a year; we know how much each picture's going to cost; if we go over the figures we're not going to get any profits.' In a nice way, he was bawling us out. I said: 'Hector, you're going to eat your words.' I said: 'I think we're making an unusually good picture. I think you're going to see, when it's finished, that it won't be a program picture. It will be something special.' He said: 'We make specials; we know when we're going to make a special. We don't figure that program pictures like this are going to cost anything.'

"I told him: 'Let's see what happens! Later on, when we have a hit, you're going to come to Joe and me and you're going to apologize for this conversation.' He said: 'If that happens, I'll be very happy. But I don't believe it will.' Well, Zukor and Lasky thought *Morocco* was so terrific that they put it into Grauman's Chinese Theater; it was the first Paramount picture ever to go into Grauman's! Turnbull came and apologized to us. He was OK.' "

Von Sternberg's assistant, Henry Hathaway, who later became a famous director, says of him: "He was miraculous. In *Morocco,* he just had a rail and a piece of deck and a curtain and fog—and there you were on board ship. He took an old Mexican street on the Universal back lot and said, 'Bring me some eucalyptus poles and palm leaves,' and then we had *Mogador!* His 'desert' was at Guadalupe, just a little tiny piece of beach with sand dunes. Marlene I remember walking up the beach while hairdressers and makeup people went crazy. She was a good sport, and I remember she insisted she take off her shoes before she joined the mule train. Realism!

"Dietrich was coddled as a star by Joe. She was held up to us in glory. You'd have to walk over and say to her secretary, 'May we have Miss Dietrich, please?' She always had to have a limousine the length of a city block and a chauffeur in a blue uniform with an embroidered cap and an elegant tent made of silk and fit for a sultana. Their romance, if it was a romance, never showed. Joe never even *touched* her on the set. She seemed to be just another person to him."

Morocco, according to von Sternberg, was seen years later by the pasha of Marrakesh, who said to him, "You must have spent weeks on location in my city."

Years later, Al Hirschfeld and Dolly Haas went with Marlene to see *Morocco* at the Museum of Modern Art. Al said to her, "Marlene, how did you get that expression, that wonderful expression at the end of *Morocco* when you kick your shoes off and make your way into the desert to follow Gary Cooper?"

"I did what Joe von Sternberg asked me," Marlene replied. "I counted from twenty-five backwards!"

Because of the Paramount block-booking system, in which the exhibitors demanded two Dietrich pictures a year, Marlene was rushed into another movie immediately, *X-27,* later called

Dishonored. It was about a spy, formerly a prostitute, who betrays her country for love of a worthless man.

Reminiscent of Pola Negri's famous vehicle *Hotel Imperial,* the film begins with a typically chauvinist von Sternberg title: "X-27 might have been the greatest spy in history—if she had not been a woman." X-27 is an ardent Austrian patriot, capable of driving her lover (Warner Oland) to suicide when she discovers he is a traitor, yet also capable of setting a Russian flyer (Victor McLaglen) free because of her passion for him. Like Amy Jolly, X-27 is defeated by circumstances, talking of her "inglorious life"; early in the film she looks forward to a "glorious death," which she achieves when she is shot down by a firing squad. After the young lieutenant refuses to give the order to shoot, she uses her one or two remaining minutes to put lipstick on her lips and straighten her seams. It is a madly novelettish conclusion to another wholeheartedly romantic work.

Again the film is autobiographical: a woman who has lived freely and adores her country gives her complete devotion to a militaristic martinet. It is filled with abstruse personal references and jokes: X-27 is the widow of a "Captain Kolowrat," a startling reference to the fat Count Kolowrat who produced *Café Electric,* wanted Marlene to make love to him, and died happily after seeing her legs once more. In the big disguise scene, Marlene revives the hair style of a maid in an early film she made with William Dieterle, *Man by the Roadside.* A costume ball echoes one she attended in Berlin in 1930. Victor McLaglen's uniform and bearing resemble those of Marlene's stepfather, Eduard von Losch.

Once again, this brilliant film shows von Sternberg's ambiguous attitude toward his star. He photographed her in a series of images even more voluptuous than those in *Morocco,* from the shimmering rain that drenches her at a street corner in the opening sequence to the delicate shadows and beams of light that embellish her in the last crazy scene when she makes up her face before the firing squad. Knowing how fascinated she was by mirrors, he inserted a private joke in which, on her way to death, she fixes her hair while viewing her reflection in the mirrorlike blade of a ceremonial sword. Yet alongside the sexually charged images, the images of a man in heat, there is humiliation of her: she is turned into a fatuous maidservant, reduced to a romantic fool capable of betraying her country (something unthinkable for Marlene). Consciously or unconsciously, von Sternberg and his hack writers were viciously saying: "OK, X-27 betrayed Austria for a cool martinet. Marlene did the same to Germany."

In this fine movie and in *Morocco,* the script which von Sternberg dictated from behind his enormous desk was used for a paper chase, the pieces literally torn to strips in his hands and stuffed into his pocket or cast away to be whirled off by wind machines and picked up by slaves. Dietrich told me that she made up most of the dialogue and situations as he went along, and this "improvised" look often works, giving a freshness to the pictures on the screen that they might not otherwise have. But the schoolgirl-novelette level of his mind, the perverse skittishness of his treatment of character, are unmistakable.

Morocco was a smash hit and, together with the great critical and commercial success of *The Blue Angel,* released at the same time, established Marlene once and for all as one of the supreme female sex symbols. The reviews were sympathetic; the public fell in love with Marlene's wit, self-mockery, and electric beauty. *Morocco* remains one of the best pictures she made, from the opening, with the troops marching through the shadow-dappled streets of Mogador, to the scene when she rushes from her engagement party at the sound of the legionnaire drums, to the last crazy, romantic gesture of the walk into the desert. This is sublime hokum of a kind Hollywood has long since ceased to make, kitsch so entertaining that it would seem foolish to subject it to the normal standards of criticism. And in the film Marlene, laconic, bored, contemptuous in tie and tails, insolently addressing her seedy audience or losing her head completely when she finds her name carved in a table by her erstwhile lover, has never been more watchable.

The day that *Dishonored* was finished, Marlene left Hollywood for five months. It was clear that she regarded Hollywood only as a place to work, that she could find no pleasure in its night life, and that she longed to return to Berlin, London, and Paris. In London, she attended the premiere of *Morocco* at the Carlton Theatre, greeted by a line of heralds in full uniform blowing trumpets, and attendants dressed in traditional Moroccan burnouses. Her mother joined her and, according to people who were there, had some sharp Berlin remarks to make about the vulgarity of the occasion.

Marlene continued with her mother to Berlin, to see Rudi and Heidede. Heidede was sick, and Marlene was very distressed to discover that she had to go to Prague for a premiere of *Morocco* at the Lucerna Theater there. A reporter of the *Prager Presse,* a newspaper in Prague, boarded the train as it entered Czechoslovakia and found Marlene acutely uncomfortable and worried. She hadn't slept all night, had a blinding headache, and was counting the minutes before she arrived in Prague and could telephone Berlin.

Almost certainly, her worry led her to make a firm decision to take Heidede to Hollywood. After nursing Heidede back to health, Marlene went with her to the United States in April 1931. Rudi was left behind. The following year, he moved to Paris. In 1927, he had met an intimate friend of Marlene's, Tamara Matul, who had danced in the chorus of *From Mouth to Mouth,* in Rudolf Nelson's revues, and in a number of musicals. He had fallen in love with her. She had modeled herself on Marlene, plucking her eyebrows, painting them in a high arch, making her cheekbones look sunken, and dressing in similar clothes. She was one of three Russian girls, seen everywhere together: Tamara, Varya, and Hopé. Marlene was deeply fond of her.

Unstable and neurotic behind a mask of smiling charm, Tamara, with her dark hair and eyes, was a Russian beauty. She and Rudi remained together until her death in 1968. Marlene kept the apartment at 54 Kaiserallee for them until they went to Paris, letting it go only when Hitler came to power in 1933.

Marlene disembarked in New York with Heidede and her old friend Gerda Huber, whom she had brought along as a nursemaid for Heidede and a companion for herself. As she walked down the gangplank, two lawyers appeared and thrust a writ into her hands. It was from Mrs. Riza von Sternberg.

The writ charged Marlene with $100,000 for libel and $500,000 for alienation of von Sternberg's affections. The libel charge stated that Marlene had given an interview to the newspaper *Neues Wiener Journal* in Vienna in which she had said that Riza was an undutiful wife, and that von Sternberg had planned to divorce her before she divorced him. The article also claimed that Riza had attempted a boycott against Marlene's pictures.

Marlene felt she had been misquoted in the Vienna article and immediately prepared a defense on that basis. In order to help her case, Marlene telephoned Rudi in Berlin to ask him to come to Hollywood: a husband on the scene would clearly keep the gossips quiet. Rudi arrived in Hollywood, leaving Tamara in Berlin, on July 19, 1931. He said that he was looking forward to Marlene's pancakes and that she was completely faithful to him —he was a loyal friend in need, and Marlene was grateful. Marlene and von Sternberg drove with Heidede to the Pasadena station, to greet him at the train. Despite all their precautions, they were chased down the platform by a mob of the paparazzi of the time, who flashed cameras and scribbled notes while Marlene and Heidede, embraced Rudi. All three participants in the scene were dressed in white, making a pretty picture for the photographers. Needless to say, von Sternberg had made sure he was the most glamorous of the three, wearing a handmade white tropical suit, a white beret, and white-and-tan oxfords. The reporters snapped at Rudi, "Are you jealous of Marlene and Joe?"

"No," he replied. "I don't *think* I'm jealous. We shall all live in a house in Beverly Hills." He added, "I shall be here for four weeks; yes, I am glad to see my family; no, Marlene did not alienate Joe's affections; yes, Marlene and I are faithful; yes, this is a family reunion and nothing else."

The four members of the group, Marlene, von Sternberg, Heidede, and Rudi, rather oddly described in the press as "the family quartet," climbed into a white Rolls-Royce supplied by

Paramount. They drove off in a kind of *tableau vivant,* von Sternberg sitting in front with the chauffeur while Marlene, her husband, and her daughter linked hands at the back.

On August 7, 1931, von Sternberg was brought before Superior Judge Roth to answer charges of contempt of court for failing to pay Riza her required alimony, following her just-completed divorce proceedings. Von Sternberg, cold and level-voiced, testified on the witness stand that Riza had ruined his work as a director for three months by suing him, and that he had declined to pay alimony because of the misery she had caused him. The judge told him that his action in refusing alimony was illegal; von Sternberg retorted angrily that he had paid ten thousand dollars as a property settlement and twelve hundred dollars as back alimony. Riza testified under oath that he had opened accounts at several department stores in Marlene's name and had furnished an apartment for her.

The upshot was that Judge Roth decided von Sternberg had acted in contempt of court, and Riza's counsel asked for court fees, traveling expenses of thirteen hundred dollars for Riza's trip from New York, and punitive damages. Next day, Marlene and Rudi jointly announced that all charges of her having alienated von Sternberg's affections were "completely unfounded and absurd."

Marlene testified in court: "I had just landed in New York when . . . I was served with papers. . . . Those papers, although nearly four months have passed, have never been filed in a New York court. Instead, all I have heard since then have been suggestions that publicity should be avoided if these suits were settled, and I have insisted steadfastly that I would far prefer the publicity of these suits to the payment of a single penny on these absurd, false, and unwarranted charges."

Paramount was extremely unsettled by this matter and managed to persuade Riza to drop the two suits, paying her $100,000 to do so, and instructing Marlene to send her a letter of apology and explanation for the article published in Vienna. In the meantime, that summer of 1931, von Sternberg had been shooting a bowdlerized version of Theodore Dreiser's *An*

American Tragedy at Lake Arrowhead, California, and in Hollywood. The crew hated him so much that one afternoon, while he was addressing them pompously through a megaphone from a small boat, they slipped down and loosened the mooring so that he drifted away on the tide, still talking in order not to lose face until he disappeared around the corner of an inlet.

Marlene frequently traveled up to the lake to see him, acting considerately toward the nervous young Frances Dee, who played the rich girl, Sondra, in the movie.

While Theodore Dreiser attempted a lawsuit against Paramount and von Sternberg (what they were doing to his novel, Hitler was doing to Germany), the director began preparing another Dietrich vehicle. He said to studio boss B. P. Schulberg one day, "OK, so this time we'll put Marlene on a train. . . ." The result was *Shanghai Express,* in which she played yet another prostitute with a heart of gold. Dressed in black Travis Banton feathers like an exotic bird, Marlene played Shanghai Lily, a fly-by-night of the China coast who offers herself to a rebel leader to save her chilly ex-lover's life. This stuffy English bore (played by Clive Brook) announces that he was wrong to doubt her faithfulness, and at the end they are on the verge of marriage.

Von Sternberg was under pressure despite his declared intention to make no more pictures with Marlene. As if to compensate for the inanity of the screenplay, the director heaped his Shanghai Lily character with costumes, furs, drapery, all of which suggested that she must have come aboard the train with thirty-six trunks, somehow stuffed into a bedroom the size of a broom closet. Perversely, von Sternberg hid her legs throughout the entire production, but he decorated her face with rich shadows, expertly supplied by the cameraman Lee Garmes. She was forced to speak the dialogue in slow motion, like a talking turtle ("It t—o—o—k more than one man to change my name to—Shanghai Lily!" caused roars of laughter across the country and countless imitations by everyone from vaudevillians to schoolgirls.)

The actor Martin Kosleck remembers arriving from Berlin

during the rushes. "It was my first day in Hollywood, and Marlene's Rolls-Royce whisked me off to a screening room at night. Marlene waved 'hello' and sat looking critically at herself on the screen, criticizing or praising her own face and hair, and saying with great gusts of merriment, 'Oh, God! My *acting!* Now I move my eyes this way, now that way.' She stopped laughing when I foolishly said, 'That Chinese girl is wonderful.' It was Anna May Wong, playing her maid. I must have been crazy to have said such a thing. The atmosphere grew distinctly chilly after that."

Making the picture was a Hollywood nightmare. Von Sternberg, who had been wildly shouting through a megaphone, not surprisingly lost his voice. The production boss Sam Jaffe gave him a microphone instead. Von Sternberg at first rejected it, then began playing with it like a toy. He went one better, and fixed up a public address system which would have done justice to Grand Central Station. Jesse L. Lasky wrote in his memoirs: "As I entered the stage . . . I could hear the booming voice of the director reverberating through the enormous structure. . . . Joe was staging an enormous close-up of Marlene and Clive Brook, almost breathing in their faces as he gave them directions, but still talking in the microphone!"

Lee Garmes remembers, "Von Sternberg had become very vain by the time we did *Shanghai Express.* He acted out all the parts, and it became rather hilarious. First, he was Clive Brook kissing Marlene, and then Marlene kissing Clive Brook! You should have seen Clive Brook's face! His impersonation of Anna May Wong had us all in stitches. But we didn't dare show our amusement. Clive Brook wanted to be Clive Brook. Von Sternberg wanted him to be von Sternberg. For hours on end they would sit down and battle, but their voices were never raised, they'd say in a near whisper, in extremely gentle tones of voice, 'Oh, you fucking son of a bitch!' "

Shanghai Express became the biggest single hit of Marlene's career to date. The public went crazy over its dialogue, quoting such lines as "What in the name of Confucius is a coaster?" And the reply, "A coaster's a woman who lives by her wits along the

China coast." Each time this exchange took place there were yells of mirth from New York to San Francisco. Paradoxically, it was the madness of the movie that made it popular, and the dazzling images turned on the critics. The *New York Times* wrote, "Many of the scenes are so beautifully lighted that they recall etchings."

Again, Von Sternberg had created a magical, fanciful and elegant movie, another love poem to the woman who obsessed and frustrated him.

Marlene made a new friend in 1931, the handsome lesbian socialite and author Mercedes d'Acosta. She had noticed Mercedes at parties, and one night at a dance recital by Harald Kreutzberg she asked Cecil Beaton to introduce them. Next morning, she arrived at Mercedes's house on Sunset Boulevard with an enormous bunch of white roses and gave them to Mercedes's maid, Anna, saying, in German, "May I see your mistress?"

Mercedes was astonished, but asked Marlene up to her bedroom. She had never met her. Marlene confessed she had called Cecil Beaton to obtain her address. "I just wanted to bring you flowers," she said, adding that she had been concerned over Mercedes's pallor and undernourished appearance. She added that she understood her condition must be the result of loneliness; that she, too, was pining away with homesickness for Europe. While Mercedes looked at her with amazement, Marlene said, "I'd like to cook for you. I will make you well."

Not knowing what to say, Mercedes invited Marlene to a dinner party the following night, and told her new friend, "Don't use rouge. It doesn't suit you." Marlene went into the bathroom, washed her face, and never wore rouge again.

The two women became intimate friends. Mercedes encouraged her to wear slacks all the time—at the studio commisary, when out driving, or shopping in Beverly Hills. They spent weekends together at Marlene's rented Santa Monica Beach house. Twice a day, florists would deliver enormous bunches of roses to Mercedes's house. When Mercedes protested that the house had become suffocating because of the perfume of thousands of flowers, Marlene sent vases, clothes, porcelain, and furniture instead.

Marlene remained close to Mercedes for several years. When Mercedes had an automobile accident in 1934, Marlene telephoned from Paris and made sure she was moved into a better hospital room, guaranteeing payment of the bill. When they met in Paris just before World War II broke out, Marlene paid her fare so that she could escape the Nazis. In the late 1940s, when Mercedes accidentally poured cleaning fluid in her eyes instead of eyewash, Marlene saved her sight by making a special eye preparation and helping to nurse her gently back to health.

Marlene's healing qualities, her capacities as a doctor or nurse to her friends, were observed by many in Hollywood. If anyone was sick, or in need of financial help, she was the first to come to their home, tidy up, and prepare delicious German meals for them. She was always a tender and loving mother to Maria, sitting with her at the beach, taking her for drives through the hills, and instructing her in English with the aid of a governess.

When Marlene returned to Berlin in 1932, she became fascinated to learn that a novel she admired, George Froeschel's *A Very Different Woman,* had been bought by Paramount. This was the story of an adulterous wife who is almost killed in an accident; she has a blood transfusion, and discovers that the donor, a young and attractive man, is linked to her by a mysterious force. Drawn to him, she eventually dies at the exact moment at which he dies somewhere else.

Froeschel will not forget his meeting with Marlene to discuss this project: "She had luncheon with me at the Hotel Bristol, the most elegant and exclusive of the hotels in Berlin. She understood at once that this was a modern version of Tristan and Isolde; she had an instinctive grasp of every element of the novel, which she had read and understood profoundly.

"As editor of a leading Berlin newspaper, I met everyone who mattered. But of all the people then or later I ever met she was the most brilliant, the most miraculous human being I ever knew. Only one thing disconcerted me a little. She arrived at lunch in a perfect tailor-made costume. As she sat down, she spread her legs very wide and showed me herself all the way up to her waist. I was very surprised to say the least, but I managed to keep my eyes on her face, and continue the conversation. She was bright, lively, and fascinating, but we never made the picture together.

"Von Sternberg talked her out of it. He wanted to make some terrible nonsense of his own. It was a great, great pity."

In Hollywood Paramount demanded that director and star immediately prepare another picture. Since Jules Furthman was on a drunk, von Sternberg called up S. K. Lauren, a young Broadway playwright who had been shipped out to the coast, to write the next vehicle, a story about a woman who pays for her husband's radium poisoning cure by becoming a prostitute, and dragging her seven-year-old child from pillar to post through various dives. Apparently, Marlene wanted to make the film: she wanted to portray a woman with a child, which she had not done in her previous films. She had written in her *Saturday Review* article of August 15, 1931: "I want to play interesting women with many sides to their characters, because I believe that in creating a variety of characters the individuality of the actress herself becomes richer and deeper.

"I determine to assert my own personality and to remain as detached as possible from the popular conception of the screen vamp. Perhaps my resentment of this unfair method of exploitation has added a certain piquancy to the wry, mocking smile I assumed for my world-weary heroines."

Here in 1931 was the sure voice of a liberated woman crying out for depth, light, and shade in feminine characterizations on the screen. Yet ambiguously she was still drawn to the glamorization von Sternberg gave her.

S. K. Lauren, in Hollywood in 1976, says: "I couldn't stand von Sternberg. He seemed to take to me. That bothered me, because I couldn't take to him. When he gave me the plot I thought, 'This guy's crazy.' But after two Broadway flops, how could I argue? They put me to work with that racketeer Furthman, who luckily did almost no work. Finally, I finished the treatment. Von Sternberg called me into his office, about three times the size of Hitler's, and with one hand on the script went into an interminable, impressive silence which was enough to scare the bejeezus out of me. He brushed the script onto the floor. He said, very slowly, using the royal plural, 'We choose to overlook the presumption that this screenplay has ever been written.'

"Thereafter, he'd dictate everything. The result was garbage. At one point (I think we were somewhere in South America in the story) I spoke up, I had the courage of the newcomer, and I said, 'Joe, I don't like this, it's too rambling, it doesn't have any movement.' He went into a pause which lasted about fifteen minutes. 'Sam,' he said finally, 'You're talking to a man who is the world's greatest master of movement.' It sounded like he was a laxative. I said, 'Shit!' under my breath and left. He didn't even hear me, he was lying back gazing up at the ceiling or some damn thing.

"After several weeks we still hadn't licked the script. We went from Hollywood to Palm Springs. Palm Springs was a hell-hole of a one-horse town in those days. No air conditioning, and a hundred and thirty-five degrees under the shade of an agent's promise. I used to spend the afternoons dodging through the sagebrush to avoid von Sternberg and I'd come slap up against Harpo Marx.

"We went back to Hollywood. We had written sixteen lines which didn't get into the picture. In desperation, we asked Furthman to think of something. He arrived next morning with a description of a background. He read it aloud to us. It was about a brothel. I was amazed at the literacy of it. This guy was such a slob. When he got through I said, 'Jules, that's a fine piece of writing.' And von Sternberg said, 'It ought to be. It was fine when Zola wrote it in *Nana*.'"

The script finally completed, von Sternberg took it to Schulberg. Lauren and Furthman tagged along like dogs behind their master. Schulberg banged the script up and down on his desk, screaming, "This is the godammedest piece of shit I've ever read in all my life! Furthman, you're off the lot! Get out!

As for you, Lauren, I'm ashamed of you. We bring you all the way from Broadway and you crap on our heads!" Lauren didn't dare tell him that every word of the script had been dictated by von Sternberg.

Next day, Schulberg hired three more stooges to write a new screenplay. Von Sternberg left at once for New York, announcing he had left the picture. Back in Hollywood, Marlene told Paramount she would not work unless von Sternberg directed her. Schulberg called her to his office and told her that Richard Wallace, a journeyman contract director, would take over at once. She said, "I won't work with Wallace." "OK," Schulberg said. "We'll suspend you."

On April 27, 1932, Marlene was struck off the Paramount payroll. She had been ordered to work on the set that morning, but had refused to clock in. She had declined even to send a note to Schulberg explaining her recalcitrance. Schulberg announced that lawsuits would be filed against both star and director, pointing out they were both humble employees, drawing paychecks like anyone else, and that they would be treated as such. They had breached their contracts in a "completely arbitrary fashion" and would "be punished accordingly."

In New York on April 28, von Sternberg told a press conference, "I will return to Hollywood and my profession in a few days. But it probably won't be at Paramount. Yes, they threaten eternal excommunication or something like that if I go elsewhere, but I don't think they can prevent it. I don't anticipate either of us will have any trouble." Paramount retaliated by saying that Tallulah Bankhead would take over Marlene's role immediately. Tallulah delivered a characteristic remark: "I always did want to get into Marlene's pants." Told that the studio would sue him for $100,000 damages, von Sternberg made an equally characteristic observation: "I think they're trying to humiliate me by asking so little."

Five

A Kidnap Threat

In Los Angeles, Marlene set up house in Bel Air in 1930 and then, in 1931, in Beverly Hills. Heidede, who now became known as Maria, told *Ladies' Home Journal* many years later: "I loved California immediately because it was so sunny. We lived in a wonderful house that was surrounded by trees, like a park. I had lots of animals—a German shepherd dog, a monkey, several cats, two sheep, a parrot, and an aviary that held two hundred birds." *Ladies' Home Journal* added: "The house seemed to have been built for parties and Dietrich gave them once or twice a week. Maria, in hand-sewn organdy, would sit on the stairs while the orchestra played and beautiful people dressed in their beautiful best danced past her."

While still on suspension by Paramount, Marlene had the worst scare of her life. Rudi had returned to Paris and his job of dubbing foreign versions. Gerda Huber had gone back to Berlin to continue work as a free-lance journalist with a series of articles on Marlene's life. Marlene was living at a North Roxbury Drive house on the corner of Sunset Boulevard with Maria and a temporary nursemaid. One morning she opened her mail as usual.

One of the letters grabbed her attention. It was made up of single letters cut out of newspapers and pasted onto sheets of paper. It was very brief. It read:

> YOUR DAUGHTER WILL BE KIDNAPPED UNLESS YOU GIVE
> US $10,000. HAVE THE MONEY BY MAY 16. LEAVE YOUR
> CAR IN FRONT OF YOUR HOME AND PUT MONEY PACKAGE
> ABOUT SIX INCHES FROM REAR ON REAR BUMPER. KEEP
> SILENT. DON'T BE CRAZY. QUICK ACTION. WANT ONLY $5
> AND $10 BILLS. LINDBERGH BUSINESS.

On the reverse the note read:

> BETWEEN OURSELVES. BELIEVE YOU US WE WILL JUST
> HANG ON.

As soon as she read the notes, Marlene called Chief Blair of the Beverly Hills police and District Attorney Buron Fitts, who came to her house immediately. She then called von Sternberg, who sent her an armed bodyguard. Marlene telephoned Rudi in Paris. She instructed Maria and the nursemaid to keep to the floor in case somebody tried to fire through the windows. Blair and Fitts spent the night at the house. Blair told *Photoplay:* "She wanted to be in on everything. At the dinner table, she kept jumping up from the meal to wait on us, though she had adequate help. And all night, she kept rushing to the kitchen every hour or so to make coffee for the men. It seemed to give her great satisfaction to do things personally. She felt that she was helping."

There were no attacks on the house. Next morning, another letter arrived, which read:

> YOU CAN DECIDE FOR YOURSELF. YOUR GIRL OR DEATH
> NOTICE. WHAT ABOUT IT. LINDBERGH BUSINESS.*

The reverse of the note contained the words:

> MARLENE, MARLENE. WOMAN, YOU WOULDN'T TAKE THIS
> CHANCE.

Blair and Fitts decided that the notes were those of an amateur. Further notes meant for her were accidentally sent to the

---

*The kidnapping of Charles Lindbergh's baby was currently in the news.

wife of an importer, Mrs. Egon Muller, whose own child was threatened with kidnapping, in notes accidentally sent to Marlene.

Marlene selected two bodyguards who worked in shifts. She had iron bars placed over the windows, which are still on the house. The doors were double-locked; a special iron gate was double-padlocked, an electrical alarm system installed, and a German police dog stationed in the entrance hall.

Maria's nurse was armed. Marlene herself kept a gun in a drawer. One night, a ladder was found outside the nursery window.

On May 16, the day the would-be kidnappers demanded the money package be left on the car, the police put a package of dummy dollars on the rear bumper. Twenty-five FBI men hid in the bushes and watched. Nobody came to collect the money.

Blayney Matthews, Chief of the District Attorney's Extortion Detail, followed a line which detected the whereabouts of the crooks in Chicago. Marlene believed that too much newspaper publicity had scared the criminals off. She issued a statement to the press:

We have received threatening letters from time to time, but at the request of police remained silent. Necessary measures were taken to safeguard the child as well as myself with bodyguards. As long as the police have given out the details there's nothing left for me to do but admit it.

The crooks were never caught. Some years later, after Marlene had vacated the house, a young prowler was caught in the grounds, who claimed to have been the original would-be kidnapper. But it turned out that he, too, was a hoaxer.

This unpleasant episode had an unfortunate repercussion. Because of her need to protect Maria, Marlene never sent her daughter to school in California. Maria told *Ladies' Home Journal:* "Instead I was taught at home by two tutors, one English, one German. From nine to twelve, I had lessons, and lessons again from one to three-thirty, sometimes in the house, sometimes in the garden under the trees. Every afternoon I had a tennis lesson or a piano lesson or a dancing lesson or a swimming lesson, all at home. I was never permitted to leave the grounds."

While housebound at North Roxbury Drive or at the beach, Maria began eating excessively: chocolates, cakes, and ice-cream sundaes. As though to compensate for her lack of friends, she stuffed herself until she became obese. She also became excessively morbid, studying numerous books on disease and writing about suicide. On the very rare occasions when she was permitted to leave the house, she was still under armed guard. Marlene tried to make up to Maria for her isolation by discussing her own clothes and scripts with her daughter, and allowing her to help in the selection of jewels she wore in her pictures.

Martin Kosleck recalls a curious incident of this period: "Rudi and his mistress Tamara were staying at the house. One day, Marlene came home and found them showing pornographic pictures to little Heidede. Marlene was absolutely furious. She screamed and ranted. Heidede said sweetly, 'The cartoons in the *New Yorker* are much prettier.'

"The child had an odd sense of humor. I told her I had a cat, and she said, 'You're much too poor to have a cat!' I can't pretend I liked her.

"Marlene was worrying because the child was so big. She seemed even more worried about her premature height than her weight. She sent her to a Dr. Matson at Santa Monica for treatments. They didn't do any good."

During the kidnapping scare, the quarrels between Marlene and von Sternberg and Paramount continued unabated. Early in May, a special meeting of the Conciliation Committee of the Academy of Motion Picture Arts and Sciences was called to consider the differences of actress and director with the studio, simultaneously considering James Cagney's battle with Warner Brothers. Studio spokesmen revealed that they were totally dissatisfied with von Sternberg's original story from the beginning, since it contained unsympathetic treatment of Dietrich's star image. In one sequence, she was shown shoving her child under a table in a sleazy café, while she attempted to allure a man for a night of commercial sex. She was also made to humiliate herself in many scenes, which appeared to reflect the director's conflicting feelings of hatred and love for her. The matter was never satisfactorily resolved. But when it was made clear to von Sternberg that he would be blackballed in the industry if he did not proceed with work on the picture, he was forced to proceed.

When Marlene went to the premiere of *Grand Hotel* at Grauman's Chinese Theater during this period, the crowd yelled, "Stick to it, Marlene! Don't give up! Fight to the finish! We're for you!" The crowd broke through the rope, and surged forward, almost crushing her in the rush. As they did so, a woman screamed out, "Von for all and all for Von!"

In midsummer 1932, von Sternberg reluctantly started work on *Blonde Venus,* having redictated the entire script to Sam Lauren. It became crazily elaborated, with settings in New York, Paris, Baltimore, and Galveston. The story made even less sense than before: at one stage, the heroine gives all her money to a woman in a flophouse and immediately afterwards manages to pay her fare across the Atlantic. Marlene had to appear dressed up as a gorilla to a chorus line of female Fuzzy-Wuzzies, stripping off her gorilla arms to disclose braceleted wrists and singing brazenly "All night long / I don't know right from wrong." "Lesbian" touches were added, including the character of a butch female nightclub owner angrily dismissing Marlene, who says to Marlene, in a typical von Sternberg joke, "I have a kid myself." In a scene backstage in a seedy cabaret, a floozy announces herself to Marlene with the words, "My name is Taxi Belle." Marlene replies, "Do you charge for the first mile?"

Marlene's dressing room was completely redesigned by the famous art director Wiard Ihnen at vast expense, with rich carpeting, satin drapes, and oval mirrors. It was some sixty feet long and thirty feet wide, with hallway, living room, dressing room, bathroom and makeup room. It cost over $300,000. It was obviously von Sternberg's deliberate act of anger against the studio and became known as "Von's Revenge."

Wiard Ihnen, today the husband of the dress designer Edith Head, observes: "Marlene didn't get excited, rave about it, or anything like that. She looked at it, examined every inch of it, and simply nodded her head. It was her throne room, she was the queen, and it was up to the standard she required. That was all."

Ihnen continues: "Sam Jaffe, production manager at Paramount, quit over that picture. Von Sternberg not only demanded absolute silence on the set, he would permit no visitors. There was a huge sign to that effect hung outside. I walked in one evening to check out how things were, I stood at the back of the set, very silently, so Joe wouldn't even notice me, and I was the art director!

"In walked Jaffe. He strolled over casually and talked to Dietrich, who was standing to one side in her white tie and tails. They began laughing together. Von Sternberg turned around and looked at these two. He said coldly to Sam, 'What are you doing here?' Sam spluttered, 'But I'm the *boss!* The production manager! Hell, Joe, *you* know that!'

"Von Sternberg's voice was ice. He said, 'Didn't you read the sign outside?'

"Jaffe replied, 'Yes. But—' Von Sternberg turned on his heel and snapped at the crew, 'All right, wrap it up! Our production manager has broken the rules!' It was about four o'clock in the afternoon, hours before shooting was supposed to end. Sam Jaffe was furious; shooting should have ended at six.

"Sam went out of his mind. He literally ran off the sound stage to see Manny Cohen, the studio chief. He told Manny what had happened. Manny decided not to take action against von Sternberg: they'd had enough trouble already, and they needed the picture badly. The exhibitors were screaming. They had block bookings in those days, and the picture was way overdue. When he couldn't get his own way, Sam quit immediately. When I went into his office later, he was cleaning out his desk.

"After that, Sam became von Sternberg's agent. It's a crazy business."

The writer S. K. Lauren says, *"Blonde Venus* took *forever* to shoot. I'll tell you why. There was a scene in which Dietrich was picked up for streetwalking and taken before a judge. The actor who played the judge, Cliff Dempsey, had to say the awful line, which I'm glad to say was von Sternberg's, not mine, 'You are an unfit woman to be the mother of a minor child.' The line was redundant anyway. Well, poor Cliff Dempsey couldn't get it right. He kept saying, 'You are an unfit woman to be the mother of a miner's child.' Von Sternberg kept yelling, 'The child's father wasn't a miner! He was a radium specialist!' So Cliff Dempsey said, 'OK, so my name is Madame Curie.' Von Sternberg was not amused. He made Dempsey say the line a hundred and twenty-five times, and each time Dempsey deliberately got it wrong. At the end, an automobile went by at the crucial moment and you never heard the line.

"The gorilla scene also had to be done a hundred and twenty-five times. Marlene was in the gorilla suit for *days*. Finally, the 'gorilla' slumped over. Marlene had fainted! And all B. P. Schulberg could say was, 'Get the ape back in action. We're over budget!' "

Dick Moore, who was age six when he played Marlene's little boy in the picture (and was then known as Dickie), says in his New York office: "I never forgot anything about that picture. Marlene and von Sternberg—how they would yell and laugh and scrap and fight! They had an extraordinary freedom with each other, an openness; they could—and did—say exactly what they thought, and that kept them close together.

"In one scene, Marlene was supposed to walk in a room and throw her hat on the bed in a gesture of exhaustion. She refused to do it. She said it was bad luck, like wearing green socks, whistling in a dressing room, or quoting from *Macbeth*.

"She was a good sport, she was good-humored about it, she wasn't angry, or defiant, or anything, but she was quite firm that she wouldn't do it. I watched them both with my child's eyes wide open! Then they switched to German, when they saw I was listening, and they rattled on and on about it." Finally, Marlene won. Somebody wheeled in a couch, and she threw her hat on that.

"I remember the absurd publicity campaign of the time. Tallulah Bankhead was on the lot making *The Devil and the Deep,* with Charles Laughton, and the studio kept putting out releases which read, THE WOMEN IN DICKIE MOORE'S LIFE: WHICH WILL WIN, BANKHEAD OR DIETRICH? I had no idea what that meant.

"Marlene gave me a model boat. It was about two thirds the length of my desk today, a perfect model of an ocean-going yacht. You cranked it up, the propeller turned, and you could launch it. It was a very sophisticated toy. She sent her chauffeur in the Rolls with it. I was overwhelmed by this magnificent present. The only problem was, I had no place to float it. I guess she assumed our family had a pool, but in fact we had nothing of the kind.

"So I put it in my bathtub. The engine whirred, the propeller turned—and the boat sank."

Dick Moore continues: "I didn't see Marlene again for fourteen years. I was a GI in the war and I'd been injured in battle. I was laid up in the hospital near Los Angeles and I guess she read about it in the papers. Now at that time I had a king-sized crush on June Haver, the musical star. I was lying in my bed asleep, having a beautiful sex dream of holding the gorgeous blonde goddess June Haver in my arms. I woke out of this highly exciting dream, and through the mists of my pain and sickness I could just make out a golden-haired, beautiful woman sitting at the foot of the bed.

"I reached out to embrace her and I said, 'Oh, Miss Haver, how wonderful of you to come and see me!' The beauty got up and walked off without a word. It was Dietrich. I wonder if she ever forgave me."

Blonde Venus, entertainingly silly though it was, was a complete flop. Von Sternberg left for the West Indies, to shoot a new series of backgrounds for his long-delayed circus subject, *The Lady of the Lions,* in which he wanted Marlene to play a lion tamer. It was a characteristically bizarre expedition. Everywhere he went, von Sternberg kept saying, "I want to shoot a hurricane. Is one coming?" And when they said, "No," he turned away disappointed.

Hurricaneless, von Sternberg returned to Hollywood. Meanwhile, Marlene went to New York, where, according to an English friend, Major Donald Neville-Willing, later the owner of the Café de Paris, she met the English millionairess racing driver, Jo Carstairs. Miss Carstairs was a very different kind of Joe, famous for her blonde crew cut, Jack Dempsey shoulders, and tattooed body, as well as for her wit and charm.

Major Donald Neville-Willing recalls that Marlene renewed her Hollywood friendship with Tallulah in New York. "One night at the Ruban Bleu, a very, very dark upstairs nightclub, Marlene was wearing long gloves. Tallulah called across, "What's with the gloves?" Marlene smiled, called for a waiter, took the gloves off, put them on a plate, and sent them over to Tallulah."

In Berlin, in 1932, Marlene had a busy time. Hubsi von Meyerinck used to say: "That was when Goebbels propositioned Marlene to be the biggest star in Germany. I hear she spat in his face. She must have sat down to do it."

Karl Hartl remembers: "She invited a group of us to come with her to a café on the Kurfürstendamm, and she gave wonderful bonbonnieres to my wife, myself, everybody there, including Willi Forst, Hubsi von Meyerinck, and others of our gang. She was warm, generous, and adorable. It was just a few months before Hitler took over in Germany."

It was to be Marlene's last visit to Berlin for thirteen years. Disgusted with Hitler, she refused to go back while he was in power. Later in the 1930s, she had to arrange to meet her mother (who had moved from Berlin to Frankfort) in Switzerland. Unfortunately, neither her mother nor her sister Elisabeth seemed interested in moving to Vienna, Paris, or the United States.

Berlin that fall of 1932 was as beautiful as ever: the chestnut trees a blaze of green against the opulent gray buildings, the restaurants alive with violins and witty conversation, the lakes around the city forming a ring of bronze in the sunlight. But it was a fool's paradise at the end of an era. When von Sternberg went to Berlin to try to set up productions with UFA, it was on the eve of Hitler's becoming chancellor, and the Jews were already leaving for Paris, where Marlene spent several weeks visiting, among others, Maurice Chevalier.

In London that year, Marlene was walking in Soho with her close friend Hans Kohn when she said, "Just wait a minute." She walked over to the prostitutes' "beat" and began parading up and down, a veil over her face. Not a single man propositioned her. After half an hour, she crossed the street and said, "You see! Here I am, and not a single man is interested in approaching me. I'm a complete flop as a prostitute!"

When Marlene returned to Hollywood, she discovered that the studio, furious with von Sternberg for his recalcitrance and extravagance and even more furious over the failure of *Blonde Venus,* had decided to cast her with another director. Von Sternberg urged her, if he couldn't work with her, to choose to work with Rouben Mamoulian, who had made his name with *Applause* and *Love Me Tonight.* The subject the studio chose for her and Mamoulian was Sudermann's *Song of Songs,* a favorite of hers. But she was appalled by the script. The studio had to sue her for $185,000 to make her do it. The novel was reduced to drivel in the script, which dealt with a peasant of the kind she had parodied in *Dishonored,* who falls in love with a sculptor, only to be taken in charge by a lecherous baron. As the maid is carried into a cottage on the baronial estate by her riding instructor, her foot knocks over a lamp and the cottage catches fire. She vanishes—not in a puff of smoke, but into a nightclub—where she sings "Johnny," in a large black feather hat. She winds up marrying the sculptor. Penniless, she looks forward to a life of baronless bliss.

Nobody liked this example of imbecility. The British actor Brian Aherne recorded in his memoirs that, meeting him for the first time, Marlene said, "Why do you, an important actor from Broadway, come here to make this silly picture? I have to do it, because Mr. von Sternberg has walked out, and I am left without any protection. But you! Are you crazy?"

Aherne was much too shy to tell her the truth: he had accepted the part in order to have a date with her.

Aherne recorded a strange episode toward the end of shooting. Mamoulian could not find a script page which would cover the last scene. He begged the coauthor of the screenplay, Sam Hoffenstein, to provide one. Hoffenstein could not. Everyone sat around trying to decide on the finale. Finally, Aherne came up with a typical actor's solution: an immensely long speech to be uttered by himself. Marlene went back to her dressing room to bake a cake while the studio reached a decision. The end result was that Mamoulian wrote his own scene and nobody was satisfied.

Two curious incidents took place during the shooting. On March 28, 1933, Marlene was riding sidesaddle through a forest near Calabasas accompanied by the actor Hardie Albright, when a snake darted under her horse's hooves. The horse reared, and she was thrown to the ground on her head. She suffered from concussion, and from headaches for several weeks.

A week later, one of the maids at Marlene's Santa Monica beach house, convinced that Marlene was romantically involved with Aherne, wrote (according to Martin Kosleck) a lewd sign on a wall. "The sign was in German," Kosleck says. "It read, THERE IS FUCKING IN THIS HOUSE. Marlene called von Sternberg, who immediately drove over and made very one of the servants come out and write the same message on the wall one by one. Soon the entire wall was covered in the dirty words. Finally one of the maids hesitated before applying the paintbrush. Von Sternberg cross-questioned her. She broke down and confessed—and he handed her over to the police."

In 1933, the new Motion Picture Production Code was introduced, making it impossible for prostitutes to be played as heroines on the screen. This must have come as a considerable shock to von Sternberg, whose peculiar psychology, it seems, could accept Marlene in films only as a prostitute. When Paramount signed him to a new contract early that year, he began to prepare for her a script based on the life of Catherine the Great of Russia. But typically, he removed the empress's statesmanship almost entirely in the writing, changing her into a mere heartless seducer of men.

In his earlier films with Marlene, von Sternberg had, as we

have seen, shown her characters to be feminine and filled with tender feelings despite their dissolute lives. But it is clear that by 1933 von Sternberg was falling out of love with Marlene, realizing at last that he could teach her everything except to learn to love him. Paul Ivano, the veteran cameraman who had accompanied him to the West Indies for the ill-fated circus picture, says, "Joe was very strange all through that trip. He suffered from insomnia, and seemed to be on the verge of a nervous breakdown. He was convinced he was losing Marlene and he was miserable. I have no idea whether his feelings had any basis in reality."

The script about Catherine the Great, by Manuel Komroff, brutally portrayed the empress (Maria Sieber played her as a child), selecting her personal guard for their physiques, riding her horse up the palace steps, and subjecting her people to a complex variety of tortures, culminating in the casual murder of her husband behind a looming statue in the court. Von Sternberg was viciously commenting on the fact that his star was the empress of Hollywood, that he believed she was free with her favors, and that she was harsh and inconsiderate with her inferiors. Nothing could have been further from the truth. That she permitted herself to be savaged in this fashion says much for Marlene's loyalty and devotion to the man who had made her an international star. And once more, paradoxically, von Sternberg was to lavish great care upon lighting her, making her look more ravishingly beautiful than ever before.

Von Sternberg crowded the movie with vulgarly obvious but still exciting visual symbolism. The empress's wedding scene is extraordinary, Catherine seemingly fluttery and virginal, soft and yielding behind her veil, her fiancé tall and powerful in tight-fitting black, his body deliberately emphasized by the clothing, behind him a series of enormous phallic candles. The movie is crammed with sexual images: gaping mouths, eternally opening doors, cannons being wheeled into position, sheets turned down, furs, hair, gloves. Only the impotent grand duke played by Sam Jaffe is shown as limp and weak, accompanied by slackening drapes and broken icons.

Made in defiance of the Motion Picture Code, *The Scarlet Empress,* as the film came to be known, was von Sternberg's best picture since *The Blue Angel.* It is a visual and aural *tour de force,* absurd and extravagant but executed by a master hand.

Before it began shooting, both Marlene and von Sternberg had made odd, inconsequential trips to Europe. Disaffected with Hollywood, von Sternberg had spent the early spring of 1933 in Berlin, oblivious of the fact that Hitler's advent would render him, as a Jew, quite helpless as an artist in the new Germany. His lack of a proper grasp on reality, so clearly indicated in his scripts, was never more in evidence than when he went into discussions with UFA. Erich Pommer had left for London, and Max Reinhardt had moved from Salzburg to London. It seems incredible in view of the political circumstances that von Sternberg was disappointed at his failure to make a new career in Berlin. He returned dejectedly in May to make his new deal at Paramount.

On May 28, 1933, just under three weeks after Marlene also signed a new contract with Paramount, elections in the free city of Danzig resulted in a victory for the National Socialists, who captured thirty-nine out of seventy-two seats in the German senate. On June 20, the Nazis took over the government and began establishing their revisionary policies. In late May, Marlene sailed for France. She began her Paris visit by attending the opening of *Song of Songs;* at the end of the showing, she emerged from the curtain, and to her astonishment almost nobody applauded: personal appearances of this kind were not customary in Paris.

Marlene mingled with a fascinating group of émigrés who lived at the Hôtel Ansonia in Paris: Peter Lorre, Franz Waxman, Frederick Hollander, Jan Lustig, and the gifted lyricist, Max Kolpe (later Colpet), who spent much of their time playing cards and trying to learn French while they sought to establish themselves in the French film industry. Marlene recorded new songs for Polydor, some of them composed for her by Waxman and written by Kolpe, the two men driving out to her sumptuous retreat at the Hotel Trianon to work with her.

She would greet them on the steps, exquisitely dressed in Schiaparelli creations, her golden hair blowing in the wind, her blue eyes shining. In the suite, she would sit with them for hours going over the music note by note, perched on the arms of chairs, chain-smoking, sipping at champagne.

At the end of a hard day's work on her songs, Marlene, according to Walter Reisch, liked to relax, not at the fashionable tourist traps or the more elegant restaurants such as Tour d'Argent or Maxim's, but at the Russian Chez Korniloff, at Little Hungary, or at Chez Luis, a Czech restaurant which specialized in *Topfenknödeln,* dumplings filled with cottage cheese. She liked to lunch at two, and dine at ten at night. Often, she would go in the kitchens of these foreign establishments, and help prepare the food.

She clearly fell in love with Paris, which she had first visited in 1931. The orderly beauty of the city, the wide avenues with their lush plantings of trees, the somber gray nobility of the Arc de Triomphe, the cafés with their gay awnings, the bustle of the Champs Élysées dazzled her romantic spirit. She responded to the severity and discipline of Paris as well as to its voluptuous pleasures, and she became more and more a Parisienne, the logical side of her nature softened and warmed in the golden light of a Paris summer.

But even in this seemingly peaceful environment of smart women and bustling men, of tiny cars buzzing like insects, there was trouble in the air. A year before her visit, President Paul Doumer had been murdered in cold blood by a Russian émigré. Shortly after her departure, the Stavisky case would throw the country into an uproar, and would be followed by violent rioting in Paris. She must have been more aware than ever that the world had not been at peace for more than brief periods from the day of her birth.

On September 20 Marlene returned to America, refusing to say anything to reporters about Nazi Germany, probably because she did not want to imperil the lives of her mother and sister. She had helped Rudi and Tamara in Paris, and he seemed comfortably settled with Paramount. Maria was still under armed guard, being trained by governesses in Hollywood.

Back in Los Angeles, Marlene continued to be friendly with Mercedes d'Acosta, Martin Kosleck, and Hans von Twardowski. She went into extensive costume fittings with the neurotic Travis Banton, courageously enduring the suffocating weight of period clothes under hot lights for *The Scarlet Empress* costume tests. In his house in a New England forest, John Lodge, who played Count Alexei and later became ambassador to Spain and Argentina as John Davis Lodge says: "I was amazed by the energy and resolution of Marlene, and her complete dedication to conveying the director's vision. She cared nothing for her own comfort, she endured everything, and von Sternberg was incredibly painstaking in making sure that her every movement went like clockwork. Unlike everyone else, I admired von Sternberg as a man. He was very good to my young children, and I think behind that mask he was a tender and suffering human being."

Sam Jaffe, who played the Grand Duke Peter, does not agree: "I was disgusted by von Sternberg's treatment of Marlene. There was a gigantic dinner party scene. Von Sternberg shot it over so many days that the boar's head at the center of the table began to decay. It stank terribly. Finally, Marlene could take it no more. She fainted. People kept saying, instead of rushing to her aid, 'She's putting it on!' But she wasn't. Somebody came along with some smelling salts. I understood German, and I heard him saying to her in that language, 'Would I make you do this if it wasn't necessary?' and 'You must go ahead, for the good of the picture.' At last she complied. But it was hell for her. She asked him, 'At least can't we have a new boar's head?' So far as I was concerned, von Sternberg was the boar. Or bore.

"I remember he made Louise Dresser, who played the dowager empress, go around blowing out candles over and over again as though she had a thousand birthdays. He would scream, 'Less breath! Less breath!' 'All right!' she finally said, 'There ain't no more breath!' She walked off the picture. Von

Sternberg wanted to replace her, but he wasn't allowed to. When she came back on the set, she looked him straight in the eye and said, 'No more candles!'

"Von Sternberg was boom crazy. At first, he hadn't liked the idea of booms, but once he got used to them he couldn't stop. In the big dinner scene he liked to ride over the table on this great boom as though he were on horseback. One day he yelled, 'Everyone out! I want an empty stage!' They all left except for one man, a little red-faced man sitting in the corner. 'Didn't you hear what I said?' von Sternberg yelled. 'I said, "Clear the stage!"' 'But Mr. von Sternberg,' the man replied faintly. 'Have you forgotten? I'm the cameraman.'

Sam Jaffe continues: "There was a scene in which I was supposed to give a speech beside Louise Dresser's coffin. He made me do it thirty-seven times. Finally, he said, 'It's got to be right this time! If it isn't, if you can't do it, I'll change the scene. I'll have you come out and spit, instead of giving the speech!'

"I said, 'If I do spit, it will be right in your eye!' I snatched off my Harpo Marx wig he had given me and glared at him. He said, 'You'll never work in pictures again.' I replied, 'Thank goodness for that. I work on the stage, I just come out and do pictures when I'm between engagements. *You* work in pictures.' He took me for a walk the whole length of the sound stage and back, up and down. He gave me a long lecture on aesthetics, and said, 'Mr. Jaffe, I wonder if you have any idea how important I am. Why, I have seventy million followers in Japan alone!'

"I said, 'That's wonderful, Mr. von Sternberg. Christ only had twelve!'"

The public was unable to accept Marlene as a villainess who did not discover true love in the last reel, and *The Scarlet Empress* was a box office fiasco, losing a fortune. A British version of the same story, starring Elisabeth Bergner and inferior in every way, had beaten it to the punch. B. P. Schulberg was attacked by Adolph Zukor for having permitted the picture to be made. He was dismissed and replaced as head of the studio by Ernst Lubitsch.

Richard Kollorsz, designer of the icons in *The Scarlet Empress*, says, "Both von Sternberg and Marlene left an unforgettable impression on me. Von Sternberg said to me, when we did *Shanghai Express*, 'I want the train to come on looking like a dragon.' I didn't know what on earth he was talking about. I told him so. He said, 'Figure it out for yourself.' So I put a dragon's face on the front of the train, breathing fire, and he took one look at it and said, 'OK.' I don't think he had the slightest idea what he wanted in the first place.

"Generosity was not his middle name. He said to the accountant's office, referring to Peter Ballbusch, who did all the magnificent sculptures for *The Scarlet Empress* film except for a couple I did myself, 'There'll be thirty-five dollars a week for Mr. Kollorsz and twenty-five dollars a week for Mr. Ballbusch.' What the hell, it was the middle of the Depression.

"I remember when I first met Marlene. She said to me, 'Do I look perfect?'

"I told her, 'Yes, but your breasts are icebergs.'

"She looked astonished. 'Why do you say that? All of my body is warm.'

" 'Miss Dietrich, your breasts *are* icebergs. So many men have been wrecked on them!'

"She was incredibly proud of her daughter. Her daughter was roly-poly, like a little dumpling. Marlene said, 'She's a princess! Her figure is absolutely perfect! You're an artist; you should appreciate it!' To my amazement, she stripped Maria naked and the ten-year-old child stood before me in her birthday suit. She looked even more like a dumpling. I said, 'She's flawless. The Venus de Milo in miniature!' Marlene smiled and hugged me. And then she said, 'And watch your language in front of her!'

"Von Sternberg carried on like crazy. Whenever we said anything against the picture, he'd say, 'A good dog doesn't shit in its own kennel!' Whenever he would quarrel with Marlene, he'd clear the set completely. He'd say to me, 'In ten minutes I want Moscow.' I'd tell him, 'You can have the Winter Palace in ten minutes. Moscow takes fifteen!'

"I remember when we ran the rough cut of *Empress*. We had

worked for months like hell. She arrived with her chauffeur, her housekeeper, and her maid; and we all sat and looked at the picture. I remember her pacing up and down restlessly, her high heels clicking on the floor.

"Finally, she went out, and click-clicked up and down outside. Von Sternberg said, very loudly so she could hear, 'This would be a great picture. If you took the actors and actresses out of it!' "

Six

An International Star

By 1934 Marlene was established as the most glamorous of international stars. In the midst of the Depression, with millions on the bread line, she represented for countless women a wish fulfillment fantasy of unlimited wealth (she was the third highest-paid person in the nation, earning at least $350,000 a year), and of beauty, elegance, and style. Whereas her only serious rival as a female star, Garbo, lived in secrecy, and never dressed up, Marlene flung herself headlong into the public life of a rich woman. Critics poured ecstatic prose over her: the leading British journalist James Agate wrote: "As for Dietrich, she makes reason totter on its throne," and that was typical of journalists' responses in most countries of the world.

She spent money on a royal scale. She bought the finest dresses—from the great couturiers of Paris; she traveled by drawing room on trains, in deluxe suites on steamers, and in chauffeur-driven limousines; she stayed at the Lancaster or the Trianon in Paris, the Waldorf Towers in New York, the Bristol in Berlin. Her beach house was the guest cottage of Marion Davies's multimillion-dollar estate in Santa Monica. She gave her makeup woman, Dotty Ponedel, a house; she gave others who pleased her gold cigarette cases, bracelets, sets of luggage.

A famous hostess of the mid-1930s, the Chinese princess Tai

Lachman, wife of the impressionist painter and film director Harry Lachman, says: "Marlene was constantly at our parties; indeed, we were constantly at hers. She entertained, as we did, on a very lavish scale. The rooms at these parties were filled with flowers. The men wore tuxedos and the women were decked out in rubies and diamonds. Marlene was always at the center of attention. I remember, one night, I saw her, leaning against the wall, in white, sipping a glass of champagne—with a single petal of a white rose floating on the surface. It was a Scott Fitzgerald image: unforgettable."

Mrs. Samson Raphaelson, wife of the well-known playwright and screenwriter, says: "Marlene always arranged to make a tremendous 'entrance,' escorted by a famous and handsome movie star, walking down the stairs—at one time, in a sailor suit which was the sexiest thing you ever saw—or in gold lamé lounging pajamas. Nobody could move in backless dresses as she did: every man in the room was looking at her, and the women were *furious!*

"She would stand with a long cigarette holder, count ten, and then materialize, like the most beautiful ghost in the world. Our social set agreed: there was no one to match her."

A typical little scene of the period would be at a jeweler's on Fifth Avenue: a knot of excited shoppers forming as Marlene made her way to the private office suite of the manager, to make a selection of cabochon emeralds from satin-lined boxes.

Her generosity and free spending were such that, according to Hans Kohn, she never invested in anything. In 1934, she traveled all the way to the Hague to discuss buying annuities and life insurance policies, with Kohn, a banker, but despite his most urgent warnings she neglected to follow his advice. She spent everything she had. She owed back taxes. Her agent, Charles Feldman, begged her to at least buy a house or apartment buildings, but she could not be bothered.

At home, when not working, she would rise very late, go to lunch with friends at some currently fashionable establishment, spend the afternoon shopping, and then prepare herself in a stunning evening gown for nightclubbing or dining. She was often at the theater, in London, Paris, and New York, rushing backstage like a fan with congratulations when she saw an actor or actress she admired. She read voraciously, swooping down on the leading bookstores and ordering cartloads of books to be delivered to her. She preferred simple, precise novels and poems.

She never kept a large staff. She usually had at least one maid —several German ones in her rented homes in Beverly Hills and at the beach—and her chauffeurs were highly prized. But she did not maintain the kind of huge household which so many of her contemporaries found necessary. She was generous to her servants.

She typed her own letters, unevenly, using two fingers, emphasizing important points in red ribbon or capital letters, and inserting numerous question marks and exclamation points.

She listened to music for hours, mostly French composers of the turn of the century, and operas. She studied minutely the results of her horoscopes, done after 1939 by Carroll Righter. She also studied the horoscopes of her friends and lovers, and made matches from horoscopes as well.

She used to cook for von Sternberg, and for Hans von Twardowski and Martin Kosleck. She would go to their homes to prepare the dishes. Von Sternberg had a fantastic Neutra steel house in San Fernando Valley, with a moat around it.

Since she never exercised—was rarely seen walking in Central Park and could not even be imagined on a bicycle—her slimness was a mystery to everyone: she ate like a trooper, and often filled herself with chocolates. She did not diet until after the war. Her explanation was that she smoked several packs a day and only slept four or five hours in a night. Her dramatically pale, washed-out appearance, beautiful when she was young, can also be explained by this.

It would be futile to try to "place" any part of her life in terms of the life lived by ordinary mortals; to the press she was a Helen of Troy, a Cleopatra. She tried constantly to give the impression that she was just an ordinary hausfrau like anyone else. Sometimes, to prove it, she would get down on all fours and scrub her floor in an evening gown before going out to a party.

In those years, Marlene's relationship with Maria became more and more heavily charged. By being so protective towards Maria, insisting on bodyguards around the clock, keeping her home from school, and regulating her swimming and tennis lessons, and by displaying to her child her own lacquered beauty every day, Marlene unwittingly set up a love-hate relationship with her daughter which was to persist. In interviews over the years, Maria told reporters of her consciousness of being fat, and not as beautiful as her mother. She had the strain of spending time with her father, whom she scarcely knew, and the giddy, unbalanced Tamara, at their successive apartments in Paris; during one very awkward summer, she lived, according to Hans Kohn, with Rudi, Tamara, and Marlene at the Hotel Lancaster.

She was also aware, she wrote, of her mother's extraordinary list of beaux, never forgetting how her mother, a ravishing, gilded beauty, would bend down and kiss her good night: Maria would breathe in the expensive perfume, catch the shine of blonde hair and gems, before Marlene left her to go out with her latest date for an evening of nightclubbing or dinner at a Russian restaurant with caviar and violins. The little girl could not mingle with children of her own age. It was an unnatural existence; and it is astonishing that Maria grew up to be the elegant and well-balanced woman she is today.

Marlene left for Europe yet again in early 1934, resuming her Paris friendships; she was particularly close to Billy Wilder, an old friend from Berlin who was making his first venture into French film production with *Mauvaise Graine,* starring Danielle Darrieux. On her way back to the States aboard the Île de France in April, she was invited to join a group in the dining saloon. The men stood up as she came to the table in shimmering white sequins, down the great staircase under a blaze of overhead lights, into what John Malcolm Brinnin described in a history of Atlantic shipping as "a vast mausoleum done in three shades of gray marble from the Pyrenees that was additionally illuminated by 112 motifs of electrified Lalique." She was appalled to notice as the men rose that she would be the thirteenth at table. Superstitious as ever, she turned to leave. Suddenly, a handsome broad-shouldered man with a chunky, red-cheeked face blocked her path. He said, "Don't worry, Miss Dietrich. I'll be the fourteenth." He was a writer who had managed to crash into first-class. His name was Ernest Hemingway.

She had read and liked his work, and after dinner, they strolled up to the deck and chatted. She told him about Maria's morbid preoccupation with books about disease, and she recited a poem Maria had written about a suicide. Hemingway was admiring of the poem, and fascinated by Marlene. They became friends at once. There was no question of a romantic liaison, either then or later. Hemingway told his friend and biographer A. E. Hotchner that sometime afterward there might have been a romance, but "the Kraut" (as he always called Marlene) was involved with "that worthless R——." This was presumably a reference to her relationship, further on in the 1930s, with Erich Maria Remarque.

Shortly after Marlene returned to Hollywood, von Sternberg began work on *Capriccio Espagnole,* a version of Pierre Louys's decadent novel, *The Woman and the Puppet.* Since the setting was Spanish, von Sternberg characteristically hired a writer who had a Spanish-sounding name, the distinguished novelist, poet and playwright, John Dos Passos, author of *Manhattan Transfer.* Dos Passos's books *1919* and *The 42nd Parallel* had flopped commercially. This fastidious, high-strung man was suffering from rheumatic fever. He needed sunshine and money, and he decided to accept the offer. He flew out from New York to Salt Lake City and changed planes to an ancient trimotor that flapped its wings like a vulture. The flight was rough and he spent most of the journey being sick in his hat.

He staggered drunk off the plane and collapsed in a heap at von Sternberg's feet. Then he rose, shook von Sternberg's hand

and said, echoing a widely held belief, "Joe Stern of Brooklyn, I declare!" (Although the director had grown up in the United States and had added the "von" to his name, he had been born Josef Sternberg in Vienna.) Von Sternberg remained silent during the drive to the Hollywood Plaza Hotel. That night, the manager of the Russian restaurant downstairs sent up an entire balalaika troupe to entertain the Great American Author, who was groaning in bed, holding his head in agony and saying "Thank you, thank you" in Russian several times over, in the hope they would leave. They stayed all night, while Dos Passos tried to distract himself by writing a long letter to Hemingway.

Hearing Dos Passos was sick, "that nice German hausfrau" as the novelist called Marlene in a letter to Hemingway, sent him flowers. Hating gladioli—her favorites—he tossed them in the wastebasket. Von Sternberg came by each day and went through the motions of working out dialogue while he had another writer doing the real script behind Dos Passos's back.

Von Sternberg finally threw away both of these scripts and prepared one of his own.

The screenplay became von Sternberg's most personal attack on Marlene to date. Paradoxically, it is her favorite of the pictures she made with him, because in it she is most captivatingly photographed. She played Concha Perez, a temptress who destroys men. At least in *The Scarlet Empress* there was the excuse that power had corrupted Catherine, that a stupid girl had been ruined by the acquisition of power and by the wicked court (Hollywood). Unlimited access to money and sex which royal authority (stardom) had brought to her had wrecked a star's character. But Concha Perez is evil from the start. She is heartless, cynical, utterly devoid of feeling. Lionel Atwill, as her lover, is modeled on von Sternberg, even down to the mustache and the thin, hard line of the lips. Concha's implacability is conveyed in the opening shot, when Antonio, another of her admirers, bursts a balloon with a slingshot at a carnival right in front of her face and discloses an expression of complete indifference. Von Sternberg wrote in his memoirs that an air pellet was used to explode the balloon, and that Marlene did not

Marlene's parents,
around 1897.
(*Courtesy Deutsches
Institut für
Filmkunde*)

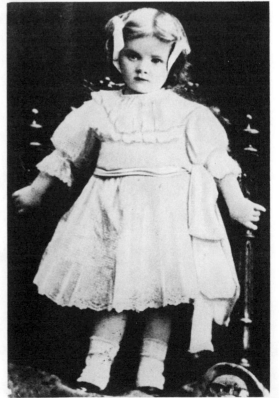

Marlene at age six.
(*Courtesy Deutsches
Institut für Filmkunde*)

Marlene (at left) leads school players in "La Paloma", Berlin, 1916. (*Courtesy Max Kohlhaas*)

Auguste-Victoria School, graduation class of 1918. Marlene is second from right in the bottom row. (*Courtesy Max Kohlhaas*)

Marlene with her newborn child in front of her apartment building, 54 Kaiseralle, Berlin, in April 1925. This photo postcard was sent by her husband, Rudi Sieber, to friends for Easter. (*Courtesy Mia May*)

Marlene in *It's in the Air*, 1928. (*Courtesy Max Kohlhaas*)

Marlene in *The Blue Angel*, 1929. (*Courtesy Deutsches Institut für Filmkunde*)

Von Sternberg (at left) directing Marlene and Emil Jannings in *The Blue Angel*, 1929. (*Courtesy Max Kohlhaas*)

Von Sternberg in the Berlin apartment of Erwin Piscator, 1929. (*Courtesy Riza Royce von Sternberg*)

"Von for all and all for Von"; Marlene, Heidede, Rudi, and von Sternberg, Hollywood, 1931. (*Courtesy Max Kohlhaas*)

Marlene with Maurice Chevalier and Gary Cooper, 1932. (*Courtesy Deutsches Institut für Filmkunde*)

Marlene as Concha in *The Devil Is
Woman*, 1935. (*Courtesy Deutsches Institut für Filmkunde*)

Marlene in her thirties.
(*Courtesy Deutsches
Institut für Filmkunde*)

Marlene with Jean Gabin in *Martin Roumagnac*, 1946. (*Courtesy Deutsches Institut für Filmkunde*)

Marlene with Erich Maria Remarque, Hollywood, 1948. (*Courtesy Max Kohlhaas*)

The Big Lift: Marlene entertaining the troops, 1945. (*Courtesy Max Kohlhaas*)

Marlene with von Sternberg, 1948. (*Courtesy Max Kohlhaas*)

Marlene with her daughter at Gertude Lawrence's funeral, 1953. (*Courtesy Max Kohlhaas*)

Reunion in Berlin, 1960: Marlene and von Sternberg. (*Courtesy Max Kohlhaas*)

Marlene on the
London Underground,
1973. (*Courtesy* Daily
Express, *London*)

disclose by the flicker of an eyelash any feeling of terror as the pellet was fired.

His memoirs make clear that the director thought of Marlene in the same terms as he thought of Concha Perez. It is also clear that this was a classic example of sour grapes: since he could no longer hope to obtain her emotional interest in him, he assumed she had no emotions. The film became disappointment disguised as art.

As always in his scripts, von Sternberg portrayed the world of officialdom, of the grand bourgeois and the military, as a world of idiocy and corruption. The movie not only condemns Marlene, it condemns Hollywood and the society which buys the Hollywood product. The struggles between Concha and the von Sternberg-like Pascal reflect Marlene's battles with her mentor, but not those humorous battles which their contemporaries recall. Here there is a struggle to the death. Von Sternberg's most bitter comment on Marlene is shown in a song, "Three Sweethearts Have I," which includes the line "To all three I'm true / And I could be as true to you."

Joel McCrea, who had just made a great hit in *Bird of Paradise* with Dolores Del Rio, was originally cast as the younger romantic lead, Antonio. He recalls: "I didn't know Dietrich. I hated the director. He did forty-seven takes of me and I walked off. I went down to see her in her dressing room and she said, 'I'm sorry to hear you're leaving. He treats me badly too, he calls me "You cow" in German!' Cesar Romero played the role instead. He was much better than I was. He looked more like a matador—I looked like a New York policeman!"

Cesar Romero says: "Joel McCrea evidently disagreed with Mr. von Sternberg on a few things and Mr. von Sternberg disagreed with him, and Joel walked off the picture. They had to get someone to replace him right away because they were already in production. All I knew was that the casting office at Universal called me and said, 'Go to Paramount studios and ask for so-and-so.' I went! They took me to the stage, and I walked into the scene where Joseph von Sternberg was directing Dietrich. A beautiful, magnificent set. Von Sternberg said to one of his assistants, without even saying hello to me, 'Grab him, and put a costume on him!' They put this costume on me and he sat me at a table, gave me a few lines to read, turned the camera, and said, 'OK. You'll do. Fine.' Next thing I knew, I was playing opposite Marlene Dietrich!

"He was not, to put it mildly, the nicest man in the world to work with. He was a little Napoleon. He was a little man and he ruled the stage like a little king. It was to be the last picture he made with Marlene Dietrich and it was the end of their Svengali-Trilby association. He used to bawl her out by the hour in German. Marlene would cry. And cry. She had a German maid who used to stand on the sidelines. I used to watch the maid's reactions to what von Sternberg was saying. He must have been saying terrible things to her because the maid used to start back in horror and clasp her hands to her face. He was rather sadistic. He would make you do tiny things over and over and over again.

"I had one simple thing to do, I had to run down a flight of steps. I had these high-heeled Spanish boots on. He said, 'Do it again, please, a little faster.' It was agony—I had to run, run down these stairs. Finally he had me jumping the steps, five, six at a time, until I tripped and fell smack on my face! Then he said, 'OK, that's enough!' The next day we went in to see the rushes. I saw myself run down the stairs a hundred times—and I heard him say to the projectionist, 'Print take two!' "

Despite the glittering images, the compositions in depth which recalled the work of Spanish painters, *The Devil Is a Woman* (Lubitsch's title for *Capriccio Espagnole*) was an artistic failure. The audience could not relate to a woman without virtue, and refused to accept Marlene as an inhuman creature. Moreover, political trouble threatened the very existence of the film. The ambassador from Spain reported to his superiors that the film was a travesty of Spanish life, and an insult to the Spanish police and governing authorities. The United States State Department was so aggravated by fears of a collapse of Spanish-American arrangements for mutual trade that the master print was ritually burned in Washington in front of the Spanish ambassador.

The Spanish government banned the movie and said that

unless all other prints of the picture were withdrawn no Paramount film would be permitted to enter Spain. Adolph Zukor crumbled under the pressure, and toward the end of 1935 the film was permanently withdrawn.

In the meantime, B. P. Schulberg left Paramount under a cloud, moving over to Columbia. Lubitsch became production manager, and later head of production. He hated von Sternberg. Not only were they temperamental opposites—the one witty and urbane, the other obsessive and solemn—but Lubitsch resented von Sternberg's continuing insolence toward him. When he had complained of von Sternberg's extravagance in supplying a large crowd scene in *The Scarlet Empress,* von Sternberg had called him and said, "But, Mr. Lubitsch, I got that scene out of the vault. You shot it yourself in [your film] *The Patriot."*

The last day of shooting of *The Devil Is a Woman,* von Sternberg barely talked to Marlene. When the final shot came, he snapped, "Cut. Print it." And he walked off without a word.

Marlene was shocked almost to tears by his callousness. It is possible that his anger resulted from the fact that she had been dating the recently arrived great German director Fritz Lang, a brilliant but autocratic martinet of picture making who had resisted every effort of Hitler and Goebbels to make him stay in an important position in the Nazi film industry.

Von Sternberg left town following the disastrous previews of *The Devil Is a Woman.* He had not wanted to work with Marlene after his first two pictures because of the difficulty of directing a woman he loved, and who would never love him. After this last picture together, he went into a professional decline. His career never recovered from the loss of his greatest inspiration. She quickly proved that she could be good without him, that her message to him on her photograph, "I am nothing without you," was modest and wrong. He should have written the same words on his photograph.

From the days in Berlin when Marlene had mingled with White Russian émigrés and had filled her apartment in the

Kaiserallee with icons and white baroque furniture, she had been passionately pro-Russian. When she returned to Hollywood in 1935, she met a remarkable man. He was Alexander Vertinsky, who towards the end of the czarist régime had obtained a vast reputation singing about unfaithful or unrequited love in a strange, haunting voice, filled with melancholy and tender regret. He sang in a Pierrot costume, his face white with powder and his eyes like coals in snow. His most famous songs were "Magnolia" and "The Mad Organ Grinder." He gave more than three thousand concerts and became a millionaire in rubles before he was forced to flee Russia for Paris and New York and Hollywood. Penniless, he was reduced to performing in seedy dives which catered to poverty-stricken Russian immigrants.

He met Marlene in Los Angeles, and fell hopelessly in love with her; and after futile attempts to become involved with her he wrote a savage poem about a hopeless adoration for a movie star. Entitled "Good-bye," it was dedicated to her. A sample passage, translated by Mischa Allen, reads:

> Night falls. There must be songs.
> Kisses. Help me undress . . .
> The lights go out.
> "Tommorrow we will shoot at dawn.
> I cannot, now . . ."
>
> It's better at the last
> To put an end to this sublime
> Love affair—and with a sigh
> Breathe "Good-bye."

According to the *New York Times* obituary, Vertinsky drifted from America to Shanghai, and then returned to Russia at the invitation of Stalin, who forgave him his political background because of a passion for Vertinsky's recordings, played over and over again in the Stalin household in Moscow. Mischa Allen, Vertinsky's translator in Canada, writes: "While in Moscow in the 1960s, Marlene Dietrich paid a visit to Vertinsky's grave and placed flowers on it."

In 1935, Marlene traveled to Paris, Switzerland, and Vienna. Those who knew her at the time feel that she must have been hoping that some part could be found for her in an Austrian film, perhaps directed by Willi Forst, who was now prominent as a filmmaker. While in Vienna, she embarked on a new intimate friendship, formally conducted and elegant as any in an Arthur Schnitzler play, with Hans Jaray. Jaray was a gifted and handsome actor, director, and playwright, a household word in Austria in those days. Of noble Hungarian ancestry, half-Jewish, witty and intelligent, with a flawless, slender body, he was everything a woman of culture and distinction could wish for.

Marlene frequently visited his impeccably furnished apartment at 33 Reisnerstrasse, with books, paintings, carpets, and curtains which she, with her highly developed aesthetic sense, most warmly admired. The relationship did not last a long time, but it was enclosed in joy; it ended, as it began, in luminous affection.

Although Vienna was not the gay and glittering city that legend imagined it, the city offered superb theater: Hans Jaray's performance in *Cissy*, in which he first attracted her attention, causing her to go backstage, was one of its most refined pleasures. There were teas at the Sacher Hotel, drinks at the Bristol Bar, or evenings mingling with the fashionable crowd at the Imperial. But Marlene much preferred the out-of-the-way places, the small cafés where the cooking was good and where violins were played on the long summer evenings, before Hitler moved in and the Jewish Berlin émigrés moved en masse to Paris.

She formed a warm friendship with the gourmet and author of cookbooks, Ludwig von Karpathy, who taught her many secrets of Hungarian-Viennese cooking which stood her in good stead. She learned to prepare the finest dumplings and the best goulash her friends ever tasted—probably because of von Karpathy.

Back in Hollywood during this period, following the collapse of her relationship with von Sternberg, Marlene met and, according to his daughter and widow, became emotionally involved with the great fallen silent star John Gilbert, who had been ruined when, because of the inadequate recording techniques of the day, he had sounded awkward in a sequence of an early talkie, *His Glorious Night.* Many people believe he had been sabotaged by his boss, Louis B. Mayer.

According to the star Eleanor Boardman, a double wedding had been arranged for Garbo and Gilbert and the director King Vidor and Boardman, at Marion Davies's beach house in Santa Monica. Garbo had failed to turn up, and Gilbert had flung himself to the floor in an outburst of disappointment and rage. Mayer said, "Why don't you just fuck the dame and forget all about marrying her?" Hysterical, Gilbert seized Mayer, dragged him into the marble bathroom and began to strangle him. Mayer's lieutenant, Eddie Mannix, dragged the two men apart. In a scene which Clifford Odets later duplicated in a play, Mayer got up off the floor and told Gilbert he was through, even if it cost the studio a million dollars a year. It almost did, because a few days before Gilbert had signed a contract with Mayer's superior, Nicholas Schenck.

Marlene had, of course, heard of Gilbert's decline, and when she met this fragile man in 1935, she felt all her maternal instincts acutely awakened, and longed to do what she could to resuscitate his spirit. Knowing that his contract with MGM had finally run out and he had made a flop picture at Columbia, *The Captain Hates the Sea,* she begged Lubitsch at Paramount to help him out by giving him a new deal. Lubitsch, despite his many differences with her and his hatred of von Sternberg, trusted her judgment and agreed to test Gilbert for the role of a jewel thief opposite her in his next production, *Desire.* This was to be directed by Frank Borzage, and to begin production in February 1936.

It is curious to realize that Marlene was following Garbo in a relationship with Gilbert. She loved Gilbert's daughter Leatrice. She encouraged Gilbert when he told her that, knowing he could not live much longer because of the degeneration of his body from alcohol, he would revise his will. With his servants as witnesses, he left his ex-wife Virginia Bruce two $50,000 annuities. He left the bulk of his estate to Leatrice, saying, "She has filled a great void in my life."

No sooner had she helped Gilbert prepare his role for *Desire*, dried him out, worked on a lighting pattern for his face to disguise the lines and wrinkles, and seen him sail expertly through the tests and still-photo sessions, than Marlene received a brutal shock.

One weekend she was sitting by the pool of his house at 1400 Tower Grove Road when he dove in and swam. Suddenly, he began thrashing about in agony. He had had a heart seizure. She managed to ease his suffering while the servants called an ambulance. He recovered, but Lubitsch unhesitatingly struck him from the cast list of the picture, claiming that he dared not risk a major production by using someone who might not last through the film.

Marlene's healing instincts were foremost in her relationship with Gilbert. She twice succeeded in getting him off the bottle, only to see him slip back. She evidently knew his hypersensitive temperament, and how difficult day-to-day living in the merciless Hollywood environment must be for him. Her tenderness, gentleness, and consideration for von Sternberg had been wasted. But here was a man who needed her and respected her, who did not look down on her, who had the kind of poetic and romantic spirit which was mirrored in the softer side of her nature.

One day, Garbo came to the door of Gilbert's house in a battered roadster. Marlene opened the door herself and was astonished to see Garbo there. Gilbert went out to the car and talked to Garbo for an hour. From the look of them, it seemed he was begging Garbo to take him back. According to Leatrice, Marlene was horrified and immediately decided to leave the house. She fled; and as soon as she did, she again met Gary Cooper and began dating him.

Leatrice recalls, "Marlene was unable to resist Gary Cooper. The moment father found out, he went to pieces again, and didn't stop drinking until the day he died. One day, Marlene went over to play tennis with him at his house. He fell down in front of her with some kind of seizure, and the real shock was, much of his hair fell out. His hair lay on the court. I think she really panicked then and realized what she had done. Her guilt was terrible to see."

It came as a severe blow when, on the morning of January 10, 1936, one day after Gary Cooper was announced for the leading role of *Desire,* John Gilbert died of a heart attack. Marlene experienced acute emotional distress, crying helplessly. She was, Leatrice says, convinced she had "killed" him. On January 11, she arrived at the funeral accompanied by her dear friend Dolores Del Rio, John Barrymore, and Gary Cooper. Marlene tripped and fell in the aisle, sobbing loudly. She sank into a pew and threw herself on Dolores Del Rio's shoulder, weeping again. She managed to pull herself together sufficiently to view the cedar casket with its gray broadcloth heaped high with her gift of her beloved gladioli. But she broke down completely when Reverend Dodd spoke the words of the Psalm: "The Lord is my shepherd, I shall not want."

After the funeral, Marlene became tough and practical. She was convinced that John Gilbert's new will, which she had seen being written, had been suppressed. The published will left Virginia Bruce the bulk of the estate, including his house, real estate, and common stock amounting to almost half a million dollars. This was the residue of his savings after the stock market crash of 1929 had taken most of his personal fortune.

As soon as she saw the announcement of the terms of the will in the *Los Angeles Times,* Marlene told her chauffeur to take her to the home of Leatrice Joy, the mother of Gilbert's daughter Leatrice and a former star of silent pictures, who had married and divorced him some years before. Arriving at Leatrice Joy's front door without warning, Marlene shook the newspaper in her hand and said, "This will is an outrage! Jack revised his will! He left almost everything to young Leatrice! You must hire a lawyer immediately and get hold of the missing will!"

From Leatrice Joy's house, Marlene immediately went to

Gilbert's, and was horrified to find it had been ransacked from attic to cellar. Souvenir hunters had swept through everything, picking up a large number of objects. She grabbed the servants and demanded to know why they had permitted this sacrilege, where the police were, and what had happened to the revised will. They kept repeating over and over like automatons, "We don't know nothing."

All of John Gilbert's belongings were put on auction, except for a few items retained by Virginia Bruce. The will was never discovered, and the earlier one was adhered to. Marlene went to the auction and bought two double-bed sheets for $700 the pair.

Marlene, discovering that Leatrice, Jr., had been left only $10,000, and loving the child as only she could love children, virtually adopted her. When she went to Europe after making *Desire,* she sent the little girl beautiful gifts, including stuffed animals, a gold bracelet, and many other things. For three years, she remained devoted to her. She would sweep up to the child's house in her Rolls, dressed in a cloud of silver fox, dripping with cabochon emeralds the size of plover's eggs, and whisk her off in the car as though it were a fairy carriage, with its deep white fur rug, its makeup compartment, and built-in sound system playing her favorite songs.

Leatrice, Jr., says, "She called me whenever she was in California and took me to openings of films—*Snow White and the Seven Dwarfs,* and *The Country Doctor,* with the Dionne quintuplets. She begged Darryl Zanuck to let her play the mother or the nurse in *The Country Doctor* for nothing, or even a walk-on, just to be near those five glorious babies! She was a very sentimental lady.

"After the premieres she would take me to her great kitchen and cook scrambled eggs or give me fudge or cookies she had baked. She was always sending me boxes of candies from a Viennese confectioner in Beverly Hills. She gave me a star ruby pendant on a thin platinum chain, which unfortunately was stolen when my mother's house was burgled, and when I was heartbroken because I lost the gold watch my father gave me on our last Christmas together, she had an exact duplicate made, even to the engraving on the back in an astonishing, minutely accurate duplicate of my father's own handwriting, 'To my darling Tinka.'

"Our friendship lasted two and a half to three years. After her deep involvement with Erich Maria Remarque in 1937 we saw less of each other, and I was in boarding school; but I shall never forget for a minute how Marlene, then one of the greatest stars in Hollywood, took the time and trouble to lift a rather plain little girl out of the dismal despair I was in after father died, and helped me make the painful journey into adolescence, playing as well as she could the role my father might have played. I will always be grateful."

Seven

Towards
World War

Desire, with Gary Cooper replacing Gilbert, was shot in late February and March, 1936. Marlene showed no trace of her grief, and gave a most adroit comedy performance. She played a jewel thief who steals a pearl necklace from a Parisian jeweler, only to be shamed by a Peoria hick engineer into returning the gems. She is married to him while on parole. Directed by Frank Borzage under Lubitsch's careful supervision, this was a delicious light comedy, airy and refreshing by contrast with the more claustrophobic von Sternberg vehicles.

Yet again the movie contains elements of biography. The Parisian setting echoes Marlene's numerous visits to that city. Street addresses of shops and salons are only slightly altered from those she would frequently visit there. Her favorite gladioli are in two scenes. By a perverse joke, she is seen driving recklessly throughout the picture, although it was well known she couldn't drive. The emphasis on jewels refers to the fact that she was building up a large collection, not from gifts to her by men, but from gifts she had to buy for herself. Transvestite jokes, often applied to her, are woven into the dialogue: she describes a duped jeweler as preferring nightgowns to pajamas because he "imagines he is a schoolgirl."

Immediately after *Desire* was finished, Marlene was rushed into a remake of the old Pola Negri vehicle, *Hotel Imperial,* about a maid in a wartime hotel who shelters a soldier and falls in love with him.

The director was Henry Hathaway, a tough and feisty young man whom Lubitsch very much admired. Hathaway says, "I had just made a picture called *Peter Ibbetson*, and Lubitsch was crazy about it. He asked me to come and discuss the script of *Hotel Imperial* with him. I liked it very much.

"At that time, Dietrich was in box-office trouble: she had deteriorated because of her treatment by von Sternberg. She was considered quite a clotheshorse, but not an actress. I disagreed with that. I though she was a damned good actress.

"I blamed her decline on von Sternberg. My idea for *Hotel Imperial* was to start with a shot of a long, wide hallway, and a woman scrubbing and mopping the floor. She has dirty hair and dirty clothes; she is wearing old carpet slippers. She's a slob. As she gets the guy and hides him and as she falls in love with him, she gets progressively prettier. Then you see Dietrich in all her beauty coming out of the cathedral married, with the Uhlan swordsmen framing her on either side. She has become completely transformed.

"It was a wonderful idea. The first time she wore a clean apron, it would have astonished and excited the audience. It would have driven them wild!

"Lubitsch loved the idea. She herself viewed *Peter Ibbetson*, and approved me at once. She asked me, 'Do I have to look *very* hideous?' I said, 'Yes, as ugly as it's possible for you to be, at first. No lipstick, no powder, matted hair, a complete slob!' She became more and more excited!

"We started the picture. Each time we began rehearsals she was a little more dressed up than I wanted her to be. I always won, because I'd go to Lubitsch and he would tell her what to do. It was in her contract that he would continue as producer even though he was head of the studio. She'd come on a scene, and she'd want to fix her ugly hair, and I'd say, 'Not yet, for Christ's sake. You can be beautiful later! Halfway through the picture Lubitsch was fired; he got into a fight with the big boys, and he was dismissed; he was gone.

With him gone, she misbehaved. She came on for a scene of scrubbing floors with her lipstick on, her hair perfectly groomed, and I was horrified. I said, 'Jesus Christ! You can't do this!' She told me, 'I have the say now that Lubitsch is gone. 'I told her, 'You haven't got the say. I'm making the picture and I don't want to spoil the idea I have, that you only get beautiful because of love.' We had a hell of an argument. I said to her, 'You're not supposed to be beautiful until next Thursday.' And she'd say, 'Please—can't it at least be *Wednesday?*' I told her, 'No,' and the next thing I knew she'd gone.

"As I said, in her contract it stipulated that Lubitsch was to produce the picture. Unless Lubitsch was back on the lot to produce the picture, she was legally right: she needn't make the picture. Paramount had a big problem. She even walked off the lot. They were furious with her. She had become a monster of her own making. Von Sternberg had demanded so much for her, her price was so high, she was a problem. They said to her, 'Lubitsch is not coming back.' She said, 'If Lubitsch is not coming back, I quit.' So I said to them, 'Look, forget her. *Just forget her!*' They did. They said, 'We'll take Margaret Sullavan and use Dietrich for the long shots.'

"I was happy with Margaret Sullavan. She was marvelous. She didn't care how ugly she looked. We worked about three or four days. She wasn't married; she was going with Henry Fonda. She and Hank were kids who had grown up in the theater and who were very playful. She had a water pistol and she'd squirt him in the face with it, and he'd scream laughing and squirt her and they'd fall over. He'd rib her about her ugly hair and face and costume, and she'd chase him and he'd chase her in and out of the scenery!

"They fell over a pile of wires, which we call a spider, and rolled over on the floor, and she found she'd broken her *arm!* The studio bosses called me and said, 'Do we have to get Dietrich back? Can't you have Maggie Sullavan wear a sling?' I said, 'God's told me twice not to finish this picture. A heroine with an arm in a sling scrubbing a floor and going to her wedding in a sling? It's *ridiculous!*'

"The picture was canceled. A couple of years later, in 1938, the producer Walter Wanger, who was a good friend of mine, called me one day and showed me the stuff I'd shot with Dietrich. He edited it and he had about three or three and a half reels of it. It was *good.* The progression of it was fantastic. Marlene'd be making the bed of the man she loved, and when she turned around and faced the camera she looked just a little bit better. When she fixed a little meal for him in the cubbyhole, she looked marvelously authentic. I looked at Walter and I said, 'Jesus Christ. We were wrong to let her go. She's an *actress!*' Walter said, 'I've shown it to Dietrich, and she loves it, and says she'll finish it now if you'll direct it.' I said, 'Tell her to fuck off!' That was the end of it. She had humiliated me and the company and I couldn't forgive her. Later, Robert Florey made *Hotel* Imperial and Billy Wilder reworked it as *Five Graves to Cairo*.

"In 1938, I saw a picture Rouben Mamoulian had made, *Applause*. I had begun to feel a little guilty about not finishing *Hotel Imperial* with Dietrich. Maybe, I thought, I should have patched things up with her. *Applause* was the story of an old burlesque dancer whose daughter was ashamed of her, a reworking of *Stella Dallas,* first made in 1925.

"I didn't think Helen Morgan had been good as the mother, or that the picture, although quite OK, had been that well made. I thought it would be a marvelous chance for Dietrich to play a nonglamorous role. I told the company and they were happy with the idea of remaking any of their old things. But when I mentioned Dietrich, the studio bosses said, 'Oh, Jeeezus!' 'Now *wait!*' I said, 'Look, she's learned her lesson, she's down and out, and she wants to do a picture with me, she's apologized, she even wants to finish *Hotel Imperial.*' They let me talk to her, I told her the story, and she said, 'Yes, it's interesting. I'd love to work with you. I'll let you know if I decide to do it.' One day, the new Paramount boss Y. Frank Freeman called me in and said, 'What did she say?'

"I told him, 'She'll let me know.' Wednesday he asked, 'Did you hear from her?' I said, 'No.' Thursday and Friday, the same question, the same reply. On Monday, he said he had finally had word from her. I went down to his office and he said, 'You won't believe this.' She came in with von Sternberg and said she liked the property. She marveled at it, it was a good chance for her, and she would make it, but only on the condition that von Sternberg directed it. I sent her home! Soon after, Paramount canceled her contract."

After *Hotel Imperial* was discontinued Marlene obtained a loan-out arrangement so that she could appear for David O. Selznick in a version of Robert Hichens's novel *The Garden of Allah*. Selznick's files show that he had planned this picture with her back in the summer of 1935, and that she had discussed the possibility of costarring with John Gilbert in it. Marlene's close friend Gregory Ratoff, a brisk Russian émigré director and actor, had acted as a go-between in the negotiations.

Despite the fact that Selznick had been dismayed by most of Marlene's pictures with von Sternberg, he felt she would be perfect for the part of Domini Enfilden, a former convent girl who falls in love with a lapsed monk in North Africa. He cast Charles Boyer as the monk, since Boyer had also become available following the collapse of the *Hotel Imperial* project.

The director was Richard Boleslawski, a former Russian lancer, dashing and colorful, who had built up a major reputation in the previous four years. Selznick called Marlene into his office, in a building modeled on Mt. Vernon, for a furious pep talk. He told her he understood her pictures ran over schedule and budget because of her fanatical attention to hair, costumes, and makeup. She told him, "It's not true. I want to make this picture quickly. I have to get to England. I've been signed to do a picture there, *Knight Without Armor*, for Alexander Korda."

Selznick lectured her interminably, telling her that, while he had admired her performance in *Desire*, he did not feel she had the capacity to make an audience cry. He also told her that he felt she worried too much about her profile, and about the lighting of her cheekbones.

The meeting evidently bored Marlene. The writer Gavin Lambert recalls, "For years Marlene used to play a game. Her friends had to name the one person in the world each would not go to bed with even if their childrens' lives depended on it. She invariably named Selznick."

It is not quite clear why she undertook to make the film, since she despised the script from the first. Joshua Logan was flown from New York to supervise the dialogue direction. No sooner had he been introduced to her than she said, being unable to pronounce *r*'s "Have you wead the scwipt? It's twash, isn't it? Gawbo wouldn't play the part. She said she didn't believe the giwl would send the boy back to the monastewy. She is a vewy clevew woman, Gawbo! She has the pwimitive instincts—dose peasants have, you know."

As though to imitate von Sternberg, Boleslawski dressed up in britches, jackboots, and a hunting jacket to take off into the desert near Yuma, Arizona for the shooting in temperatures of 135 degrees. There, Marlene had to utter inane dialogue day after day. She told me in 1965, without the *w*'s, "That screenplay! I swear I said, 'Only God and I knows what is in my heart!' a hundred and five times. Finally I said to Josh, 'Can't Charles Boyer say it the hundred and sixth time?' "

In his autobiography, Logan goes on to tell a hilarious story of the making of the picture, with everyone getting tangled up in the accents and in the miserable lines. Forty years later, reading the book, Marlene told her friend, the fashion designer Ginette Spanier, "Josh makes us all sound so illitewate!"

In tents in the suffocating desert, Marlene was still literally burning a candle (or two) for John Gilbert. She had pictures of him everywhere.

In the course of a brief romance with Selznick's production manager, Willis Goldbeck, she was sitting on the sofa one night when a wind blew out the curtains and a candle on one side of Gilbert's portrait fell over. "I guess Jack is telling us what he thinks of us," Goldbeck said.

According to Logan, Marlene hated the director, and longed for the work to end. Everyone was ill except her, and begged her to intercede with Selznick to get them back to Hollywood. Marlene found a solution. Right in the middle of a scene, she fainted. Selznick was forced to withdraw the company.

Selznick was furious with Marlene when he saw the rushes. He wrote to Boleslawski on June 17, 1936, saying, "Would you *please* speak to Marlene about the fact that her hair is getting so much attention, and is coiffed to such a degree that all reality is lost. Her hair is so well placed that at all times—when the wind is blowing, for instance, or when Marlene is on a balcony or walking through the streets—it remains perfectly smooth and unruffled; in fact, it is so well placed that it could be nothing but a wig."

Unhappily, by the time he received this note, the director was too sick to care. He had drunk infected water at a spring and had fallen gravely ill. His widow recalls that this huge and bearlike man came back from location reduced to less than ninety pounds. Within a few months, he was dead.

Despite the fact that she did not admire his work, Marlene was, as always, exquisitely kind to Boleslawski and did her utmost to save his life. Nothing could save the picture. It was a box-office disaster.

Most of the reviews were vicious. Today, the film, for the first half, at least, is very entertaining, designed with flair and directed with strong pictorial feeling. It is a glorious example of High Camp nonsense, visibly sent up by Marlene in every scene.

Marlene left for England five days after the picture was finished. She caused a great deal of talk aboard the *Normandie* —walking on a private terrace on the play deck in pajamas while tourists gazed at her. She joined the officers for lunch in the mess hall, danced with the captain and told jokes at his table, and won five months of free drinks at the 21 Club for Ham Fisher, creator of Joe Palooka, because she invited him to her private four-room suite for cocktails. His friend had bet he couldn't get invited.

Vogue magazine reported: "She had a suite called Deauville. She had blue satin upholstery and a baby grand piano, swathed herself in green chiffon, and painted her toes and fingernails green to match her emeralds. The captain took Maria up to the bridge and let her blow the ship's whistle at noon. Among the craziest press releases from the *Normandie* was one which had Marlene complaining about the rough sea. 'A thousand pardons, madame, I'll see it doesn't happen again,' the Captain said. Within twenty minutes, the sea was flat."

On board ship, Marlene watched *Desire* and was photographed smiling adoringly at her own image. Marlene planned to practice at the piano in her suite, until she found it was out of tune, and the ship's company did not include a piano tuner.

She arrived at the Dorchester in London creating a stir as her thirty-six suitcases were carried through the lobby. She became friendly in the first couple of days with Frances Marion, the Hollywood script writer who had been engaged to adapt *Knight Without Armor* from the novel by James Hilton. Together, the two ladies entertained Marlene's costar, the fragile and asthmatic Robert Donat, at afternoon tea at the hotel.

Donat, flustered by Marlene's beauty and made dizzy by her exotic perfume, twice upset his teacup and spilled the buttered crumpets on the floor.

The late Frances Marion told me, "She evidently felt that if she could get into a relationship with him she could help him with his sickness. Since she was just over John Gilbert, I knew she was looking for another man.

"But something happened in the middle of tea which turned her to ice. She discovered he was married. He didn't have the slightest idea, I'm sure, that Marlene would be attracted to him, and therefore he mentioned his wife quite innocently, assuming that she knew about it all along. I knew from her eyes that she instantly decided to lay off. As a strict rule, she would never get involved with a man who had a wife.

"During the picture, Donat was off for two months with a terribly severe asthma problem. When he was finally well enough, he came back to a darkened sound stage. She had arranged for all the lights to be turned off. Suddenly the lights went up and she led the entire cast and crew in toasting him in champagne. Then she said, and only she could have thought of it, 'Hooray! Knight Without Asthma!' "

Marlene created a sensation when she first walked onto the set. She was wearing a white bathrobe, was followed by two maids carrying towels, and walked slowly towards a large marble bubble-bath tub. She was supposed to have worn flesh-colored tights under the bathrobe, but had rejected the idea. As a result, a normally indifferent crew had become uncharacteristically attentive, and adjoining sets were emptied as additional technicians suddenly appeared. Feyder ordered dozens of takes, and with each of these Marlene was completely naked for a couple of seconds. Just as she completed the sequence, she slipped on the soapy floor and fell with an undignified scream. Jack Cardiff, the cameraman, reported later, "What does a gentleman do when a world-famous beauty is lying stark naked at his feet, unable to get up? Everyone was much too embarrassed to help her and, still naked, she limped off to her dressing room, accompanied by her hairdresser and two hopelessly flustered maids."

Maria was sent to Brilliamont, the most exclusive girls' school in Switzerland. Heavy at age twelve, with puffy cheeks, Maria still suffered miserably from self-consciousness and from the contrast between her pudgy appearance and her mother's slender beauty. After Maria was placed at the school, Marlene moved from the Dorchester to a flat in Grosvenor Square, two floors below Douglas Fairbanks, Jr.'s, penthouse. She dated him frequently. They spent many weekends at the country house of the merchant banker Sir Constantine Benson, where Marlene prepared most of the meals. She urged the insecure Fairbanks to risk his career by accepting the difficult part of Rupert of Hentzau in Selznick's *The Prisoner of Zenda*, a part which was to make him more famous, and for which she supervised the curling and dyeing of his hair. Fairbanks says, "Marlene's decision for me was the right one. She was a glamour girl with brains. Amusing and unpretentious. Not at all the mystery character. A gallant, straightforward girl full of ideas."

While Marlene was in London, von Sternberg was directing the ill-fated and never completed *I, Claudius* for Korda. She saw him on and off, and remained devoted to his talent. One

Sunday, there was a violent thunderstorm. She had a severe cold, but insisted on going out in the Rolls, with von Sternberg, Rudi (who had come over from Paris), the singer Richard Tauber, and the writer Walter Reisch, to see her old friend Claudette Colbert's film *Under Two Flags* at the Tivoli Theatre in the Strand. She had learned that a French actress, who had been replaced at the last minute by Colbert, was still visible in some of the long shots. All through the screening, she kept jumping up and down saying, "There she is! There's that French actress!" Several people, not recognizing her voice, turned around and told her to be quiet.

After the show was over, the rain had gone and the sky was clear. Marlene dismissed the Rolls and the little group walked back towards Piccadilly.

As they strolled along, they gradually became aware they were being followed. Nearing the Burlington Arcade, they turned around. They were astonished to see a very large and menacing pack of prostitutes. The streetwalkers encircled them completely and pinned them against a wall. The leading prostitute strolled up to Marlene, looked at her in the eye, and unhesitatingly stripped off her left shoulder-length green glove.

Marlene was frozen with astonishment. The men seemed paralyzed. The prostitute walked off with the glove, swinging it triumphantly.

Suddenly another woman appeared, and ripped off the other glove. Marlene, with her usual cool, did not express anything. Now a third woman stepped forward and stripped off her blouse. Then the prostitutes left.

Marlene laughed when she got home. Walter Reisch recalls that Marlene said, " 'You see! They wanted souvenirs of me! They've seen all my pictures! They think of me as the queen of all the prostitutes!' "

Knight Without Armor, released in 1936, an elaborate story of the Russian Revolution, lost the producer a fortune. Marlene was named "box-office poison" by the motion picture exhibitors, along with Katharine Hepburn and Bette Davis. She laughed at the announcement, and apparently decided to move to Europe to make pictures in Paris. That she still intended to become an American is clear, because in 1937 she stood in line with carpenters, plumbers, and scrubwomen in the Los Angeles Federal Building to take out naturalization papers.

She gave her birth date incorrectly as December 27, 1904, and smiled while the clerk, visibly unsettled by her presence, kept dropping his pen in an effort to enter her vital statistics on the necessary form. Barely able to suppress her laughter, she announced that her eyes were blue and her hair blonde, that she was five feet eight inches tall and weighed 124 pounds. She gave her wedding date as May 17, 1923, whereupon the clerk gave up completely, wiped his glasses, upset an ink pot, and dropped a handkerchief on the floor. With a considerable effort, he pulled himself together and announced it would be two years before Mrs. Sieber could become a citizen. Delighted by the clerk's statement, Marlene walked past the large and whispering crowd which had gathered in the corridor, and with her manager, Harry Eddington, and her lawyer, Loyd Wright, swept off to her limousine. Two years later, she made the final arrangements; and in November 1939 she cast her first vote on the set while working in the film *Destry Rides Again*.

Die Stürmer, official organ of the Nazi party, ran a photograph of Marlene taking her citizenship oath before a Jewish judge, and denounced her with the words: "The German-born film actress Marlene Dietrich spent so many years among Hollywood's film Jews that she has now become an American citizen. Here we have a picture in which she is receiving her papers in Los Angeles. What the Jewish judge thinks of the formula can be seen from his attitude as he stands in his shirtsleeves. He is taking from Dietrich the oath in which she betrayed her Fatherland."

As if to celebrate her decision to become a citizen, Marlene went to more parties that year than ever before. At one event, she appeared in a costume representing Leda and the Swan, the swan wrapped so realistically around her that she appeared to be making love to herself. At another gathering, she danced with Mrs. Lubitsch dressed in a costume representing a shotgun wedding, complete with gun and dummy husband. At Basil Rathbone's, she daringly appeared in black top hat and white tie and tails, with her close friend Dolores del Rio accompanying her as her bride. She often led the male line for the costume prizes, and frequently won.

It was apparently in a party spirit that she embarked on filming *Angel*, directed by Lubitsch from a script by Samson Raphaelson.

Angel was the story—again set in Paris as well as in England —of the wife of a diplomat who falls in love with a man of the world. Samson Raphaelson says, "I never read the play it was based on. Lubitsch came to New York and told me the story. I never felt it came to life. I never asked myself the question, 'What really happened between the wife and her handsome friend? Did he let his pants down? Did she strip? Since she was older, did she blindfold him in the afternoons?' And then, Marlene's part, it was just a beautiful vacuum. Lubitsch was the best actor I ever saw, the best director of dialogue, but he needed a writer to do a character in depth—and I failed him."

The cameraman of *Angel*, Charles Lang, says: "Lee Garmes had laid down the pattern of lighting for Dietrich, with a traveling spot very, very high above the camera. I simply followed this. At night she would watch the rushes and say, 'No, this isn't right, that isn't right.' She'd criticize or praise, assessing herself as a painter would his own painting. It was extraordinary how objective she was about herself. It was as though she were not herself—that she saw herself at one remove. Of course, we had to use soft focus in those days, because the makeup on her was so very heavy that she would have looked artificial and harsh. She was terrified that her nose would show; she said it was a ski-run, Bob Hope *thing,* and she *never* permitted me to show it!"

Marlene's costar Melvyn Douglas recalls, "I had not met her before. We met for the first time right there on the set. She was cast, I was cast, and we simply *got to work!* Instead of the glamour gal she was exploited as being, I found her to be a very friendly homebody—what the Germans call gemütlich.

"She was always bringing little buns and cakes on the set which she had baked at home; she passed them out in the afternoon and we'd sit having coffee or tea. She was much prouder of her culinary than her histrionic abilities.

"She brought her daughter on the set when the child was on vacation from school. I remember this very large girl bouncing up and down on Mama's lap! Lubitsch had some difficulties with her. She played this woman who was supposed to be the most ladylike of English women, the wife of Lord Somebody-or-other, who's a member of Parliament, living in a great mansion —a fact which made the picture amusing: here was the essence of ladyhood going off with a man for three weeks to a rendez-vous in Paris!

"I think Marlene was very conscious of the fact that she was a sex symbol on film, and was used to playing ladies of easy virtue. Ernst wanted to maintain the ladylike front; there was some conflict between them as he reminded her constantly, 'This is a *lady* you're playing, not a *demi-mondaine.*'

"Maybe she just automatically slipped back all the time; I don't know. She was *tremendously* meticulous about her hair, makeup, lighting, jewelry, and costumes. I'd never been so impressed. She knew exactly where the lights were to be set for her. I remember one rather amusing episode. We were doing our first scene together. As we were going through the re-hearsal it seemed to me that she wasn't really looking at me. It seemed that she was sort of glancing out of the corner of her eye. I wondered what the hell she was up to. Maybe she was looking at some other member of the cast. Suddenly I looked in the direction she was looking in and right by the camera was a very tall cheval glass, a mirror, and she was checking herself in this, instead of making eyes at me. It was quite disconcerting, and my vanity was hurt. It was like a *ménage à trois.*

"The stagehands adored her; they had been on her every picture; she knew all their names, the names of their wives and children; it was like old home week every day! She and Garbo, with whom I played *Ninotchka*, were entirely different. Marlene was and has continued to be much more 'with it' in the sense that she was a part of the actual, day-by-day, growing world. Garbo was quite the opposite; she was off on cloud nine, all by herself, a curiously detached sort of person."

Angel, released in 1937, was another flop at the box office; and Marlene left via New York for France, her contract canceled.

On the train to New York, she ran into Noel Coward and Katharine Hepburn—who told her that she, not Marlene, was the worst box-office poison. Marlene laughed. "No, no, Kate! I'm the biggest poison!" she shouted.

Hitler approached her with the gift of a Christmas tree, presumably implying that she could be the queen of a million Christmas trees if she wished to be. Goebbels and von Ribbentrop both made overtures on his behalf, but she rejected them both with disgust.

During the 1930s, Marlene became very close to Erich Maria Remarque. He fascinated her. Like her stepfather, he had served in the First World War, which had provided the inspiration for the masterpiece which made him famous, *All Quiet on the Western Front*. A Roman Catholic by birth, he had had a colorful background: he had worked as a stonemason for a cemetery, he had flown an autogyro, he had test-driven high-speed automobiles, he had become an authority on tropical fish, and had an astonishing amount of inside information on the Nazi party which had put him on Hitler's most-wanted list since 1933. He had been among the first to buy Impressionist painters when they were selling at very modest prices, and his house on Lake Maggiore in Switzerland was by 1937 a showplace of French masterpieces. He had had a bad first marriage and had divorced and remarried. His friends called him "Boni."

He was built like a quarterback, with broad shoulders and narrow hips, fair hair, and a clean-cut, strong-boned, handsome Aryan face. He loved music, and often amused friends with stories of having played a pedal organ in a lunatic asylum. Though a brilliant conversationalist, he was fiercely shy and reserved, had only given three interviews in his life, and was terrified of the press. Like Marlene herself, he was intellectually gifted and given to periods of melancholia and despair. He was not an optimist. He found life, despite his looks and fame, a burden.

He escaped from life's pain by going to terrible Paris night-clubs, including one in which the showgirls used to catch coins between their legs thrown by the male customers. He was a poor lover, often unable to achieve erections because of his drinking; but he was constantly seen in the company of other women, as well as Marlene.

Remarque was morose by nature, filled with memories of his early life, when he had a fierce struggle to survive. Each new book presented him with crushing problems. Often he would sit at his desk from nine in the morning through the entire day without being able to write a single line and could not work until two or three in the morning. He felt such despair that he had to be locked in his room to prevent him from giving up entirely and going skiing or swimming. He could not shake off the feeling that he had wasted his life. Despite his success and passion for art he felt that human existence was futile, a series of antic gestures between darkness and darkness.

A lapsed Catholic, he no longer believed in God and the Devil. After the torment of writing a book was over, he cared nothing for the praise and blame of critics, hoping only to obtain only more financial security. He returned all gifts that appeared to come from fans, except those which obviously were given with deep feeling, such as images of saints from Mexico. Only occasionally could he find release from his misery. In his book *The Road Back*, he described a boy who lay down in a field, exhausted and wretched, and then a brilliantly colored insect perched on a single stalk. This renewed his belief in life. Only the thrust of life, life asserting itself against impossible odds, could provide him with a feeling that something could be clung to in the great abyss of space.

Remarque hated to be alone too long with his desolating thoughts. He might go mad. He might not be able to write again. He might be weighed down by an infinity of futility. His favorite phrase came from Beethoven, "When we are seventy years old we shall be able neither to affirm ourselves nor see ourselves; we shall then begin, little by little, to try to get somewhere."

Although Marlene and Remarque never discussed their relationship with anyone, it is not difficult to understand what drew them together. First of all, there could be no doubting of Marlene's understanding of the pacifist message of his novel *All Quiet on The Western Front*. *The Road Back* (about the unhappiness of a group of disbanded soldiers) and *Three Comrades* (a study of the hopelessness of the post-war generation) meant a great deal to her also. She understood the agony of war because she had lost her stepfather in it. All through the absurd Hollywood years, the garish parties, and the traveling across the Atlantic, she had seen the Germany she had loved disintegrate. Yet her attitude toward the suffering of human existence was quite different from Remarque's. Whereas he looked at life with despair, barely relieved by his conviction about the reviving powers of nature, she believed that man had a destiny to stand up and to assert himself, through duty, honorable acts, and kindness to others, in the face of the universe.

Her love of Goethe proved still to be an inspiration, and she never forgot the message of *Faust*, the visionary beauty of the hero's journey from hell to heaven.

There can be no doubt that, apart from his physical appeal, she was drawn to Remarque's unhappiness as a nurse might be drawn to an invalid. Her healing effect on him was quite considerable, though he was not directly responsive to it. Theirs was a loving friendship, which he oddly echoed in his novel published at the end of the war, *Arch of Triumph*, in which he is dimly seen in the illegal German doctor Ravic, and she, more in her twenties persona of a struggling actress, can be discovered in the character of the girl, Joan Madou, with whom Ravic falls in love. One can only regret the fact that she, with her toughness, tenderness, and melancholy, did not play the part in the film version, instead of the cheerful, self-assured Ingrid Bergman.

There has been much speculation about the extent of Marlene's influence on the writing of *Arch of Triumph*. It seems that she inspired the first description of Joan Madou: "Ravic first noticed her when she was almost beside him. He saw a pale face, high cheekbones and wide-set eyes. The face was rigid and masklike; it looked hollowed-out, and her eyes in the light of the street lamps had an expression of such glassy emptiness that they caught his attention."

Another passage suggests Marlene's personality: "My head is made of silver [Joan Madou is speaking] when I think of both of us and sometimes it is like a violin. The streets are full of us as if we were music, and from time to time people break in and talk and pictures flash by like a movie, but the music remains. That always remains."

There is a moment in the book which is pure Marlene: "She tried to force her way through [the open door] with an armful of giant chrysanthemums. He did not see her face. He only saw her figure and the huge, bright blossoms. 'What is that?' he said. 'A forest of chrysanthemums. For heaven's sake, what does it mean?'

"Joan got the flowers through the door and flung them with a flourish onto the bed. The blossoms were wet and cool and the leaves smelled of autumn and earth."

Music and flowers, laughter and sadness, the sound of a violin, the faint shiver of rain through dripping trees: the book perfectly hits off a romance in Paris on the verge of a world war.

Denver Lindley, Remarque's favorite translator, says: "There's no question that Marlene, as the model for Joan Madou, desperately wanted to play the part in the film, made in 1948. But I don't think Remarque wanted her to do it.

"He sent her the final manuscript in Paris in 1946. She read it, and wrote to him that not only was it a beautiful book, but he also wrote better letters than Jean Gabin.

"Remarque showed me her letter and said, 'I'm not surprised she said that, because I had written to her that she should be Joan Madou. Also, I'm a professional writer. And what's more, I didn't mean what I said!' "

One day in 1938 Marlene was at Fouquet's with Remarque

when a thin, pale, almost blind man caught her attention. He was waiting with two friends, a man and wife, to be seated at a table.

The woman turned to her impulsively and asked, "Are you Madame Dietrich?" She replied, "Yes. And may I ask who you are?" "My name is Mary Colum; my husband, Padraic Colum and I do a little writing." "Oh, of course I have heard of you," Marlene continued. "I'm sure you would like to meet Monsieur Erich Maria Remarque."

Mrs. Colum said, "And this"—she indicated the almost blind man—"is Monsieur James Joyce."

Marlene was astonished. Her eyes opened very wide, she paled, and clutched Remarque's arm. Remarque, too, was enormously impressed. A moment later, the waiter announced Marlene's table. He thoughtfully placed the Colums and Joyce next to her. She talked with great intelligence about her love of *Ulysses* and *Dubliners*. Joyce said, "I saw you in *L'Ange Bleu.*" "Then, monsieur," Marlene replied, "You saw the best of me." Joyce was as fascinated as she was.

The songwriter Peter Kreuder remembers those Paris days vividly in his memoirs. He used to stay in a hotel near hers in Versailles and go over every day to work with her on the songs. She had a concert grand in her suite, a splendid Bechstein on which he could tinkle away. They worked day and night. Marlene was inexhaustible. Her favorite was a number with lyrics by Walter Reisch, "I can only give you a couple of flowers / Only flowers / Nothing else."

One evening, he recalled, when Marlene was busy, Kreuder taxied to Paris and wandered about the Champs Élysées. He went down a small side street and entered a bar where he had a few drinks. Finally, very late, he left, and looked for a cab. A large car rolled up and stopped next to him. A beautiful girl was at the wheel. She smiled to him. She was offering him a lift. He ran through the rain, and climbed in. She said, "Where to?" When he told her "Versailles," he thought she would decline. But she nodded happily, and, flirting obviously, swept him off towards his destination.

Part way there, she suddenly drove off the route. She made

off towards St. Cloud. They arrived at a large house. A maid took him to a large oval room with an immense bed at the center. The girl disappeared, promising to return in a few minutes. Kreuder noticed a small table next to the bed, with champagne on it cooling in a bucket, and two glasses. The girl returned, exquisitely naked. Kreuder stripped off his clothes and enjoyed an hour of intense pleasure with her. He wrote, "It was the most brilliant theatrical staging I have ever seen for an experience of sex."

At last, the girl said farewell with a kiss, and told him a taxi was waiting to take him to Versailles.

Next day, Kreuder writes, he had to return to business commitments in Germany. At the end of their last day's work, Marlene seized his wrist and put a golden wristwatch on it. She thanked him warmly for his songs. The wristwatch bore the legend, "Marlene, Paris, 1937." She told him that that evening would be a celebration, a farewell party for him. She would be taking him to a very special club she knew. With her entourage, he was driven in one of a fleet of several cars through Paris.

En route, they turned off towards St. Cloud. They reached a large house. They went into a circular corridor with small rooms leading off it. Each room had a table with drinks on it. They took their places. The lights went down. There was just the faintest glimmering of illumination. Marlene, her companion, Remarque, and all the others, turned their stools around as if at a signal. They looked through small apertures let into the wall. Kreuder peeped through one of these slits. At first, he could see nothing.

He experienced a shock of recognition. He saw an oval room, a huge bed, and beside the bed a table, with champagne cooling in a bucket. A maid opened a door, and a middle-aged man entered. The man stripped, and lay on the bed. The door opened again. Now Kreuder knew. It was the naked girl he had slept with. He was horrified to realize that he had been the object of a sex show the night before, and that perhaps Marlene had been watching him! He fled, his chair fell, and he vomited in the corridor. When he returned, feeling ill, Marlene said,

"What's the matter?" She was laughing so much, Kreuder writes, that the tears ran down her cheeks. The whole crowd, led by Marlene, toasted him uproariously in champagne. Her mocking laughter followed him as he fled down a long corridor to the street.*

In 1937, behind the superficial glamor and the shine of expensive shops, there was an agony in the air of Paris, the sound of a death rattle. The Munich crisis and riots in the streets brought the sting of winter even to the summer heat. There were massive strikes and the franc collapsed. In September 1938 there was more unrest. The Daladier cabinet failed to solve any problems, and on November 30 there was a twenty-four-hour general strike.

Despite the deteriorating situation in Europe, it is doubtful if Marlene or Remarque foresaw the collapse of France. Remarque, drinking heavily, became particularly difficult. Max Colpet visited the couple at the Hôtel du Cap at Eden Roc in the south of France, where he found her distraught over Remarque's frequent absences. Colpet wrote in his memoirs that on one occasion Marlene called him in the middle of the night and begged him to help find the missing novelist. She mentioned that Remarque had a tendency to drive his sports car recklessly along the cliff roads, and might have crashed.

Colpet searched every bar he could find. He was about to give up when on a sudden instinct he made his way into a local homosexual night spot. There he found Remarque, drunk and ordering calvados, an apple brandy he favored, with shrill gay people gathered around him.

Remarque was not homosexual. He had evidently wandered into this place without knowing what it was. Colpet rescued him and drove him back to the Hôtel du Cap. Marlene was overwhelmingly grateful. "At last I can sleep now," she said.

Remarque continued to sneak out in this fashion, hoping Mar-

---

*(This description is based on Mr. Kreuder's memoirs, *Nur Puppen Haben Keine Tränen* (Munich: R.S. Schulz, 1974).)

lene wouldn't notice, but she always did. In his more sober moments, they spent time with her friend Noel Coward, whom she had first met in 1935 after telephoning him from Hollywood to England to tell him how much she admired his film *The Scoundrel.* She also saw a good deal of Somerset Maugham and Darryl F. Zanuck, head of Twentieth Century–Fox Studios, who discussed the possibility of her playing Lady Esketh, a British society woman, in *The Rains Came*, a role subsequently played by Myrna Loy.

The English millionairess Jo Carstairs was very much in evidence, her fair, cropped hair, her powerful figure, and electric personality intriguing Marlene constantly. Jo talked about her island in the Bahamas, Whale Cay, and of the magical white house she was building for Marlene there. Marlene would become a kind of princess of that lovely tropical island, with a staff at her command. Marlene politely declined.

Playing tennis, lying in the sun, Marlene seemed unaware she was on the edge of a volcano. She and Remarque were both in Hollywood in the late spring and early summer of 1939, and a picture of them taken in a nightclub shows her particularly depressed. Remarque hated Hollywood, the empty streets at night, the ugly studios, the atmosphere of empty-headed greed. To avoid the gossips, they traveled by different ships to and from Europe.

Rudi came to America, and frequently went out with her, von Sternberg, and Remarque both in Los Angeles and New York. There was an odd little storm in a teacup at Delmonico's nightspot in Manhattan when Marlene arrived in a white-hooded monkish gown, designed by Travis Banton, and a society woman, Mrs. Dudley Ritts, arrived in the identical gown. Marlene stormed out.

A more serious event took place when she returned to France on the *Normandie* on June 14, 1939. Government agents seized her luggage and held Rudi, insisting her property be held as security against back taxes of $284,000. It had been in the papers that Marlene earned the third largest salary in the nation, after William Randolph Hearst and Mae West. While the luggage went up and down from the wharf and the French Line officials screamed that the sailing might have to be canceled because of the tide, reporters swarmed about Marlene's cabin, demanding information. Finally, she handed over her collection of jewels, including her famous emeralds, as security, and the ship was permitted to sail.

In the late summer of 1939, she and Remarque were back at the hotel at the Hôtel du Cap, discussing a new film: *Dedée d'Anvers*, a story of low life to be directed by Pierre Chénal, with Jean Gabin and Raimu. She became friendly with Gabin, and with Chénal's wife, the beautiful actress Florence Marly. The guest list at the hotel that season was a roll call of Marlene's favorites: Jo Carstairs and her secretary Violla Rubber, Joe Kennedy (an intimate friend), his son Jack, Gabin, von Sternberg, Remarque, Rudi, Tamara, her daughter Maria. Remarque and von Sternberg used to play tennis on the long, golden afternoons, while Marlene, Chénal, Marly, Gabin, and Raimu held script conferences around a table in one of the salons. On one occasion, Florence Marly remembers, Marlene noticed in mid-discussion that one of von Sternberg's shoelaces was undone; she sank to her knees in her delicate green dress and did the shoelace up while the others looked at her in astonishment.

It was during those weeks that Marlene received a telephone call from the Hollywood producer Joe Pasternak, who, having met Marlene when she had prepared *The Blue Angel* in Berlin, decided she would be perfect for a part in a new picture. Pasternak's screenwriter Felix Jackson remembers the circumstances of writing the script:

"Pasternak wanted to do a Western with Jimmy Stewart, who had come over from doing Capra pictures at Columbia. He told me to look at the old Tom Mix picture *Destry Rides Again*. Could we remake it? It was the story of the son of a sheriff who returns to a western town to avenge his father's killing. I saw the picture, and I said, 'You can't do that with Jimmy Stewart. Tom Mix was beating people up all the time. Jimmy's forte is to be passive. You can't do some 'shootin'-tootin' thing' with him. I said, 'Let's reverse it. Let's do a story about a man who doesn't believe in guns.' And I decided to add a woman to the story. The girl in the original picture was dull. Pasternak said, 'Do you think you could write a character for Marlene?' Her career was all shot to pieces. I called the character Frenchie, because Marlene had been living in France. She wasn't really salable any more but we took a gamble."

Joe Pasternak says, "Like Felix, I knew Marlene was box-office poison and that nobody wanted her. I was worried about what von Sternberg had done to her. He had turned her into a waxen image. I had met her in Berlin and I knew she wasn't like that. She was tough, down-to-earth, real. She wasn't a mannequin in a shop window.

"In the original movie, the girl was a frail, silly little child waiting for her man to come home. I decided to make Marlene the equal of Destry in looks, drive, and personality. She should be more than than able to take care of herself—Marlene was all of that! But she must be unpredictable, underneath, like a cat. And she must be able to fight without inhibitions, with another woman, pull her hair, tug her clothes, and finally get a bucket of water in her face, and take it all on the chin. That Marlene could do.

"The bosses at Universal were completely against having Marlene in the picture. They didn't think she could draw flies. Her picture in England, *Knight Without Armor*, had been a terrible flop. She was finished, wasn't she? The exhibitors had said so, hadn't they?

"And as for Jimmy Stewart! How could I cast this weak, skinny, frail kid with the soft face? Why, Destry was a powerful, broad-shouldered masterful male! What a disaster!

"But thank God the success of some pictures I had made with Deanna Durbin had ensured that everone took me seriously. They finally cracked. OK, I could have Stewart and Dietrich, but let it be on my own head if they flopped!

"Jimmy I signed at once; he wanted to do a Western very badly. Then I called Marlene in the south of France. Joe Kennedy came on the line. He said, 'If it's a part in a picture, she isn't interested.' I asked to talk to her. She said, 'Why do you want me?'

"I was astonished. 'Because of the wonderful work you've done. I know you'll be great in this picture I have for you.'

"There was a long pause. 'OK. What is it?' She didn't sound at all enthusiastic.

"I took a deep, deep breath and said, 'It's a Western.'

"She roared with laughter. 'Oh, no! You must be crazy!'

"I said to her, 'Darling, please trust me. It's a marvelous part. You'll be sensational.'

"Another long pause. 'I guess you haven't heard, my friend. I'm box-office poison.'

" 'You won't be after this picture is finished.'

" 'I'll let you know.' "

"She didn't. Days went by. She talked with von Sternberg. He told her to do it. So did Rudi Sieber and Jo Carstairs, and Remarque. She called me back. She'd do it!"

The extraordinary collection of people at the Hôtel du Cap took off together for Paris. Marlene, Remarque and von Sternberg, with Jo Carstairs and Violla Rubber, dashed off to see Mabel Mercer, who was performing at the time at the Olympia, and insisted on holding up the *Queen Mary* for several hours to catch the performance. According to Violla Rubber, Jo Carstairs had so much money and influence she was practically Miss Cunard White Star Line and was able to obtain passages for everyone. Remarque stayed behind to sort out some complicated problems vis-à-vis his wife, while Marlene and the others continued to New York.

Jo Carstairs sent Violla to Hollywood to take care of Marlene, and they moved together into bungalow 10 at the Beverly Hills Hotel. When Remarque arrived on a blacked-out Queen Mary four days after war broke out, he also traveled to Hollywood and, according to Ms. Rubber, checked into Marlene's bungalow. "He used to sit at night writing in a tiny cramped hand to the tune of classical 78 rpm records while Marlene smoked and walked about, her nerves screwed tight," Ms. Rubber recollects. The neighbors—Mr. and Mrs. Herbert Marshall—grumbled about the noise.

Their relationship was threatened: Remarque's wife Ilsa arrived on another of the last ships from Europe in an attempt to affect a reconciliation, but she was diverted to Mexico, where she remained.

In September, worried about her mother and sister in Germany, Marlene reported for work on *Destry Rides Again.*

Joe Pasternak says: "When Marlene arrived at Universal she said, 'What's this, putting me in a Western?' But when I explained to her she would be more physical, more real, more down-to-earth than she had been, more the real Marlene, in fact, she shrugged and said out of the corner of her mouth, 'Well, OK.' Also, she needed the money!

"She took one look at Jimmy Stewart and she began to rub her hands. She wanted him at once! He was just a simple guy; he loved Flash Gordon comics—that was all he would read. So she did something incredible—the most incredible thing I ever saw.

"She locked him in his dressing room and promised him a surprise. The surprise was that she presented him with a doll, which she had had the whole studio art department come in over a weekend and make up for him—a life-size doll of Flash Gordon, correct in every detail! It started a romance!"

On the set Marlene hugely enjoyed rolling her own cigarettes, a technique taught to her by Joe Pasternak, shooting crap, and cutting up for the director, George Marshall. Most of all, she relished the big fight scene, in which she fought with her rival Una Merkel in a barroom. Miss Merkel remembers, "I had never met Marlene. We were introduced in costume on the first day of work, in the saloon set. I had never raised my hand to a living soul, and I'm sure she hadn't either. There were two stunt girls on the sidelines. Marshall said, 'There'll be no rehearsal. You just go in and do whatever you can. Try it! And we'll keep shooting as long as you can keep up the fight! If it gets to be too much for you we can get the stunt girls in and they can finish the rest of it.'

"Neither one of us knew what we were doing but we just plunged in and punched and slapped and kicked for all we were worth! They never did call in the stunt girls. She stepped on my feet with her French heels and the toenails *never* grew back.

She was stronger than me. She was very powerful and I was very thin. Luckily I have a remarkable constitution. I was bruised from head to foot! When it was over, I looked like an old peach, green, with brown spots. And I *felt* rotten, too.

"At the end of the scene, Jimmy Stewart came in and dumped a whole bucket of water over us. He did it in a long shot and then he had to do it over for close-ups, and then *Life* magazine wanted pictures so they did it over again! He dumped water on us for *hours*.

"I had to go to the hospital for a couple of days. My Dr. Branch wanted to be sure I had no internal injuries. She was scarcely bruised at all!"

Eight

A Soldier in Skirts

Destry Rides Again reinstated Marlene as a major star. Her performance of Frenchy—witty, earthy, sexy—earned her the best reviews she had received since *The Blue Angel*. At last the bloodless, languid image of the vampire woman von Sternberg had created had disappeared, and the real Dietrich emerged. Here was a woman who made her own rules, who took the man she wanted and died for him at the end. Here was a woman, also, who was aware of her body, who knew to a fraction the erotic effect she created. She was a kind of benign reversal of Lola-Lola, a creature who did not exploit men or destroy them, but who conferred strength on them, who taught them how to live.

It was a clever stroke of Marlene and Pasternak to hire Frederick Hollander to write the songs. "You've Got That Look That Leaves Me Weak" and the unforgettable "The Boys in the Back Room" with lyrics by Frank Loesser were masterpieces of popular song, comparable with anything Hollander had done before. Marlene, who, incredibly, had done little or no singing in pictures for several years, sang wonderfully in these numbers, dressed in the costume of a saloon moll, her legs better than ever. At the age of thirty-eight, her voice was no longer the high-pitched instrument it had been in *The Blue Angel* and *Morocco*. It was now reminiscent of Claire Waldoff in its husky, uninhibited vulgarity and pizzazz.

Marlene was pleased that many of her friends had settled in the United States. Rudi and Tamara were in New York, along with Hans Jaray. With Billy Wilder, who had arrived in Hollywood some years before, Marlene worked hard helping refugees to settle in their new environment. Among these were the novelists Leonhard Frank and Thomas Mann.

Remarque kept appearing on the set of *Destry Rides Again* with new dialogue for Marlene which was emphatically not suitable for a Western.

Marlene used to visit the Princess Duya in Santa Monica, a gypsy who worked in a tent covered with astrological signs, next to a tea-leaf reader, a crystal gazer, and a phrenologist.

The Princess was almost a hundred years old, and was said to share her one tooth with her sister. Marlene followed her advice religiously, sitting in a moldy chair while the Princess read her palm.

Marlene sent Frederick Hollander to see the Princess. He crossed the gypsy's palm with silver, and she said, peering at him intently, "Things are not so good." Disappointed, he got up to leave. Seeing that she was losing a potential customer, the Princess motioned to him to sit down again. She picked up his hand, peered deeply into the palm, and said, "And they're not so bad, either!" Delighted, he stayed to hear a glowing account of his future. Just as he turned to leave, he heard the Princess humming a tune. It was "Falling in Love Again."

Marlene became very friendly in those months with John O'Hara, whose novel *Butterfield 8*, published in 1935, had been given to her by James Stewart. Marlene had understood the character of the unhappy girl in the book. O'Hara wrote later, "From that moment on I had great respect for her, where before I had had only—only?—a boyish lech. It was along about that time, too, that Dorothy Parker, a friend of Marlene's, told me that Dietrich had asked her to look at some short stories she had written. Dorothy took on the task with some trepidation, and was pleasantly astonished to find that the stories were good."

Another new friend was Carroll Righter, the astrologer, a tall, pale man with heavy, blunt features.

Righter was a student of Evangeline Adams, the Boston astrologer who began her career when she accurately warned the owner of the Windsor Hotel, New York, that his establishment would burn to the ground. Before long, Caruso, Mary Pickford, and J. P. Morgan had become her clients. Righter, son of a well-to-do Philadelphia Main Line family, was originally trained for a career in law, settling in Hollywood after doctors gave him six months to live and his horoscope indicated he had "physical protection in the Southwest." Crippled by a back ailment, he followed the stars so carefully he was dancing within the year.

When he met Marlene, he identified her as a Capricorn, and analyzed her character so expertly she immediately hired him to do her chart. From that moment on, she never accepted a script, took a plane, or entered into a love affair without his advice. Whenever she met a man she was attracted to, she had the man's exact hour of birth written down and sent over or telephoned to Righter.

Righter's career bloomed, due to Marlene's recommendations of him to her famous friends. He hired a man as butler because he was a Libra and a woman as cook because she was a Virgo, and hired four full-time secretaries and a mathematician. When Marlene called him, he would often say, "Oh, hello, Capricorn, how good to hear from you. Don't forget to be careful of that difficult Scorpio." He always maintained his clients' charts within easy access of his bed so that they could call him any hour of the day or night. He began to give parties, to which he invited only people born under the same sign. The appropriate zodiacal animal was on the lawn to greet the guests. Thus Marlene found herself greeted rather unflatteringly by a goat. Taurus parties involved bulls on the lawn, although Righter ruled against having scorpions running about for his Scorpio parties. He selected crocodiles instead.

The moment the box-office results from *Destry Rides Again* —in 1939—came in, Joe Pasternak whipped up another vehicle for Marlene. This was *Seven Sinners*, in which she was cast as Bijou, a kind of torch-singing Sadie Thompson of the South Seas who was constantly getting men into trouble. She was costarred with the young John Wayne, as the handsome naval officer

Bruce, and with Broderick Crawford as the former seaman, Little Ned. Tay Garnett was chosen to direct.

Garnett describes how Marlene first met Wayne: "We had a problem. Our plot was *Madame Butterfly* with a twist. A singer fell for a naval lieutenant; then, realizing she would ruin his future, she left him. We needed a tough he-man type who could use his fists, and decided to borrow him from Republic. His name was John Wayne. Marlene had the choice of all her leading men. I decided not to mention Wayne to her, but simply to place him in the Universal commissary where she couldn't miss seeing him. He stood between us and our table as we walked in for lunch, chatting with a couple of actresses I had set up. She swept past him, then swiveled on her heel and looked him up and down as though he were a prime rib at Chasen's. As we sat down, she whispered right in my ear, 'Daddy, buy me that!' I said, 'Honey, it's settled. You got him.' Then, at a prearranged signal, Wayne came to the table. If you didn't know what was gonna happen you'd be as blind as a pit pony. Their relationship got off like a fireworks display. They were crazy about each other, but every man on the picture wanted her. I did, but she wouldn't lay."

Broderick Crawford recalls, "Joe Pasternak was so mad about Marlene he kept begging her to go to bed with him. Finally, she said, 'I'll go to bed with you when Hitler is dead.' On a certain day in 1945, he called her and said Hitler was dead and it was time to collect. She replied, 'Hitler is alive and well and living in Argentina!' "

Tay Garnett adds: "Marlene was beyond any actress I've ever known in giving of herself all there is to give. There was no one like her. She was a fiend for work. It was characteristic of her that whatever she did, she did it with both barrels. There was no such thing with her as doing anything halfway. She'd be in a rehearsal and she'd say, 'Put another scrim on.' 'Tighten that up, just a wee bit.' Or she'd say, 'That setup was too high for me, for a close-up. Take it down about six inches.' She knew to a fraction the best angle on her face, because she had learned everything from von Sternberg.

"We hit it off immediately. There was a great rapport. She

had a nice sense of humor. She was the most generous person who ever lived. At the end of a picture she gave away gifts— she gave the prop man a huge hi-fi console, and she gave me a watch. She had it designed and made by Flateau. It was beautifully inscribed.

"She took orders like a soldier. She loved the scene when the saloon was wrecked; she wanted to be in the thick of it, hitting people on the head with vases! It was glorious for her!"

Seven Sinners, released in 1940, was another hit, and the Hollander-Loesser songs, "I've Been in Love Before," "I Fall Overboard," and "The Man's in the Navy," were uproarious. Bosley Crowther in the *New York Times* wrote, "Miss Dietrich's Frenchy in *Destry* was an Arno sketch of countless sultry barroom belles: her Bijou Blanche in *Seven Sinners* is a delightfully subtle spoof of all the Sadie Thompsons and Singapore Sals that have stirred the hot blood of cool customers south and east of Manila Bay. If Miss Dietrich and her comedies were just both a little broader, Mae West would be in the shade."

The other leading critic of the day, Howard Barnes of the *New York Herald Tribune,* wrote, "If anything, she is even better than she was in *The Blue Angel.*"

The next Pasternak vehicle, *The Flame of New Orleans,* released in 1941, was less successful, and Marlene told me why: "The director, René Clair, was too autocratic and haughty, and he couldn't get along with the crew. He wasn't interested in their little problems, their wives, and their children. As a result, they didn't give of their best. A pity."

The movie was not successful, despite Marlene's entertaining performance as Claire Ledoux, who impersonates a countess in the New Orleans of 1841. The movie was too artificial and strained, and does not wear well today. Marlene was much more at ease on loan-out to Warner's in *Manpower* (1941), a delightful absurdity in which she played a clip-joint hostess on the outskirts of Los Angeles who is fought over by the rugged men of Pacific Power and Light. George Raft and Edward G. Robinson as the rival linemen conducted a real-life struggle over Marlene, easily won by George Raft as the handsomer of the two.

Early in 1941, Marlene had a new distraction. The great French star, Jean Gabin, whom she had met in Paris, and had profoundly admired in his films *Quai des Brumes* and *Le Jour se Lève*, arrived in Hollywood in answer to a contract offered him by Darryl F. Zanuck at Twentieth Century–Fox which Marlene, who knew Zanuck, may possibly have suggested. Gabin had worked in minesweepers and in the army; and while on leave in the fall of 1939, he narrowly escaped being seized at his home in Dreux near Paris, fled to Cherbourg to rejoin his unit, and had just managed to leave his car when it was blown to pieces.

Moving through a shell-shattered countryside, he acted as a kind of Pied Piper for a group of children, leading them to safety over a three-week period during which he only slept twice in a bed and lived on what he could find in the fields. After the armistice he went to the south of France for eight months until the Vichy government finally gave him permission to sail for America.

There could be no doubt that his story moved Marlene, adoring as she was of children, and fascinated and impressed by bravery. She took charge of Gabin from the moment he arrived and checked into the Beverly Hills Hotel, entertaining him at parties (which he did not much enjoy), having her chauffeur take him to the various beauty spots, and walking with him on remote beaches. But he was tormented by a feeling of guilt that he was enjoying the sybaritic pleasures of life in Southern California while his nephew was in a concentration camp and his niece had to stand in line for six hours for 120 grams of meat a week in Occupied France. A moody, sullen, taciturn man, he was offended by what he felt to be the mindless opulence of Beverly Hills and Bel Air, the endless talk about sex and money, the crude movies, and the crude men who made them.

She and Gabin were seen everywhere—at the premiere of *The Young Mr. Pitt*, at Ciro's, at the Mocambo, at the Biltmore and other night spots—while Remarque dropped out of the picture.

In late 1941, when Marlene had her fortieth birthday, their romance began in earnest. Gabin was tall and powerfully built, with a boxer's shoulders and chest; Marlene told the journalist Carlos Clarens many years later, "Gabin had the most beautiful *loins* I've ever seen in a man, that final point in male beauty, where the torso joins the hips." His hair was prematurely gray, almost white, his face deeply bronzed, and his eyes bright blue.

Gabin loved the bustle of ports, the smell of the sea, the clank of cranes, the roar of locomotives, and the tooting of ships' horns. He loved the land, the fields, the creatures of the land. He always longed to retire to the country, and when he finally did so, it was to a magnificent estate near Laigle in Normandy. He liked to mix happily with farming folk and peasants in the overcrowded, noisy village taverns.

Gabin was not an easy man to know. He could be stingy, mean-tempered, and harsh. He was not an intellectual. He despised opera and ballet, which Marlene loved. His early struggles had been similar to Marlene's. He had been forced to work in the Folies Bergère, in vaudeville, in operettas, on a cabaret tour of South America, and in bit parts in movies. After a disastrous early marriage, he went through a long period of sadness and isolation in the midst of a steadily escalating career. With his stubborn, strong face, somber eyes, and tight-lipped mouth, Gabin was an actor of great interior resources, suggesting a severe self-discipline and indifference to the trappings of stardom. His eloquence was that of a workman, animal and instinctive.

He was to the marrow of his bones a man of the people, who never forgot that he once worked as a cement mixer at twelve francs a day. He acted from his gut. He despised intellectual pretense. He was fond of describing himself as the French Spencer Tracy. Whereas Remarque had attracted Marlene because of his uncompromising, austere intellect, Gabin clearly drew her by reason of his earthy, perhaps rather stupid, but constantly alive peasant quality, his sheer manly virility.

Marlene used to dress up as a maid in a *diamanté* apron to serve him; she would prepare dinner to his exact specifications. Their friend, the actor Marcel Dalio, recalls that she even used argot when addressing Gabin, saying, "Mets ton popotin là." (Literally, "Put your fanny there.")

According to Dalio, Gabin rented the house of Garbo for a few months in 1942. One night, Gabin noticed out of the corner of his eye a ghostly figure, like Fantômas in the old French silent serials, flitting by the window of the dining room while they were eating. A moment later, Marlene noticed the figure at another window. Gabin decided it was a prowler, and went out to have a look. He could see nothing.

Night after night, Fantômas reappeared and disappeared with equal rapidity. They were unable to determine what was going on. But one night, Fantômas was a little too slow. Gabin noticed the face and said to Marlene, "It's Garbo!" She had apparently been watching them to make sure they didn't damage anything or in any way disturb the furnishings of the house.

Frequently, the director Jean Renoir and his wife used to drop over to see Marlene and Gabin. Renoir recalled: "Marlene was so extravagant in her patriotism she would sing 'La Marseillaise' in nightclubs. Gabin didn't like that. He would complain and she would say, tapping his forehead, 'This has a hollow ring. That's why you're so attractive. Your head is quite empty. You haven't got a thought in your head. Not a single one! Don't change!' "

Renoir continued: "Marlene was always asking [my wife] Dido to go with her to the ladies' room. Dido was horrified! She thought it meant a pass! Then she realized Marlene simply wanted to show her legs to her, so she could say how beautiful they were! No pass." He added in his autobiography, "[Showing her legs] was simply the enactment of a ritual. But it must be added that the worship of Marlene's legs was perfectly justified."

During her romance with Jean Gabin, Marlene continued to see John Wayne. Since Gabin tended to be possessive, one can guess that this must have caused him considerable anguish. As a liberated woman, Marlene managed to make her own decisions. She and Wayne went to football games and prizefights, they fished and hunted, and they drove north up the coast to Santa Barbara and San Luis Obispo. Unlike other actresses he worked with, she was a good sport, and liked solid American food, including broiled steaks and grilled fish. The columnists

capitalized heavily on their relationship, especially Louella Par-
sons, who became gaga as she drooled over their dating in
exotic locations. They acted in a new movie, *The Spoilers,* together in the full glare of publicity. At one stage, they had a kind
of fistfight in which she was knocked to the floor, but got up off
the ground and kissed Wayne on the mouth right in front of the
unit. As with all her relationships with men, this was a liaison
of companionship rather than passion, a brotherhood of the
spirit.

Whenever a screen fight was called for with Wayne—and
fights were frequently called for—Marlene always plunged in
with a will, elbowing, kicking, and scratching him until she was
covered with bruises, and they both laughted at the results. As
in *Destry* and *Seven Sinners,* she could be what she really was:
tough, down-to-earth, full of humor. The pleasure to be gained
from seeing these Wayne-Dietrich films today is the pleasure of
seeing Marlene acting without pretense, having a glorious free-
for-all among the boys.

In 1941, Marlene's agent Charles Feldman, made a deal
whereby an old friend of hers, the director Mitchell Leisen, and
Marlene were sold to Columbia as a package to make a comedy
called *The Lady Is Willing.* In his authorized biography by
David Chierichetti, Leisen said, "She gave one of her best performances . . . she sits crying with a little baby in her arms, and
you see a real actress. She could cry hysterically on cue, but she
didn't think that was enough. She said she had been up all night
(in the script) too, so she sprayed a horrible fluid into her eyes
until they were all red and puffed up, and then she really let go
and sobbed."

After only a few days of shooting, Carroll Righter advised her
not go to work, as he was sure she would suffer an accident. She
called Leisen to tell him she couldn't go to work that day, but
he insisted she do so. She asked her chauffeur to be extremely
careful on the way to Columbia. There were no collisions. Just
as she was entering the set for a scene, carrying the baby,
walking very slowly and carefully, she stepped on the child's
little red fire-wagon toy and fell over on her back. She twisted

her body to protect the baby, and in the process broke her ankle.

Fred MacMurray recalls, "Marlene was amazing. She never showed her pain, and wouldn't go home. She had to be mounted on a small 'dolly' to give the impression we were walking together against a back projection of a street. She managed to move her shoulders to suggest she was in motion normally. Then something crazy happened. To show we were going down a slope, the set had to be cantilevered. Without warning, Marlene and the little 'dolly' took off! They vanished in the wings! She picked herself up off the floor, put on some orthopedic shoes, and came back and did the scene without the 'dolly.' Is there anyone like that?"

Leisen had to perform miracles to cover her movements. To conceal her limp, he would have her start with one step, cut to MacMurray looking at her, then cut to the other step. Because the set was filled with mirrors, these tricks had to be most skillfully arranged. Often there were so many mirrors, that the director, script girl, and assistant had to lie on the floor below the frame line. Occasionally, Marlene and Leisen quarreled. He remembered, "I was maddened by her endless fiddling around with the lights and with her hats and costumes. It slowed up production terribly. And then I think Fred MacMurray was embarrassed by her. She was crazy about him, and wanted him. But he was very happily married and there could be no question of a romance."

Marlene liked Leisen enormously, and went with him to New York to help him give support to two of his protégés who were appearing in a Broadway show, *Let's Face It.* Anxious to do her best to promote *The Lady Is Willing,* Marlene decided to draw attention to herself at Grand Central Station by leaning on a cane in a pair of trousers. She attracted enormous crowds wherever she went. When she arrived at the theater, the fans burst in, swept down the aisle, and overwhelmed her. She was forced to run through an exit door. She managed to get a cab, but the fans wrenched the door off. She told them to calm themselves and signed autographs for half an hour before she went back to her suite at the Waldorf Towers.

In 1942, Marlene rented a home in Westwood, an unpretentious house with a view of the golf course. She lived casually,
with two beautiful Persian cats. She had a rumpus room filled
with all kinds of oddments: an ice-cream freezer on a Ping-Pong
table, an ironing board, a broken candelabrum, a globe of the
world, and scattered books. Gabin was equally informal, and
enjoyed the mess. She spent hours listening to a radio program
called "Mr. Anthony," and playing her favorite record, *Rites of
Spring*, on the phonograph. She chain-smoked, breakfasted on
one cup of black coffee, and laughed when she caught Göring
or Goebbels on shortwave from Germany. She would listen to
Goebbels's ravings, and say to Gabin, "Nuts to him!"

In 1942 Marlene was waiting for permission to go overseas to
sing for the troops. She accepted an invitation from the Office
of Strategic Services to sing American songs with German lyrics
on shortwave broadcast to the Third Reich. What the record
reveals is that singing in German, Marlene assumed an intensity
and vibrancy seldom found in her English-speaking recordings
of the period. "Time on My Hands," "Mean to Me," and "Taking a Chance on Love" assumed an entirely different meaning
with German lyrics.

Marlene liked to imagine what would happen if the Germans
—or some disease—"got" her and she died. She liked to tell the
story of her own funeral. Rudi would be responsible for the
arrangements and would select the guests and pallbearers.
Douglas Fairbanks, Jr., would appear in naval uniform with a
wreath from Queen Elizabeth of England; Gabin would be
propped up in front of the door of the church, a cigarette
dangling from the corner of his mouth, refusing to talk to anyone; Gary Cooper would be yawning; James Stewart would be
asking whose funeral it was; and Remarque would be at the
wrong church. As she told the story, it became more and more
elaborate and risqué.

During the early 1940s, Maria, living apart from Marlene, still
heavy in her late teens, decided to become an actress. Marlene,
perhaps remembering her own family's resolute opposition to

her career, and filled with love for her daughter, encouraged Maria in this ambition. It is strange to note that Maria also went to the Max Reinhardt drama school, established now in Hollywood, where the great director had fled from the Nazis. Reinhardt was very impressed with his young pupil. He had apparently quite forgotten that her mother had worked under the supervision of his Berlin assistant Berthold Held.

Maria was determined not to trade on her mother's fame, and rejected the names of Dietrich and Sieber. At first, she called herself Maria Marlowe, until she discovered that Julia Marlowe had been the name of a famous actress. She finally chose to be called Maria Manton, and appeared in an outstanding performance of the Keith Winter play, *The Shining Hour*. The *Los Angeles Times* critic wrote of her, "The smoldering beauty of this lovely auburn-haired girl, with her ingratiatingly rich voice and intelligent inflection, would seem to bring great promise for a desired theatrical career. She was nervous at first and evidently rather shy, but soon overcame these momentary restrictions."

The critic kindly overlooked Maria's weight. Marlene had worked miracles with her clothes and makeup to lessen its obviousness. With Jean Gabin, Marlene used to attend rehearsals and performances, gently criticizing and praising.

The Reinhardt school failed, because the students were incapable of the discipline called for, the discipline of learning every aspect of theater. They discovered quickly that looks and a good body were not enough for Reinhardt, and by most Hollywood standards they were enough. As a result, most of the pupils drifted away, and new management took over, when the school became known as the Geller Workshop. There, Maria was extremely active, performing outstandingly in Sidney Howard's *The Silver Cord* and in Lillian Hellman's *The Little Foxes*. She fell in love with the British actor Richard Haydn, delighted by his quick wit and charm, but the engagement did not last. She then met a promising fellow performer at the Geller, Dean Goodman, who had also directed plays—and still does, in San Francisco.

Marlene was in New York on a war bond tour, when Maria telephoned her to tell her she had fallen in love with Goodman. Goodman says, "I was at the time (as well as acting) working as private secretary to Madame Ouspenskaya, the brilliant Russian actress. I met Maria several times while I was appearing in Frank Vosper's *Love From a Stranger*. She was heavy, but I thought rather attractive, and I sensed how eager she was to find a husband. She told me how unhappy her childhood had been, how she had been shunted between the States and France and Switzerland during the 1930s, and about being under armed guard because of the kidnapping scare.

"We dated a good deal while I was making a movie called *Top Man* with Donald O'Connor at Universal. We used to drive up into the Hollywood Hills above the Bowl and look down on the city lights and kiss. It was very warm and very romantic—before the smog.

"I think she wanted me first. I accepted her proposal of marriage. Miss Dietrich returned from New York, but I know she was against the marriage. A friend who was living at her house had made mischief, and accused Maria of marrying a man who was having an affair with Maria Ouspenskaya and was a homosexual. Maria Ouspenskaya was very old, very small, and extremely ugly!

"Maria and I had to have somewhere to stay. We couldn't go to a hotel as rooms in wartime were at a premium and we had very little money. We stayed at a friend's apartment. I had a call from Miss Dietrich's lawyer, and he summoned me to his office. Maria was very nervous, and waited outside in the car when I went in. He offered me money, but I refused it saying, 'No, Maria is working and so am I. We can get along.' He told me, 'I'm embarrassed to be asking you these questions. But did you have an affair with Madame Ouspenskaya? Are you a homosexual?' I denied both charges. When he saw that I couldn't be bought and that I would admit to nothing, he said, 'I think it would help a great deal if you would talk to Miss Dietrich. Don't you?' I told him, 'I'd be very happy to.' 'It'll all work out,' he said.

"I called Marlene. She answered the phone with her famous 'Hello—o—o' and said, 'Wait a minute, I want to close the door.' Evidently, she didn't want anybody to overhear her. Then she said, 'I think you should know at the beginning, I'm not going to support you.'

" 'Miss Dietrich, I've never asked for anything,' I told her. 'And maybe you haven't thought of the possibility that someone might love your daughter.'

"There was a very long silence on the other end of the line. Then she said, 'We—e—ll, maybe it'll work out all right. I hope so.'

"Maria and I were married in Hollywood soon afterward. Marlene did not come to the wedding. We sat on a balcony well into the night, Maria in a pink negligée, I in new pajamas. Maria found a forty-five-dollar-a-month apartment in Westwood. While I was working in the Donald O'Connor film during days, Dietrich herself came over in a furniture van with some things she had taken out of storage. She cleaned and painted and scrubbed floors and fixed up the kitchen. A woman living there saw her through a window and said to the manager, *'My God! That can't be Marlene Dietrich!'* And the manager replied, convinced, 'No, it's our new cleaning woman.'

"I never actually met Dietrich. She was doing her magic act in Las Vegas at the time with Orson Welles, I think he sawed her in half. I went on tour with a play. When I returned I realized there was no hope for the marriage. Maria no longer loved me. I asked her for a divorce, and she refused, saying, 'Mother and Father never divorced. They always feel, "We'll be together when we're old." '."

Maria moved to New York, and finally did agree to the divorce. Marlene was clearly relieved. Maria appeared in the play *Foolish Notion*, starring Marlene's old friend—or friendly rival —Tallulah Bankhead.

In late 1943 Marlene appeared in the musical film *Follow the Boys,* to be cut in half onstage by Orson Welles as she had been in Las Vegas. She also made an appearance as Jamilla, a haughty inhabitant of old Baghdad in the ridiculous but amusing *Kismet,* with Ronald Colman, under the direction of William Dieterle.

In the spring of 1944, the Treasury Department instituted a round-the-clock series of programs to present a flag to employees of the California Shipbuilding Corporation. Marlene rose at three A.M. to make the first presentation, for the graveyard shift at four A.M., accompanied by Howard D. Mills of the California Treasury staff. She appeared again at noon, and surrounded by cheering workers, including many women, she witnessed the launching of the one hundred and fiftieth Liberty Ship, named the S.S. *Ansel Briggs,* in honor of Iowa's first governor. It was only one of many appearances she made on behalf of the war effort.

Marlene was at her most energetically outgoing in this period, constantly attending social events with Jean Gabin, selling a kiss for $1,025 for the Red Cross, working in the Hollywood Canteen ladling out soup and serving doughnuts to the soldiers, appearing as a ringmaster in a Los Angeles circus.

In 1943, two of Marlene's most intimate relationships suffered a rift. Erich Maria Remarque had retained his passion for tropical fish. Marlene, who had helped redecorate his rooms in her home in Beverly Hills with Martin Kosleck and Madame Galka Scheier, had given him a present of three rare fish with the tricolor on their tails, known as "the French Fleet." Remarque put them in the tank in the dining room. One night at a dinner party, Marlene noticed to her horror that the fish were floating dead on the surface of the water. She blamed Remarque, saying, loudly, "The French Fleet is dead!"

Soon after, while attending a play in which Maria was featured, Remarque got up and went to the men's room. That was enough. Walter Reisch reports that Marlene was furious. Remarque moved to New York, where he settled at the old Ambassador Hotel.

Walter Reisch records what went wrong with her relationship with Jean Gabin. "It was at a party at my house," Reisch says, "and we were talking about opera. Gabin always used to go to sleep at the opera, and at the Hollywood Bowl concerts. It always infuriated Marlene.

"Suddenly, Gabin said, 'I don't like opera. It's stupid. Nobody sings when he's dying.' And Ernst Lubitsch said, 'A swan doesn't sing when it's dying, but that doesn't invalidate ballet.' Gabin walked out. He went and joined the Free French in North Africa. Marlene didn't see him for years."

For two years, almost since Pearl Harbor, Marlene had been begging Abe Lastfogel, head of USO Camp Shows, to send her on a tour of the war fronts. At last she got permission, and called an old friend, Anna Lee, of the Beverly Hills Hotel days, saying, "Anna, you've just come back from the front. What shall I wear?" Anna Lee replied, "The most gorgeous dress you can find. These men haven't seen a woman in a long time, and you must look as glamorous as you possibly can. Also, be sure to wear a uniform of your own design. The one they give you will make you look and feel horrible."

Marlene listened. After touring army camps, she left for New York in late February, 1944, to attend a meeting at One Park Avenue, the USO headquarters, to discuss the details of her presentation.

The master of ceremonies was to be the young Lebanese comedian, Danny Thomas. Thomas recalls: "Abe Lastfogel said to me, 'You've earned your last dollar until the war is over.' I had just played the Roxy four weeks at thirty-seven hundred and fifty a week. I thought I had died and gone to heaven. Abe said, 'How'd you like to play a bigger theater?' I said, 'There is no bigger theater. You mean the Radio City Music Hall?' He said, 'The European Theatre of Operations!' I gagged. 'And you'll have to take a slight cut.' 'How much?' 'Thirty-six hundred a week.' I gagged again. He added, 'Marlene Dietrich needs a master of ceremonies. You're it. I'll send your wife a hundred and fifty a week.'

"Patsy Flick—rest his soul—put some sketches together. I met with Marlene upstairs at Lindy's in a rehearsal room. The entertainers Lynn Mayberry and Jack Snyder joined us. We rehearsed every day, all day.

"One day we got a call to meet at One Park Avenue. We were

given ranks in case of capture. She was a colonel. We would be taken to our place of takeoff. We flew from New York in an old C-54. It had seats—that was the last time we saw seats on that tour—after that it was buckets. I got very, very airsick. Boy, how that thing jolted around! It was very rough. She didn't get sick. She helped me as much as she could, but I didn't want to know *nothing!* She was one of the most powerful people I ever met.

"We flew to Greenland and the Azores and then to Casablanca and Algiers. Our first show was in Algiers, at the Opera House. We were told not to take any notice of the paper airplanes the guys would sail down at us. There would be balloons flying around and the guys'd be busting them with cigarettes. They'd hiss, they'd boo, they'd throw anything on the stage, we were told. 'Don't make the mistake the last people did and start throwing things back,' they'd say. 'There would be chaos, riot.' I thought, 'What are we getting into?' These GIs were off on a three-day pass; they were rugged fellows, and were not exactly genteel.

"We needn't have worried. There were no balloons, no paper planes, nothing like that. They guys *screamed* when she came on the stage. They weren't ready for its being Marlene Dietrich! She was every woman in the world they were hungry for rolled into one.

"Then it happened. A bomb landed, not far away. The power failed. The men all yelled, 'On with the show!' But we had no lights. Then the audience did something incredible. Those thousands of tough, rough guys flashed all of the flashlights they had, onto the stage at once. We did the show to the flashlights. They didn't want it to end. And when Marlene took the musical saw she had had since Vienna between her legs and played it, they went completely *insane!* It was the sexiest thing you ever saw! They got down on all fours to look up—into Paradise!

"The night after the performance in Algiers, the hotel that she and I were staying in was bombed. I wanted to go down and hide in the cellar. Marlene said, 'If they hit us, they'll get what they deserve.' I didn't hide.

"We flew on to Italy. She went up to see the pilot, who flipped at seeing her legs, and said, 'Want to take over the controls?' She said, *'Achtung!'* And before anyone knew it she grabbed the wheel. And here was a woman who couldn't drive a car! Well, you won't believe this, but she actually landed the plane! It bounced up and down six stories and I left my stomach in Brooklyn! She was some kind of a lady!

"We went very close to the front lines. She made us go to places where we weren't supposed to be; we saw buildings cut in half, a half of a bathtub, a half of a horse—horrible! I kept saying, 'Miss Dietrich, where are you taking us?' Sergeants came up to us and said, 'What are you doing here? This place is mined.' She'd say, 'Never mind. I am Marlene. I can do anything I like.' She didn't mind. If she were captured she would have been executed. But she had no fear—*we* were scared shitless."

Danny Thomas continues: "We went on to Naples. It was a long drive in the dark without headlights. They called it black-out driving. I was so tired I slept in her arms. She wanted me next to her because I was the only one she could trust not to paw her. I never overstepped the limits. We had one day off in Naples. She lay sunbathing. She was naked except for a towel. I looked down, shaking. She said, looking at my knees knocking, 'Don't be such a baby.' I said to myself, Oh, my God, there she is, the most gorgeous woman in the world, and I'm just a schmuck from Chicago. The animal in me would not come out. I'd have to be a king, a general, a zillionaire to deserve such a prize! I was groveling! She laughed at me!

"She said, 'You've taught me a great deal.' I said, 'Me, a hook-nosed kid out of a neighborhood nightclub?' I knew what she meant. I had taught her comedy timing, how to hold it a beat before a punch line, how to be a good monologist. She said to me, 'When the photographers come around, why don't you want to have your picture taken with me?'

" 'I want to make it on my own,' I told her. She looked at me and looked at me, then she stood up with the towel around her, took my face in her hands, and said, 'You are a very remarkable young man. Now I understand.'

"In Italy, she was in dungarees, standing in the mess lines, trying little bits of food from each man's metal dish, and then running to the next mess line to try some more. The guys applauded her wherever she was in line. And these were guys in replacement depots. They hated anyone who had a face. They were snarlers. Their shoelaces weren't tied, their hair wasn't cut, their caps were crooked. When a commanding officer would say, 'You're not dressed correctly,' they'd shout, 'Screw you!'

"But despite that the entire complement of many thousands showed up for our performance. I'll never forget it. She and the actor Milton Frome were doing an act comparing the kissing techniques of the screen (hers) with that of the stage (his).

"I was the nervous guy who was backing towards the wings watching this. She asked me, 'Do you want to learn how to kiss?' I stammered, 'N-n-no, n-no, th-thank you!' Some of the boys began yelling out, 'I'll take your place, Joe!' They didn't know me from a can of beans! I was cowering and she said, 'Come here.' Suddenly I heard the most amazing thing I've ever heard in my life. As she walked towards me, pawing her thighs, thrusting up her breasts, there was a groan from the thousands of men. The sensuality of this incredible woman had gotten to them. She was the *female* incarnate! What I was hearing was the orgasmic cry of humans in heat. I knew what was going to happen, and I stopped the show cold: I called the MP's. They jumped on the stage with machine guns. It's a good thing they did, because the men had started to rush the stage. Gradually they sank back when they saw the guns. But we had to finish the show."

Lieutenant Colonel Robert Armstrong was Marlene's military escort in Italy and France. He says, "Marlene managed to wheedle Cadillacs to travel in out of Colonel David, head of Special Services, and General 'Jumbo' Wilson. But she always insisted on eating with the boys instead of the generals; she was a very good sport; and even when we traveled a hundred miles to an antiaircraft gun emplacement on which she was to sing for the boys, and the emplacement had moved out, leaving her nothing to stand on, she simply shrugged and said, 'All that matters is this means the Germans are retreating and the emplacement had to go with our troops.'

"She was constantly worried about her mother's being in Berlin during the last terrible bombing by the Allies, and while we were in Italy she got word her sister was in Belsen. Apparently, she said, her sister was being held as a hostage and was not at that time being ill-treated. She was a hostage because Goebbels wanted to dissuade Marlene from entertaining the United States troops.

"Marlene was fascinated by the German soldiers and kept wanting to photograph them as they came in as prisoners of war. But she was frightened to get out of her car and take pictures of them. She thought they might attack her.

"Sometimes she would perform on rough wooden platforms we would set up out on the fields, with only the headlights of jeeps to light her, or in rain under umbrellas or feeble little canvas canopies. She never had more than one suitcase for her makeup and her stage costumes. She wore GI uniform: Eisenhower jacket, regulation trousers, boots, and often a helmet or overseas cap. She never grumbled, *ever*. I think she liked being a soldier. One of the boys.

"She used to get love letters from Jean Gabin every day. He was with the tank corps in North Africa and, later, in France. She would read them with an incredible intensity, you never saw so much passion and interest in a human face.

"If ever a letter didn't arrive she would panic and walk up and down, restlessly, saying, 'Oh, God, I hope he's safe.' She was *madly* in love with him."

When interviewed by Leo Lerman of *Vogue,* in 1944, Marlene had these memories of the trip. She was allowed fifty-five pounds of baggage—a far cry from the thirty-six trunks and fifty hatboxes, not to mention the twelve dozen extra sets of fingernails bought from Woolworth's, that she used to cart with her across the Atlantic. She never forgot the flowers, especially the roses which the soldiers somehow found for her, decorating the ceilings of the hastily erected camouflage tents in which she often played. She wore four different evening dresses, designed by Irene, all sequined so that they would not wrinkle.

She discovered a passion for Erle Stanley Gardner books because they were so popular in the hospitals, and even men with gangrene could be happily distracted by the carryings-on of Perry Mason. The entry into Rome was a tremendous memory: the flowers, the fanfares, throwing cigarettes and chocolate to the people as the tanks rolled by, the crowds gazing in astonishment, unable to believe it was she. She remembered the thin domestic gin with lots of lemon that the soldiers gave her as a tipple, the wonderful steak and onions prepared over braziers in the winter snows, the open-air Italian hospitals where the patients basked in sunlight, the hospitals so clean that they answered even her exacting standards.

She told Lerman of extraordinary moments: her plane lost in a fog over Greenland, everyone aboard straining until at last they saw the one welcome break and the glimpse of ice below; a boy begging her for a scarf, which she gave him, and which he offered to GIs to sleep with for 500 francs; the beauty of Iceland, with pretty girls and spotless villages; landing in Paris on a moonlit night and rushing out into the streets where little booklets about her life were being sold, and gifts of perfume were pressed into her hands.

She remembered milking a cow in a village when the children needed nourishment and nobody else knew how to do it. She remembered Patton mapping out her route with a Special Service officer and asking her, "Are you afraid?" To which she replied with a smile, "No." She remembered living in a bombed house in Aachen. She thought of the children asking her for an autograph, and when she said, "But you couldn't possibly have seen me," they would reply, "Our mothers spoke of you. They said you were wonderful." She was amazed to discover the German troops also had her as a pinup. A German baron offered her an immense collection of her phonograph records. She met a young American who had actually lived with her mother in Berlin for many years during the war. He told her, "Your mother said during the bombing of Berlin, 'How awful it will be to be buried with all these fools!' "

Perhaps the most vivid memory was of the field hospitals. She told Leo Lerman, "I'd always sing 'See What the Boys in the Back Room Will Have' first, because that's what they all wanted, and when I'd sing they'd swoon and scream the way bobby-soxers did at Sinatra. It's a sound like wild birds flying, a sound that's wonderful and free. I'd go back to see the wounded they had been bringing in when the show began. In the time it took to do our show, they would have been cleaned up, operated on, and dosed with analgesics, and they would be lying in their beds.

"I would walk into a tent. . . . It was rather dark, with streaks of light coming in, cutting sharply into the darkness . . . a terrific silence. . . . There would be a nurse, seated there in case she was needed, motionless. . . . Absolutely no movement anywhere.

"There were rows of beds, and next to each bed stood a pole, and on that pole hung a jar, a jar of blood. . . . The only movement in the whole place was bubbling blood—the only sound, too: a little wisp of sound. . . . You stood there with actual life running from bottles into the boys; you saw it running into them; you heard it. And the wonderful thing was that they slept there like children, and the blood was running every hour of the day and night and everywhere the boys were lying wounded. . . .

"They'd come to me and say, 'There's some Nazis over there and they're sick. Go and speak German to them, won't you?' I'd go to those young bland-faced Nazis and they'd ask me with tears in their eyes, 'Are you the *real* Marlene Dietrich?' All was forgotten, and I'd sing 'Lili Marlene' to everyone in that hospital. There was no greater moment in my life."

She would never forget the experience in April 1945 (a little before the German surrender) of going to the Belsen concentration camp, where she had heard her sister had been incarcerated. No doubt Hitler would have put her mother there as well, had she not been the widow of a high-ranking army officer. He was already in a great deal of trouble with the army.

It was cold, and a black rain slanted icily through scraggy pine trees on a high hill as Marlene approached the camp in a jeep.

The miserable huts stank disgustingly. Bodies lay heaped in trenches, smothered in excrement, blood, mud, and brown water. Reached in New Zealand, Dr. Ronald Citrine, son of Lord Citrine, recalls: "Everyone was talking about it: Dietrich was in the camp, searching for her sister. We were struggling —we, the doctors, with other members of the St. John's Ambulance Brigade and the International Red Cross—to help the British officers identify the dead and the living. It was impossible. They were identifiable only by the tattooed numbers on their arms, and the master list was missing."

Marlene, with her customary unshakable courage, her determination, had to separate corpses from the living, peering into their faces in the hope that she would find Elisabeth. At last, she did find her. According to Marlene's military escort, Elisabeth had been comparatively well treated, because she was an Aryan and was of hostage status. Ronald Citrine says that Elisabeth narrowly escaped the epidemic which was announced in grim black letters at the gate: BEWARE OF TYPHUS.

Marlene scrupulously nursed Elisabeth and arranged for her to be tended by doctors, sending her in safety back to Berlin.

Marlene was stricken with virus pneumonia in Bari that year, and lay in a base hospital, suffering from severe chest pains, fever, and acute distress. She was on the danger list for several days. She was saved by penicillin, which had only just been made available by Sir Alexander Fleming. She was thus one of the first patients to use this antibiotic. She remained grateful to Fleming for the rest of his life, publicizing his efforts everywhere, and writing him heartfelt letters expressing her admiration for his genius. He in turn was a fan, frequently mentioning to the press his respect for Marlene's wit, intelligence, and knowledge of medicine.

In Italy on D-day (June 6, 1944), Marlene rushed on stage with the news of the Normandy invasion, bringing several thousand GIs to their feet for an uproarious cheer. She entered Rome in the triumphal procession of the relief troops, greeted by hysterical citizens who embraced her, unable to believe that she was actually there. She returned with her fellow entertainers to New York on June 16, still weakened by her illness, but forcing herself to give interviews to the newspapers and to appear with Mrs. Jimmy Doolittle at the Ladies Day war bond rally in Wall Street.

She returned to Europe early in September, landing first in Iceland to perform again on the musical saw, do a mind-reading act ("It wasn't hard to read a GI's mind when he looked at me," she said later) and deliver several new songs. In France and Germany, she once again slept in rat-infested ruins, helped to right an overturned jeep, and sometimes did her shows from the backs of trucks. A lifetime habit of sleeping only five hours a night—a result of insomnia rather than discipline—stood her in good stead, since she was under fire much of the time.

She again found the whole experience exhilarating, arriving in Paris carrying a prize souvenir of a three-yard-long paper-money chain made of forty-two bills from various nations, given to her by United States servicemen.

In Paris, she met her old friend Maurice Chevalier. She had been signing autographs on the Champs Élysées when she learned of the arrival of Chevalier in the city, and immediately tried to locate him. She was convinced he had been maligned by articles and newscasts which stated that he had collaborated with the Germans; and her support of him, at a time when he might have faced prosecution, was undoubtedly crucial.

She felt that the only reason Chevalier had performed in Germany was to obtain the release of war prisoners. When she finally found him, they embraced warmly, and she was close to tears with joy. Through the next three years, while Chevalier faced constant criticism, she remained his devoted admirer and friend.

A new acquaintance of those days was the haughty and autocratic General Patton, who had personally requested her appearance at various points close to the front line, after she had expressed her lack of fear of war to him. Always admiring of her art, he was never more so than when she proved to be a good soldier; and he gave her the Christmas present she was to value more than any other, a pearl-handled .44-caliber revolver which had belonged to his father and had been captured in the Mexican-American War. Ironically, she was to lose this precious gift to the United States authorities when she returned to New York in the summer of 1945, because of the prohibition of the import of firearms.

The most severe test of her courage took place during the Battle of the Bulge. Oddly, a near namesake, the German general Sepp Dietrich, was almost responsible for her capture. The area in which she was stationed was virtually surrounded by Dietrich's division. General James Gavin, of the Eighty-eighth Airborne Division, learned of her predicament from headquarters, and flew to her rescue. Handsome and dashing, Gavin was among the youngest commanders in the army, and excited the jealousy of most of his colleagues.

Marlene's friend, the lyricist Max Colpet (originally Kolpe), recalled in his memoirs that Marlene was waiting anxiously in the trap set for her, certain she would be executed, when plane motors roared overhead, she looked up, and saw a Flying Fortress. Parachutes mushroomed in the chilly air. The first paratrooper to arrive was Gavin himself. Colpet describes him kneeling with a cavalier's grace at Marlene's feet, then taking her in a jeep to a safety area. She said herself, "We didn't stop until we reached Paris."

Marlene was acutely distressed at the changes in her native country, and made a remark which was later used against her: "I guess we had it coming to us." To this day, many Germans resent her wartime criticisms of Germany; she made it brutally clear that she did not blame all that had happened solely on Hitler and the other Nazis.

Back in New York in a steaming July 1945, Marlene said, "I'm just a GI coming home." A jaw infection had knocked her out, her hands and feet had been frozen, and she had lost her uniform during a retreat. She wore a nurse's uniform with a Third Army patch and a Second Armored Division shield. On her sleeve were three hash marks signifying eighteen months overseas.

She had been named a daughter of the Seventy-first Infantry regiment, and on July 21, 1945, she welcomed the regiment home on the *Queen Elizabeth* as the ship moored at Pier 90, at the foot of West Fiftieth Street. Thousands of GIs yelled and laughed with delight as she shook her leg at them from the pier.

Marlene returned to Europe in late August. In Paris, she frequently dated General Gavin, and also caught up with Jean Gabin. Max Colpet observes in his autobiography that Marlene often got ribbed over the fact that the two names differed in only one letter, and that she seemed to be enjoying a liaison with both. There was a joke in Paris that the only difference between them was a French letter. Actually, Colpet insists, Marlene was simply flirting with Gavin, whereas her relationship with Jean Gabin had resumed. The film collector David Bradley vividly remembers seeing Marlene and Gabin strolling down the Avenue Montaigne near the Champs Elysées, where Marlene had taken an apartment (at Number 12) which she retains today. Bradley says, "It was clear they were very close. They were arm in arm; they didn't care who saw them; they laughed happily at jokes together; and they cheerfully took the Métro like any poilu and his girl friend. They were never dressed up. Marlene, looking rather pale, wore a cap or a beret, and was most often in uniform. Gabin was similarly casual, and also in a beret or bareheaded."

Marlene made the most nostalgic journey of all in mid-September, when she returned to Berlin. She was greeted at the Tempelhof Airport by her mother. Before she arrived, Marlene had written to her good friend and colleague Hubsi von Meyerinck to say she was coming, ". . . and please arrange for all those old friends who were not Nazis to be there." She asked Hubsi to set up a little party at her mother's apartment. Among those who came were Alexa von Proembsky, Hilde Korde, Walter Franck, Cornelia Herstatt, and Heinz Ruhmann.

Reminiscing about the past, the little group sat around for hours, but Marlene did not show up. Just before she was due to arrive, she had received word from the Russian authorities that she would be permitted to visit Rudi's relatives behind the Iron Curtain. The visit completed, she returned to West Berlin.

Hubsi telephoned everyone. Again, they all arrived on bicycles, and Marlene rushed in to greet them; she looked exhausted but beautiful in her uniform, embracing them one by one. Somebody mentioned Paula Wessely, a star who had been accused of collaborating with the Nazis. Marlene said, with an air of pity, "Poor Paula. If I met her, I would say, 'It is such a shame you do this. How sad you gave up your soul for a little money.'"

Somebody else mentioned Emil Jannings, the great star of *The Blue Angel,* who begged Marlene to see him, but she would not. Perhaps, she said, she could have forgiven him for working for Hitler. But she could never forgive him for denying his Jewish grandmother.

Marlene told her friends she would love to revive *It's in the Air,* with Hubsi and Margo Lion, whom she had met in Paris. She delighted them all by singing, at their urgent request, "My Best Girl Friend," with all of her old bewitching artistry.

Marlene had no sooner left Berlin to give a lecture on her films at the GI university at Biarritz, in France, than she received a telephone call announcing the sudden death of her mother. She stood in the rain among the ruins of Berlin, in black, crying gently, as her mother's remains were lowered into the grave.

In Paris, that year, Marlene saw a great deal of Ernest and Mary Hemingway. She liked Mary immediately, responding warmly to her brisk good humor and charm. The Hemingways were staying at the Ritz, and Marlene was their frequent visitor, eating like a trooper, smoking three packs a day, and relentlessly going over every detail of her tours. In her book *How It Was,* Mary Hemingway mentions that Marlene had supervised accommodations, transportation, sizes of stages and hauls, lighting and microphones, and money for her tours during the war. She used to greet Hemingway with the words, "Papa, you are the most wonderful. . . . Papa, you are the greatest man and the greatest artist."

Mary Hemingway writes that Marlene used to sit on the side of Ernest's bathtub and sing her songs to him while he shaved.

Mary did a good imitation of her, drawling huskily while Marlene fell over laughing. Sometimes Ernest used to join in the chorus, attempting "I Don't Know Why I Love You Like I Do".

Ernest's friends "Buck" Lanham and Bill Walton both came to like Marlene, fascinated by her and relieved that she made no attempt to be seductive towards them. She kept Lanham fascinated, telling of her war adventures through a heavy cold, swigging champagne. She loved to wear Bill Walton's elaborate hat, bristling with black cock feathers, and she would sit on the toilet wearing the hat, chuckling over anecdotes, while he shaved.

Marlene used to tell all concerned a new version of her funeral story, in which she would now be laid to rest in Notre Dame, with one corner of the cathedral curtained off. Ernest would ask her, "For your girl friends?" "For what would you think, Papa?" Marlene would ask.

Mary said in *How It Was*, "Marlene imagined herself lying, beautiful as always, in her coffin, appropriately placed somewhere below the high altar, and her long-time hairdresser arranging her hair for the final time, but maladroitly combing the one swirl of hair over her forehead, which was her favorite coiffure in 1944.

" 'I would rise up, take the comb from her and arrange the dip the way it should be. I should be looking my very best for my friends' last view of me,' she would say.

" 'There'll never be such a show,' Ernest might say. 'You're immortal, my Kraut.' "

Marlene became a fan that year of the great French star, Gérard Philipe, whom she saw at the Théâtre Hébertot in *Caligula*. He gave a striking performance as the demented emperor, described by the critic, J.-J. Gautier, "His movements are of a sick child, he burns, he is on fire, his voice is a nervous emanation. . . ."

Marlene evidently agreed, rushing backstage at the Hébertot to overpower Philipe with congratulations. For weeks, she sent him roses. Later, she was to admire his performance in a version of *Le Diable au Corps*, by Raymond Radiguet, in which he played unforgettably a thin, young student in love with an older woman.

Marlene spent more time in Paris in late 1945 and early 1946 than anywhere else. She was extremely friendly with Jean Cocteau, whose delicate and fastidious talent appealed to her.

The French film star and intimate friend of Jean Cocteau, Jean Marais, has vivid memories of Marlene. "Marlene and Jean Cocteau were not intimate friends but they had a profound respect for each other's talent. She frequently visited the house which Jean and I had bought together in a fashionable district of Paris. They talked often, of literature and art.

"They had first met on Jean's visit to Hollywood, when he made a journey around the world in eighty days. He was imitating Phileas Fogg, the hero of Jules Verne's fantastic novel.

"He contacted her in Paris because he wanted her to play the Princess, a symbolic representation of death, in his film, *Orphée*, based on the Orpheus legend. She would probably have been perfect; but, much as she admired him, she never seriously considered it.

"He wrote a text for a presentation I made to her during a festival in Monte Carlo. He was not sufficiently well to attend himself.

"I was very happy to deliver the text. My feelings about her were very much as Jean's were. I really came to know Marlene some years later, in about 1954, when she was living in Paris. We got together through a mutual friend, a lady who was a director of the Christian Dior fashion house. Marlene felt very lonely in Paris. As a result, I saw her very, very often. We used to go to restaurants and movies all the time together. I was living on a boat on the Seine. And she would sometimes come with friends and mingle with my friends, and cook.

"She was still in love with Gabin, even in 1954 and 1955. His house was on the Rue Francois I, very close to Dior and to her own apartment on the Avenue Montaigne. She would always want me to come with her, and sit on the terrace of a café opposite the house in the hope of catching a glimpse of him, even if it were only for a second, coming out.

"We would sit or stand there for hours and *hours*, sometimes all day. He was married, and there could be no question of their actually meeting.

"In her loneliness, in her loss of him, Marlene would drag me off to all his movies! Old, new, it didn't matter! We would sit there through performance after performance, and she would chuckle or cry, and make remarks about certain gestures of his, certain scenes, which reminded her of their love affair. I still laugh when I think of it. It was charming!

"Whenever she did see him on screen, she would make little comments, such as, 'Why does he dye his hair? He was so much handsomer when he had naturally gray hair.' But all was said, no matter what, with the utmost sweetness and sympathy for him.

"At nights, Marlene never wanted to go to sleep. She would like to talk and talk about Gabin well into the early hours of the morning; it was very difficult, because I had to start for a studio at the crack of dawn."

In Paris after the war, Marlene met Marcel Carné, who had directed Gabin in major films prewar; and the three of them would go to the Roland Petit Ballet at the Théâtre Sarah Bernhardt together. One of the young and promising dancers of the troupe was an unknown named Leslie Caron.

Marlene, Gabin, and Carné particularly admired a ballet, *Le Rendezvous,* composed by Joseph Kosma, written by Jacques Prévert, and designed by Brassai. They felt it might make an excellent film. Marlene took a great interest from the first in preparing a script with Prévert and Carné. It was felt that despite her German accent her great popularity in France would enable the French public to accept her speaking French.

A deal was made with RKO in Hollywood to coproduce the film with Pathé. A flurry of articles appeared, announcing that the famous lovers, Marlene and Gabin, would appear together, and that Prévert would write the script. Alexander Korda decided to take over at a later stage—when RKO got cold feet.

Prévert worked at St. Paul de Vence, and Carné and Gabin shuttled to and fro between the Paris and Nice railroad stations

or by automobile to work out the details, Marlene remaining in
Paris. In his memoirs, Carné described a maddening trip with
Gabin to the south of France in which he felt considerable
strain in his relationship with the irascible star. Marlene's contract called for script approval, and she immediately clashed
with Prévert on the creation of her role. Prévert and Carné
were exasperated by her suggestions, particularly one in which
she had herself descending from a carriage late at night and
paying the driver with a bank note which she plucked from the
top of a rolled stocking.

When they protested at this and other *Blue Angel* ideas,
Marlene informed Pathé that she flatly refused to make the
film. Gabin followed her. He was extremely irritable with Carné
and, acting defiantly, he decided to make a film with Marlene
for another director, Georges Lacombe, *Martin Roumagnac,*
which turned out to be a disaster.

Carné writes, acidly, "Marlene Dietrich appeared in the person, utterly realistic of course, of a Norman farmer's wife and
a petshop proprietor, a role for which she had evidently been
put into the world. . . . Perhaps the female creator of *The Blue
Angel* showed in it her talents of cuisinière, including the
method by which she was able to prepare a large salted beef.
. . . I always regret that I didn't see the film by my friend
Georges Lacombe, but only because I didn't see her cooking the
salted beef."

Marlene played a bizarre role in *Martin Roumagnac,* that of
an Australian bird-shop proprietor (Australian to explain her
horrible Hun accent). In an interview many years ago, the cameraman said, "We had a problem with those birds. Sometimes
they'd escape from their cages, circle around, and crap on Miss
Dietrich's hair!"

Daniel Gélin, a French actor who appeared in *Martin Roumagnac* remembers: "Gabin was very, very nervous about his
career, because when he left France it was with the physique
and appearance of a leading man, and when he returned he had
gray hair and a little potbelly. He was terrified of the public's
seeing him after such a long interval, making the transition

from the prewar idol to what he had become. Not only that, but he was also painfully conscious of the rising generation and of its threat to his supremacy. I remember him standing, white with stage fright, before every scene, miserable about the cameras, and hating to appear in two shots with me because I was half his age.

"Marlene looked tired after her war experiences, and was constantly having arguments with the cameraman, Roger Hubert, because she did not feel he was doing justice to her. She would worry about her appearance, but her figure was amazingly good. Occasionally, she would have two Scotches to relax herself at the end of the day.

"I remember her on one occasion wandering onto the set between scenes wearing a man's blue-striped suit and a man's felt hat, with a cigarette holder fifty centimeters long, and all of a sudden she was tossing bonbons through the air at the crew like a farmer casting grain to chickens. From anyone else, the gesture would have been repulsive, imperial, and vulgar; but from her it was charming.

"I used to go driving with her and Gabin on Sundays, through that austere, gray Paris of the immediate postwar period. We had great fun. We would all come back to the suite Marlene had at the Hôtel Prince des Galles and they would be like two young kids in love. It was delightfully absurd as he would say, 'Why didn't you, last night?' And she would reply, 'I was too tired.' He always called her, 'Grande.' To his friends, he called her, 'La Grande.' He would say, 'Grande, will you tonight?' And she would reply, with a yawn, 'Maybe. If I'm not too tired.' It was funny. . . . I used to laugh and laugh.

"At the end of shooting there was a crew dance. A kind of little *bal* where the cast and technicians got together in one of those big sound stages with the sets still up. She embraced the crew tenderly. The crowd parted so that Gabin and Marlene could dance on their own. The little, tinny band made its waltz, and they spun round and round the length of the hall under the lights. Everyone waited to see what they would do. Would it be a big romantic scene? No. He just patted her on the bottom as a carpenter might pat a waitress he was going out with. Everyone clapped. The band played 'La Marseillaise.'

"I remember Jean told me that during the war Marlene was playing near his tank brigade. A man came up to him in the tank and said, *'Ta poule* is here to see you.' He punched him so hard in the face he flew across the field. He didn't like his friend using the term *ta poule* ["your chick"].

"After Marlene left, many years later, Gabin had taken up with a younger woman, an actress.

"I was riding with Gabin in a car and we were looking at copy of a scandal magazine, *France Dimanche,* which showed the results of a photographer's having broken in to Gabin's room during this affair. The photograph showed a picture of a woman beside Gabin's bedside which the photographer had placed there. Gabin said, 'There's one person who's not going to be happy about this, and that's La Grande.' After a moment's pause, Gabin said, with a kind of verbal shrug, 'But then after all, she didn't have to leave me, did she?'

"Years later, I was in New York, and Marlene was wonderful to me. She got me tickets for *West Side Story* when they were very hard to obtain; she brought food to my suite at the hotel; and I knew it was all because of our time with Gabin. And then she said, 'How is Jean? Is he all right?' I reassured her. She had three photographs in her living room, in her apartment on Park Avenue: one of Hemingway, one of Remarque, and one of Gabin. I think the picture of Gabin meant the most to her."

The failure of *Martin Roumagnac,* which was released in 1946, put an end to Marlene's relationship with Gabin. Perhaps the chief problem, according to Max Colpet, was Gabin's jealousy. He wrote in his memoirs, "If she wore black lace, Gabin would grab her and want to know where she was going. He had a complex. He had caught his best friend in bed with one of his wives. One night, Marlene called me from her place and asked if she could spend the night in my living room. She had had a violent quarrel with Gabin and she had fled." According to some versions, Gabin had literally thrown her out.

Nine

Renewals

The war was undoubtedly the most important experience of Marlene's life. As the daughter of a soldier turned policeman and the stepdaughter of another soldier, she was at last fulfilling her destiny as a daughter of Prussia while at the same time not abnegating the anti-Nazi views she shared with Erich Maria Remarque. The masculine side of her nature, as well as the feminine, was satisfied by appearing sexily in a uniform. The most serious effect her war experiences had on her was to make her despise movies more than ever. The war also had the effect on her of making her understand that her best future lay in solo entertainment, in becoming an abstraction of the Feminine. Although it was to be some eight years before she created the work of art we now know as Dietrich-in-theater, she had clearly already laid down the basis of that great self-created work.

Meanwhile, there was the need to earn a living, and the knowledge that to do so she would have to return to the schlock factory of Hollywood. Mitchell Leisen offered her a part which was arguably more absurd than any she had played up to that time. This was the role of a gypsy who helps a crashed flier in Europe, *Golden Earrings.*

Leisen telephoned her in Paris and outlined what he wanted. She was delighted to hear from him, but dismayed by what he had to offer. She screamed, "Oh, no, Mitch, I can't play a gypsy!"

"But Marlene," he said, all in a rush, "the whole point is that this is a dirty, disgusting woman with thick, matted hair who, underneath, is so terrifically glamorous that this dull, dreary English guy has to fall in love with her."

"That sounds interesting. Maybe I'll do it."

No sooner had she agreed to return to Hollywood than the bosses at Paramount flatly refused to have her play it. "She's through, she's washed up," they all said. While Leisen slowly but surely overcame their objections, pointing out that she was now a heroine to the public because of her war tours, Marlene began visiting the gypsy encampments near the Seine, and even stayed in one of these for a week.

She arrived in Hollywood with a whole set of designs and some sample costumes bought from her gypsy friends, took one look at the "double" shots featuring her, and screamed (according to Leisen) "Those costumes are impossible! Pure Hollywood! I will have them redone!" As a result, in several long shots in the picture, Marlene's double is wearing a different dress from the one Marlene is wearing in the close shots.

Mitchell Leisen told his biographer, David Chierichetti: "Ray Milland (as the British officer) didn't want to make the picture. He didn't like Marlene; he thought he was too young to play opposite her, so he was a real bastard at first.

"He calmed down a little before the end, but he and Marlene fought the whole time. When we were shooting the scene where he first meets her as she's eating the stew, and over and over, Marlene would stick a fish head in her mouth, suck the eye out, and then pull out the rest of the head. Then after I yelled 'Cut!' she would stick her finger in her throat and make herself throw up. This whole performance made Ray violently ill.

"There was a little fire under the pot, but the water wasn't hot; we put dry ice in the pot to give off the vapors. When we broke for lunch, the prop man stupidly forgot to put the fire out. We came back, and Marlene saw the water bubbling merrily along, she assumed it was just the dry ice. She stuck her hand in and let out a bloodcurdling scream.

"She had a second-degree burn. I suggested we call it quits for the day but she wouldn't hear of it. She wouldn't even allow us to restage the scene and use her other hand."

During the filming of *Golden Earrings,* in 1947, there was a major strike in Hollywood. Paramount issued an edict that none of the actors, crew, or associated technicians was to leave the premises for the duration. The picket lines must never be crossed. Marlene and Ray Milland, still quarreling constantly, had beds set up in their dressing rooms; and by common consent each slept alone. Mitchell Leisen, who had just recovered from a heart attack (no doubt brought on by quarreling with his temperamental stars), lay on a stretcher bed in his office. Most of the others doubled up chastely with members of their own sex. This peculiar arrangement continued for nine weeks of shooting.

The picture, despite all the problems which dogged it, was an enormous hit, grossing the studio seven times its production cost of just under a million dollars. Ray Milland announced on its completion that he would never work with Marlene again, and she, perhaps wisely, said nothing.

While Marlene made *Golden Earrings,* Maria was busy in New York. She worked with Orson Welles in radio, acted on Broadway, and taught actors at Fordham University in the Bronx. Working at Fordham, she fell in love with a handsome twenty-five-year-old Italian-American, William Riva, who shared her passion for the theater and for music. On this occasion, Marlene wholeheartedly approved of the romance. Despite the fact that Riva had no money, he impressed Marlene because he appeared to be indifferent to her fame, and respectful and considerate in his feelings toward her daughter. The couple were married on Independence Day 1947 and moved into a cold-water walk-up at 1118 Third Avenue; the room was continually rattled by the elevated trains which literally roared next to the windows. It was a very dirty apartment, which Marlene, William, and Maria worked on, cleaning and painting. Marlene at first did not want to impose on the marriage by paying for a lavish home. But when after a year the Rivas' first son, John Michael, was born, Marlene insisted they move into a more comfortable house.

For $43,000 Marlene bought them a four-story home on East

Ninety-fifth Street, elegantly designed by Riva himself, with a glass front door and a hall with white motifs and decorated with large display cases of butterfly specimens. The kitchen, which Marlene helped to organize, was hung with highly polished kitchenware. The garden was very handsome; the second floor was cunningly designed to reflect the greens of the garden; and the upstairs living room was draped with gauze so that it seemed to be floating in mist. The nursery and master bedroom on the third floor were also exquisite, and again Marlene used her flawless taste in helping her daughter and son-in-law select the appropriate details.

After the war, Marlene became increasingly disillusioned with picture making, convinced that it was no longer the expression of the genius of individual persons, but rather had become a machine, a mechanical process in which the technicians had taken over the business. She told Thomas M. Pryor of the *New York Times,* "Of course, it has always been technical to an impossible extent. If you'd ever tried making love to someone in a scene and cast a soulful glance outward to see that damned microphone jiggling this way and that to catch your every breath, you'd realize how maddening it could be." She said how irritable she was when, in the middle of a perfectly good scene, after she had given her best, a sound technician announced that the entire scene would have to be scrapped, because the sound of hammering could be heard from a nearby stage. She pointed to the growing power of the unions, and the problem of minor crew members' virtually dictating the terms of production. She also expressed her contempt for actors, saying, when Pryor mentioned Gable, Power, Pidgeon, Milland, and others, "Isn't that a silly, useless occupation for a man? Imagine going to work in the morning and having someone plaster makeup all over your face. I don't think it's a man's work."

Fond as ever of radio, with its extraordinary freedom for the personality and the voice, Marlene was quick to accept the offering of a CBS contract to appear in the Ford Theater series in the fall of 1948. She also played roles on television, in very rare early appearances on the medium. She acted the Garbo role in *Grand Hotel;* and before an audience of celebrities, she gave a fine performance as Madame Bovary in a radio adaptation of Flaubert's novel. Van Heflin played her lover and Claude Rains her husband, under the direction of Fletcher Markle; and the cast and audience met for a tremendous party at the Waldorf-Astoria after the show.

In Paris, in 1947, Marlene renewed her friendship with the French fashion designer Ginette Spanier, and spent many happy hours at her apartment at 70 Avenue Marceau, near the Étoile, with its labyrinthine passages and heavily baroque plaster ceilings. She often used to ride the elevator with Noel Coward and discuss details of costumes for hours. She would also drop by Balmain's, trying on dozens of mink coats at ten o'clock in the morning. Ginette Spanier wrote in her memoirs, *It Isn't All Mink:* "I have seen her washing her own hair in my bathroom; I have seen her come back from a nightclub, her arms full of red roses. I have seen her cooking breakfast in my kitchen, doing her imitation of Frieda, the German char. . . . I have seen her come into a restaurant, a theater, with all eyes drawn to her. . . .

"Marlene is intelligent, ruthless, and quite extraordinary over clothes. She knows exactly what she wants. She knows a great deal about fitting. She also knows how a dress is made. She never smiles. She never says, 'Good morning.' She stands there in the fitting room, hour after hour, incredibly beautiful, without a smile, pinching a tenth of an inch of material here or there to show how it puckers. As the hours go by she pinches a bit lower down the dress. That is all. I have known her to have a garment fitted six times because of a seam in the *lining* of which she didn't quite like the angle."

At one point, Spanier burst out with rage, complaining that nobody in the audience would be interested in "the shadow of a seam in the lining of her dress." Marlene pointed out sharply, "If, in twenty-five years, Maria sees the picture and notices the seam puckered she might say, 'How could Mother have stood such a thing?' "

Marlene was presented with the Légion d'Honneur by the French ambassador in Washington, in recognition of her services to France. Shortly before, she had been awarded the Medal of Freedom and a Russian medal which, she laughingly told friends, had been given to her "because I drank vodka with those guys."

In 1947, Dietrich was still obsessed with Gérard Philipe. At dinner at Walter Reisch's house in Bel Air, California, with Lubitsch, the opera star Jarmila Novotna, and Novotna's daughter, she recommended Philipe as Octavian, the Cavalier of the Silver Rose, to Lubitsch for his long-delayed film based on *Der Rosenkavalier.*

She urged everyone to see Philipe in *Le Diable au Corps.* One year after the dinner party at Reisch's house, a screening of the film was arranged at the home of William Wyler, the Academy Award-winning director, and his wife, Margaret. It was November 30, 1947. Reisch says, "Lubitsch was longing to see the film and I had invited a big crowd: Mady Christians, Otto Preminger, Billy Wilder, Yvonne de Carlo, Edmund Goulding, Mike Romanoff, and many others. I went over to pick up Marlene. She was staying in an apartment house above Sunset. Lubitsch's only condition was that he wouldn't have to see Marlene's Medal of Freedom—she had been wearing it everywhere—and he was tired of seeing it on display. She would not agree to remove it. Well, we got to the house. All the people were there—but no Lubitsch.

"He never did get to see the medals. He died at two-forty that afternoon. He had been in the shower and had had a heart attack. Marlene insisted on going to his house in Bel Air immediately. She stood by the body, weeping quietly. Under her arm, she carried her latest album, which she had planned to play at the party.

"It's true, Marlene and Lubitsch had often differed. But she always had a respect for his genius, and there was always a bond of affection between these two Berliners. It's hard to believe they were born not far apart. And now she was in her prime, in her mid-forties, looking down at this great, dead director, who had been famous when she was a pathetic beginner struggling along the streets of Berlin with her violin, trying to make a living."

In 1947 Marlene was offered the part of a former Nazi living in postwar Berlin, in her friend Billy Wilder's film, *A Foreign Affair.* At first, she was horrified by the idea, thinking this must be some typically sardonic Wilder joke. She had been quite annoyed with him over an incident during *Golden Earrings.* She had contrived to lose her musical saw. When she arrived, very flustered, in the Paramount commissary and told Wilder and her other friends there about the mishap, Wilder said, "I could do with a musical saw. I could use it on some of my wooden actors." She looked as though she could have cut his head off with it, and swept out. But soon they were friends again.

Marlene spoke to Billy Wilder on the telephone, saying, "I can't play this Nazi role." Wilder had June Havoc play a scene in the picture, singing a torch song, and flew it to Marlene in Paris. When she saw it, she made up her mind. "OK, I'll do it," she told Billy.

The cowriter of the film, Richard Breen, asked Marlene, "Did you ever have an intimate relationship with Eisenhower?" And she replied, "Darling, Ike was never at the front!"

The picture was made in Hollywood. Frederick Hollander composed new songs for her, which she sang with all of her practiced authority and ease. The film was criticized for tastelessness—not surprisingly, since it made fun out of the agony of the defeated city. But Marlene enjoyed good notices, and apparently enjoyed the experience of making it.

In the late 1940s, Marlene became very friendly with the French star Edith Piaf, whose fragile figure, pinched face, and large burning eyes brought out the fairy godmother in her. She first saw her immediately after the war, when Piaf astonished

Paris audiences with her committed, passionate love songs and her off-the-cuff comments on current politics. When she met Piaf, Marlene found her depressed, worried, downcast, and on the edge of a nervous breakdown. With little confidence in her own talent, no shrewdness in choosing friends, and disastrous miscalculations in electing lovers, Piaf depended on Marlene for advice.

In her memoirs Piaf wrote: "Because of Marlene I was able to face up to my problems and overcome them. I have much to thank her for. She is one of the most intelligent women and probably the most conscientious artiste it has ever been my fortune to meet."

Later, Piaf told her biographer, "Every time I was with her I thought of *The Blue Angel*—the part where she sings in her black stockings and her top hat. Marlene was a real movie star, so perfect you couldn't believe she ate. So when she told me she liked to cook and that her favorite dish was French boiled beef, I thought she was pulling my leg!

"The two of us often had dinner together. At first I was damn careful, because I was afraid of sounding like an ass, but she gave me confidence the day she said, 'Let yourself go, Edith; for me, you're Paris. . . . And besides, you remind me of Jean Gabin. You talk like him; you eat like him; and, as delicate as you look, you give me the same feeling of strength that he does.'

"That impressed me, because as an actor and as a man, there's no one better than Gabin. I must have reminded Marlene of her big, strong Gabin the night she took off the gold cross with emeralds that she was wearing and hung it around my neck.

" 'Here, Edith, I want it to bring you luck, as it's done for me. And this way it'll get around Paris, just as it did with me.' Her gesture brought tears to my eyes."

Unfortunately, the gift did not bring Piaf the luck that she and Marlene hoped for; and, after a failed love affair, she put the cross away.

Marlene was most helpful with Piaf's New York debut at the Versailles Restaurant. She was present when Piaf stood in black taffeta on a special raised platform in front of the pale green curtains, tiny and pathetic, her colorless face lifted to the spotlight, thrilling the audience with her songs of the grimness of fate, the cry of trains late at night, the hopeless ironies of human desire. Piaf's fastidious technique, half-hidden behind a seemingly confused and tragic disharmony, stirred Marlene profoundly. She wanted to hug this poor, brilliant creature in her arms.

In 1952, Marlene supervised Piaf's costume for her wedding at St. Vincent de Paul's church in New York to the French singer, Jacques Pills. Piaf was exceptionally nervous, her face blotchy, her hair lusterless. Marlene carefully made up her face, and prepared for her a lush bouquet of new white rosebuds tied with pale blue voile. A few minutes before, a doctor had given Piaf a shot of a powerful drug to get her through the ceremony, but she had been drinking on top of it and was unsteady on her feet.

Through the entire ceremony, at which Marlene was a bridesmaid, Marlene kept looking at Piaf, willing her not to fall down or make a scene. She continued to control her through the wedding party at the Versailles and an elaborate luncheon at Le Pavillon. Intoxicated with Dom Perignon and drugs, Piaf cried as Marlene hugged her and gave her good wishes for the future. The good wishes were useless. The marriage was a failure.

Often when Piaf appeared at the Versailles, Marlene, knowing how delicately balanced Piaf was, would keep visitors at bay. If somebody rapped at the dressing room door when Marlene was there, she would open the door, peep out, and say, testily, in her special shrill, high-pitched voice reserved for such occasions, "Can I help you? I am Mademoiselle Piaf's maid!" Callers invariably fled. But one day a journalist, Robert Bré, proved more persistent. When Marlene let out her maid's harsh cry, Bré replied, "How nice. Please say hello to Miss Piaf's chauffeur, Maurice Chevalier."

In 1950, Marlene was asked by the Academy of Motion Picture Arts and Sciences to present the Best Foreign Picture award. She arrived at the Pantages Theater, and discovered that the design was a kind of hideous rococo. Lloyd Pantages told her that most of the stars would be overdressed in absurd flounces and furbelows. She told him, "If this is all going to be red, white, and blue, Mama had better be in black. And I want the dress slashed to the knee. That way, they'll see my leg before they see me." As usual, her shrewdness paid off. Much to the annoyance of several performers, she received a standing ovation that lasted ten minutes.

Aside from a brief appearance in a nightclub scene in Fletcher Markle's film *Jigsaw*, done as a favor to Markle and his wife, the actress Mercedes McCambridge, Marlene did no film work in 1948 and 1949. But when Alfred Hitchcock offered her the part of the musical comedy star Charlotte Inwood in *Stage Fright*, to be shot in England early in 1950, she accepted at once.

She arranged for her wardrobe to be designed by Christian Dior; and for her one song, "The Laziest Gal in Town," her friend Cole Porter was brought in.

Her costars were Jane Wyman, Michael Wilding, and Richard Todd. She was fascinated by Wilding. She found him witty, with a repertoire of outrageous show business anecdotes, and extremely attractive physically.

Richard Todd says, "There is no doubt Marlene was having a big affair with Michael. It blossomed during the making of the picture; I don't think they had met before. She got very frisky and Michael more and more jolly and frothy—and so it went on! She couldn't have an affair with me because I was engaged, and then married, during the course of the film. She asked me my birth date and my fiancée's, and I told her. She sent it off to Carroll Righter. He replied, 'No, no, on no account must they be married! They're not suited to each other!' She was frightfully concerned. She said to me, 'You mustn't marry that girl, your stars are wrong!' Her whole life was ruled by the stars and she was terribly worried that I was making a ghastly error.

"I told my fiancée, and she never forgave Marlene. In the long term, Marlene was right. The marriage didn't work. But I couldn't see that at the time.

"I warmed to Marlene from the first moment we met. It was at a luncheon given for her arrival, and I was very much in awe of this fable. I was as green as grass; it was my third picture; I was bewildered by what was going on. She was so kind about my inexperience; she never gave any indication that she was aware of my apprehension, though she must have been conscious of it. While she was very much a woman, she was also like a *father* to me.

"She taught me a lesson I always followed. She said, 'Never mind the taxes, earn the money.' She dinned it into me again and again. She told me, 'You can forget those people who say they can't afford to work.' She said, 'Just keep working, you'll find a way to handle the taxes.' It was her creed.

"She knew exactly what she was doing on a set every second of the time. Her heavy-lidded eyes moved almost invisibly, taking in every detail. She missed *nothing*. Hitchcock's attitude was that actors were sheep. If this particular sheep wanted a special spotlight, that was fine with the shepherd. She knew what she was doing, so he let her be. *I* didn't know what I was doing. That irritated him terribly. He never gave me any encouragement. He gave his lighting cameraman detailed instructions, and gave his assistant a chart by which the assistant plotted the moves. She loved that."

The actress Kay Walsh, who was in the film, remembers: "Marlene's figure—she was about forty-nine at the time—was still *dreamy*. But she would stuff herself all day long with steak and kidney pie. To see all that food go down into that figure—it *horrified* me. But the figure remained the same. She was under a great strain with Hitchcock but she never faltered.

"She was an absolute *district nurse* on the picture. She had a Gladstone bag, and inside it an assortment of Cartier boxes containing every kind of medical aid imaginable—not for herself, but for all those with whom she came into contact. She showed me her electrician's card, Hollywood branch. She knew more than the wardrobe people. Her dresses were sent from Paris. When they arrived she personally went to wardrobe and showed them how to iron the dresses, and how to use Sunlight brand scrubbing soap on the hem so that it would stand out. She took care of all her dresses herself.

"Hitchcock was in awe of her and she in awe of him. It made for rather a sticky beginning, but Hitch always listened to her. They were shooting a garden party scene when rain came pouring down. Hail fell. Everybody got wet. Marlene kept very cool and made suggestions for protecting the lights and cameras and putting up awnings. She got drenched, standing out there like Hitch's superior, giving instructions. Hitch obeyed."

Hitchcock expressed great admiration for Marlene. With his characteristic humor, he says, "Marlene was a professional star. She was also a professional cameraman, art director, editor, costume designer, hairdresser, makeup woman, composer, producer—and director!"

The movie was one of Hitch's least successful efforts. And it was impossible to accept Marlene as a murderess, in a cheated ending which infuriated the critics because the only way to have criticized the ending would have been to reveal it.

On October 30, 1950, Marlene sang at the Night of Stars following a Royal Command Performance of *The Mudlark*, starring Alec Guinness as Disraeli and Irene Dunne as Queen Victoria. Marlene was dazzled by Guinness's performance, and put him second on her list of Englishmen after Sir Alexander Fleming.

A few evenings later, Marlene and Michael Wilding were dining at the Caprice. Suddenly, she spotted Alec Guinness across the room. She jumped up, rushed to his table, and said without drawing breath, "You are the man I second most wanted to meet in the entire world!" He asked her who was the first. She told him it was Fleming. He replied, "I'll always take second billing if it's anyone like that."

Alec (now Sir Alec) Guinness says: "I was enchanted with Marlene. I decided that my wife and I should invite her to dinner. The question was, where? I called Kay Walsh and asked her, 'Is there anywhere in London good enough for her? She's been everywhere.' Kay replied, 'Just bear in mind she's a sturdy hausfrau. Give her a kitchen dinner at home, and she'll love it.'"

The Guinnesses extended the invitation, and told Marlene not to dress up. She arrived in a duffel coat—lined in mink. The Guinnesses were very nervous and (convinced they couldn't cook well enough for her) hired a woman for the evening. The food was disastrous. But Marlene didn't mind. She sat with them and Kay Walsh and they talked with their feet up on kitchen chairs until four in the morning. The others were exhausted, and had barely gotten a word in edgewise, but Marlene was still sparking on all cylinders. She left them cheerfully, with only two hours to go before a dawn call on *Stage Fright.* They collapsed.

In Hollywood that year, Marlene made another new friend, Hildegard Knef (later Neff). Max Colpet (as he now spelled his name) was living over Billy Wilder's garage, and Marlene was staying in the house. She used to rise at dawn after a sleepless night and scrub and clean the entire house from attic to cellar, consume two packs of cigarettes, and cook the breakfasts.

She asked Colpet to take her to Don the Beachcomber's in Hollywood to meet Knef, who had come from Germany to make *The Snows of Kilimanjaro* for Zanuck. "What's your birth date?" she asked Knef. "December 28," Knef replied. "Wonderful! You're a Capricorn!" Marlene exclaimed.

In Knef's memoirs, she describes how Marlene would deliver hampers of mushrooms, vitamin tablets, and recipes for goulash to the Hollywood Roosevelt Hotel, where Knef was staying. They went together to Grauman's Chinese Theater to see a movie. Heavily disguised and sitting in the balcony, they were surrounded by drunken sailors, who snored away oblivious of their presence.

Marlene remained close to Knef, assisting her considerably when Knef appeared in a Broadway musical, *Silk Stockings,* with Don Ameche. She worked closely with the director, the costume designer, and Cole Porter to help Knef polish her performance.

In the early 1950s, Marlene was devoted to establishing her daughter's career in those vintage years of live television. She frequently took care of her two grandchildren (there would eventually be four), while Maria was on the air. People who worked for the networks at the time recall how Marlene used to work constantly to perfect Maria's voice, movements, makeup, and hair; she came to rehearsals only when Maria specifically asked her to. *Ladies' Home Journal* reported Maria's saying: "My mother camphors my closets, and launders my babies' hand-knit wool soakers, so that they stay soft and fluffy; and she cooks for Bill and me. She and Bill are very fond of each other. Bill abominates kidneys and we never have them. But Mother cooked them one night and Bill raved about them."

Sometimes, on her way to a party, Marlene would stop by a rehearsal of one of Maria's shows wearing a mink stole and black chiffon, squat on the floor, and talk eagerly about Maria's makeup for half an hour.

Dolly Haas, the German actress, has lived near Maria for many years. "We're endlessly fascinated by events down the street," Dolly Haas says, "Marlene used to take the grandchildren for walks, disguised as a nursemaid in uniform. At one time, some Irish children attacked her grandson John Paul and she raced after them and pinned their heads to the ground until they asked for mercy. She was fiercely protective."

Max Colpet recalled in an interview in *Look* magazine that, one day, a woman stopped by to admire the baby. She cooed, chucked it under the chin, then looked up—and saw who the nursemaid was. The woman was Garbo.

Early in 1951, Marlene was in England to make *No Highway* (called *No Highway in the Sky* in the United States), in which once again she played a rather awkward version of herself, a benign version of Charlotte Inwood in *Stage Fright*. She was the musical comedy star Monica Teasdale, who is on a plane which is suffering from metal fatigue and may very possibly crash. She proves supportive of a scientist, played by Jimmy Stewart, when he deliberately wrecks a dangerous plane in a test flight to prevent any passengers from being killed in it later.

She evidently made the picture only for money, because she despised the script. She did not even seem to like the charming German director, Henry Koster, treating him coolly and failing to remember that he had met her at UFA when night after night she sat on the floor in a screening room leaning on von Sternberg's knee and watching the rushes of *The Blue Angel.*

Henry Koster says: "She calculates. She is very much aware of her beauty, her walk, the way she looks at you, the *effect* she creates. She was eager to do the right thing, and she played the part, which was not the greatest—the greatest part was Jimmy Stewart's—as well as she could. Her career was not so hot then, and I think she was glad to have the chance to make some money. She was depressed about the part. First of all, she's more personality than actress, and she had no great opportunity to develop her personality in the picture. She didn't feel she had enough exciting or impressive scenes. Also, she was up against a superb star, Glynis Johns, who had a bigger part than hers and presented her with a major problem in terms of competition.

"I found that she had genuine warmth, and at the same time she was a little bit aware of the impression that warmth would make on others. But then, so is every star, with rare exceptions —Jimmy Stewart is one exception."

Janette Scott, who played in the picture at the age of eleven, remembers: "There was a good deal of friction on the set. I remember vividly one scene where Marlene, Elizabeth Allen, and Glynis Johns all wanted to face the camera in a three-way dialogue. Had they done so, they would have faced outwards to the audience side by side! Finally, Marlene very sweetly gave in and showed her profile, which she hated. I showed my profile too, and Glynis Johns and Elizabeth Allen got their wish.

"Although I was so young, I can still remember thinking, 'I wonder why it's so important to these actresses?' Marlene was unbelievably kind to me. She went out of her way to spend time with me. I had starred with, and been around, quite a lot of big stars. Very few of them had bothered with me, because I was a child. They sometimes resented that I got equal billing. It was through Marlene that quite consciously, at the age of eleven, I was able to grasp what lens was being used, what lighting was going on, all the technicalities of picture making.

"Before that, I used to hide in the prop room and giggle and the assistant director could never find me. Marlene taught me to be serious about my craft. She took me to the cutting room and taught me about editing. I remember one of those days particularly. I was playing a scene with Marlene, and she was standing right by the camera. There was a reverse close-up on me. She whispered, 'When you speak to me, you really should hold your chin up a little bit. You have very good cheekbones, and if you just raise your chin a little bit, that light over there will hit those cheekbones and make a great deal of difference to how you look.'

"Nobody ever bothered with that kind of help before. I used to go back to my dressing room and look in the mirror after a scene, and for the first time figure out how to present myself better on film. She used to take me around the back of the camera and make me look through the viewfinder. She used to look straight in my eyes, and seem to know that all this advice would be very important to me. She made a bigger mark on my life than any human being I ever worked with in any capacity."

Janette Scott continues: "Marlene used to arrive at the studio before anybody else. Nobody ever saw her without her makeup or without her wig—ever, ever, ever. Sometimes Michael Wilding would drive her in, but they were both terribly discreet. Of course, to an eleven-year-old the idea of their romance was thrilling.

"Her star touch was impeccable. Everyone else had ordinary canvas chairs. Hers was in black velvet, with her name embroidered on it in exact replica of her handwriting. Everyone wanted to salaam."

No Highway in the Sky—released in 1951—though entertaining and suspenseful, did nothing for Marlene's career. Nor did her next film, *Rancho Notorious,* a Western in which she played an older version of Frenchy in *Destry Rides Again,* who also dies protecting her man. In this instance, the *man* was called Frenchy.

The director was the late Fritz Lang. It was almost twenty years since their romance in 1934. Years ago Lang told me, "We had a strange working relationship. She invited me to her hotel one night, and when we got into her suite, she handed me a bundle of letters.

"I took them gingerly. 'What are these?' I asked her. She said, 'They are Jean Gabin's love letters. They might give you some ideas.' I looked at her in astonishment. I said, 'The day I need any ideas from Jean Gabin, I'll give up and go home.' I left immediately. She looked disappointed."

Lang went on: "One night, Marlene called me. She said, 'Please take me out to dinner.' I replied, 'But Marlene. You mean to say you're not booked up with dates for the next month?' She said, 'Are you kidding? Men never ask me out. I always have to ask them.' I went on, 'OK. Where would you like to go?' She named a French restaurant. We arrived, and the actor-director Gregory Ratoff was there with Chaliapin's daughter. Gregory asked us to join him. Marlene seemed fairly animated, but when the dessert came, I noticed she was crying. I said, 'What's the matter, darling? Are you ill? Why are you crying?' She looked meaningfully across at Chaliapin's daughter and said, 'She's so young. She's so very, very young.'

"One night I was driving back home past the RKO Studios, where we were making *Rancho Notorious,* and I saw a flashing in my office window. I thought it must be a burglar with a flashlight. I crept up the back stairs. At last I got to the top. I stole up to my door. I pushed the door open with my foot, silently. I peered through the crack.

"I was astonished at what I saw. Marlene was standing there, taking photographs of herself in a mirror with a flashbulb. She was obviously testing herself for the next day's work. I never saw such a perfectionist!"

The film's cameraman was the veteran Hal Mohr. When she saw the rushes, Marlene said, "Hal, why can't you make me as beautiful as you made me in *Destry Rides Again?*"

He replied, "But Marlene, don't you realize? I was eleven years younger then."

Always fascinated by radio as a medium, Marlene began appearing on Sunday nights on ABC network radio in *Cafe Istanbul,* loosely based on *Casablanca,* in which she played a female version of Humphrey Bogart's Rick, the owner of the raffish cafe who tended to sing numbers in between entertaining customers. She frequently spent hours with a portable typewriter rewriting the scripts. But she could not save the show. Later, she reworked the formula as *Time for Love,* but this also was a flop.

In 1953 Rudi, who had been depressed and out of work in New York, came down with a severe attack of gastric ulcers, and almost died on the operating table. Two thirds of his stomach had to be cut out during the operation, making it impossible for him to continue with an active career. His friend Hans Kohn bought him a chicken ranch in Sylmar in the San Fernando Valley.

The pink stucco ranch was pleasant but messy. There were always ten or twenty cats, dogs, goats, and the chickens; and they all ran wild, the chickens roosting haphazardly. The tables were crowded with Tamara's mementoes, mostly small china or glass figures; and every inch of the rooms was cluttered with furniture. There were crosses, icons brought from the old apartment at 54 Kaiserallee, a fantastic conglomeration of objects. The clutter exasperated Marlene.

Rudi had several friends: Hans and Varya Kohn, Peter Gorian, the Schoop sisters—all people he had known in Europe. He had a devoted housekeeper, Eva Wiere, who after Tamara's death took extraordinary care of him. He lived peacefully on the ranch, Marlene dropping by occasionally to scrub the floors and help clean out the chicken coops, dressed in workman's overalls.

Tamara, Rudi's girl friend, lived with him there, wearing Marlene's cast-off clothing, her mind gradually deteriorating over the next ten years. She became more and more eccentric, her giddy gaiety and fits of sudden depression weighing Rudi down. He would frequently call friends and say, "Tamara is impossible today." With his poor state of health, and Tamara's horrifying decline into madness, life at the ranch was by no means as idyllic as it may have seemed.

In 1958, Joe Hyams of the *New York Herald Tribune* boldly arrived at the ranch to interview Sieber. It was the first interview Rudi had given in over twenty years. Rudi had promised Marlene he would never discuss their marriage with a reporter, but he did not have the courage to send Hyams away. When Hyams asked him if there was any special reward in being married to a movie star, he replied with a surprising touch of bitterness, "People say when they meet me, *'This* is Marlene Dietrich's husband.' Do you call this a reward?"

Sieber admitted that being a rancher was a change from studying Latin and Greek, serving in the Austrian infantry, and working in the German film studios. But it was clear that he took pride in his life of retirement, that he loved nature and the peace of the countryside. In the early 1960s Tamara's health declined so steeply she had to be committed to the state institution for the insane at Camarillo, near Los Angeles. Rudi had an almost fatal heart attack, followed by a stroke. Through these difficult years, Marlene remained loyal, flying to him constantly when he needed her and assisting him with Tamara; and when crises such as the Sylmar earthquake took place, in 1971, she was most helpful.

In May 1953, Marlene, in a ringmaster's uniform and short black pants, cracked the whip for the lions at a benefit performance opening night of the Ringling Bros. Barnum and Bailey Circus in Madison Square Garden. The lions seemed notably cowed by her presence, and she was obviously pleased by her control over the beasts.

In December, Marlene opened at the Sahara Hotel in Las Vegas for a three-week season at $30,000 a week, a record at the time. She wore a black net and sequin gown with a floor-length black net redingote trimmed with an edging of twelve feet of black fox fur. Thirty years after *Tragedy of Love,* she was still loyal to her favorite fox furs. Jean Louis designed two identical gowns, one gold and one white. Mercedes McCambridge, Billy Wilder, and Mercedes's husband Fletcher Markle were at ringside for the performance. At the end of the show, she changed into a ringmaster's outfit, with a red tailcoat and a black top hat, and wore black tights on her famous legs.

Her friend, Mercedes McCambridge, remembers: "Marlene fascinated me. She had my baby's astrological chart done by Carroll Righter—my second child. The baby died. I called her in New York to tell her.

"She said nothing and hung up. I was horrified. I thought it was callous of her. But next day, she was in Los Angeles. She had flown specially from New York. She took care of everything— the undertakers, the funeral, the flowers. I didn't lift a finger. She 'snowed' me.

"She snowed everyone. But she was the loneliest, the saddest of all. I remember as though it were yesterday—she called me up and said, 'Hello, daughter. I'm in Vegas. What are you doing?'

"I told her 'I'm sitting at home, eating a steak and watching television and I'm all alone. I don't like it. What are you doing, Mama?'

" 'You'll never guess.'

" 'What?'

" 'You won't believe this. But I'm sitting at home, eating a steak, and watching television. And I'm all alone.'

"Even when Marlene was kindest, she was least appreciated. When she visited with Rudi and Tamara, she used to come back, lean over a chair, and weep—terrible, heartbreaking tears. Tamara's increasing madness distressed her unbearably. No one knows that she supported Rudi and Tamara all those years. She sweetly gave Tamara all her old dresses. That used to drive Tamara into such a state of collapse she had to have shock treatments. There's no doubt that wearing Marlene's clothes and yet not being married to Rudi finally drove Tamara into the asylum where she died."

Ten

One-Woman Show

Almost overnight, Marlene achieved her wish: to become her own work of art. Exasperated with the ineptitude of the movies she had made in recent years (Monica Teasdale, the character Marlene played in *No Highway*, refers to them as "a few cans of celluloid on the junk heap someday") Marlene had for many years longed to return to her best métier, reestablished in the war tour with Danny Thomas: her métier as a diseuse. In this, Nat "King" Cole was greatly encouraging. Here was her true vocation: to create an image of the feminine in the abstract, yet at the same time to suggest a certain sexual ambiguity. She could herself control the lighting, the makeup, the whole atmosphere of stardom: she need not depend on others. And at last she could simply sing: she could pour out her feelings in the songs which expressed herself best. Her most characteristic moods, a somber seriousness and an antic gaiety, could be contrasted in numbers ranging all the way from a lament for lost love to "You're the Cream in My Coffee."

And she could even try to set her biographers to rights by providing a new version of her past, a Cinderella story in which the great director Joseph von Sternberg became the Fairy Godmother, sweeping her miraculously from the grim sanctuary of the Max Reinhardt drama school to the heights of *The Blue Angel* overnight. Gone were the years of struggle, of playing flappers and jazz babies in happily forgotten movies, as well as the triumphs in *It's in the Air, Spring's Awakening, Misalliance,* and *Two Bow Ties.* Gone, too, were her doubts about playing Lola-Lola because of what her family would say, and her own dislike of the part. And she made no mention of the tragicomedy of her relationship with von Sternberg, his simultaneous ill treatment and glorification of her, the peculiar tensions of their relationship.

She knew what audiences wanted to hear: a legend talking about a legend, with a legend's version of the facts. The truth would have been less comfortable and less alluring. She provided a mirage of pure beauty, not only in her figure, miraculously preserved in her fifties, the breasts high and firm, the nipples sharply outlined, the body supple and athletic, the back exquisitely curved towards the still unflawed line of the buttocks, the legs as boldly provocative as ever—not only in these physical things, but in the beauty of her musicianship, the poise and attack of her stage presence, the love that she poured out to her public.

In an increasingly vulgar era, she was the epitome of taste. She was elegance addressing itself insolently towards brutality. She was the image of pre-Hitler Berlin, with an American touch: the epitome of efficiency and self-mocking wit, tinged with cool affection. She was at once forgiving, accusing, adoring —a reminder of what had been lost and a promise of what could be attained.

William Blezard, Marlene's conductor in later years, supplies a definition of her range: "She has one and a half octaves. Her bottom note is the same as the bottom note of a viola. She has a viola register. Her phrasing is immensely subtle: she developed and popularized *Sprechstimme,* the art of speaking as though singing. She is clever at avoiding the long-held note. She doesn't need to have sustained notes, as she invests the words with special qualities and meanings. Her freedom of speech in her singing makes her phrasing inventive. She used individual variations and embellishments and, quite often, original or reworked lyrical texts. She rises freely over the accompaniment;

she releases herself in a song like a dramatic artist. She uses humor, drama, articulation.

"The words are everything for her. They are paramount. She reads and digests them thoroughly before she prepares a song. No matter how good the music is, lyrics must be written to her precise specifications, or, if they already exist, be exactly what she wants before she will proceed. She has always concentrated on the 'lie' of a song in the voice, the retaining of a particular register which does not waver. She does not have any actual key. Her voice has not changed within recent years, but it is, of course, deeper since film days. The keys of her arrangements have not been changed for the past twelve years.

"In ideal conditions, her lighting technique was based on that laid down by von Sternberg: a traveling spotlight which moved with her face at approximately forty-five degrees from above the line of her hair, augmented by special lights on the stage."

The essence of her art was simplicity. In literature, she loved the simple, the stripped down, the disciplined. The grammar of her performances was similarly uncluttered, her syntax as straight as her seams. One line ran through everything: the line of emotional truth. Whatever schmaltz she might insert into her material, she allowed none in her lyrics.

During the 1950s, Marlene developed a standard performance. In the first half she appeared in the softest and most feminine clothes, announcing that this was the part of her performance she did for men. In the second half, accompanied by a major drumroll, which kept the audience in suspense like the circus drumroll which precedes a highwire feat or a double somersault in midair, she suddenly appeared in a tuxedo, bow tie, and tall top hat, saying that this was "for the girls." She kicked her legs high with a chorus line of girls dressed in white jackets, caps, and tights. She would spread her legs on a chair and sing, daringly, "I've Grown Accustomed to Her Face," or, still more outrageously, "My Blue Heaven." Most female singers would change the lyrics of this song from "Just Molly and me / And baby makes three" to "Johnny and me" or some similar name. She rejected this compromise.

At the beginning of 1954, the Café de Paris in London, which had been bombed during the war, had reopened, and the owner, Major Donald Neville-Willing, a small, tremendously energetic man, set about preparing a startling announcement. He had decided to have Garbo appear at the club. He went to see her in New York and said, "Miss Garbo, I have something to suggest. I will pay you a thousand pounds a week to stand in my nightclub for forty-five minutes and do anything you want.

"You can recite, tell stories, sing, dance, do anything or nothing. They'll be round the block twice."

Garbo hummed doubtfully to herself. She said, "You mean, you will pay me a thousand pounds a week to do nothing?" "Yes," the major answered. "You can just stay there and look at the audience. It will be enough."

She asked, "How close will the first row of tables be?"

"Very near. We will need every inch of space to justify your fee."

Garbo grew a little cold. "Will those in front be able to see up my nostrils?"

"Yes."

"Then I won't do it!" Garbo exclaimed. The meeting was over.

Dashed that Garbo was not available, Neville-Willing called Marlene (who was now fifty-three) in New York and reminded her that he had met her with Jo Carstairs at the Ruban Bleu in the thirties. He said, "I'd love to come and see you." She replied, "Come over to Park Avenue and have a cuppa!" He went to the apartment and was served tea from the largest cup he had ever seen. The living room was completely mirrored—no wallpaper. He noticed symmetrical marks in the carpet. He knew that these were the marks of rehearsal, that over and over again she checked every move she made in the mirrors until her high heels virtually made holes in the floor.

She evidently liked Neville-Willing—his typical Englishness, his energy—and she accepted his proposal. When she arrived in London, Noel Coward met her, and prepared a verse to read for her opening.

For six hours in her suite at the Dorchester, she sang "One for my baby / And one more for the road" over and over again the first day in, while Neville-Willing twisted miserably in his chair, wishing he could go to the toilet or take a walk in the fresh air. In desperation, he ordered a plate of smoked salmon, and she ate most of it, practically in one gulp.

She worked out the whole organization of the act with her friend, the musical arranger, composer, and conductor Burt Bacharach. Neville-Willing fixed up a cableless microphone for her, which led to complications. She would be in the middle of a song and the microphone would suddenly pick up police frequencies, so that the audience could hear, across the strains of "Falling in Love Again," the message "Calling all cars! Calling all cars!"

Marlene followed a bizarre diet, eating a box of Floris liqueur chocolates in one go, starving through the day, sipping a glass of champagne in the afternoon, then eating a huge meal at midnight.

The show was an immediate hit. Coward introduced her, and the crowd gave her a standing ovation as she stepped down the stairs on midsummer's night of 1954. Kenneth Tynan, then the most famous critic in England, raved about her performance, and when he came backstage, her hand shot out of a crack in the dressing room door and dragged him inside. Later, he took her down the Thames for dinner. She was dismayed to learn he was married, to the actress and novelist Elaine Dundy, and had a daughter, Tracy. She upbraided Neville-Willing. She said, "You didn't tell me he was married! I never go out with men who are married!" But she became a lifelong friend of Tynan's, and was loving and generous to him and to his child.

She was more comfortable having lunch with another well-known critic, Milton Shulman, a Canadian who had just begun to achieve fame. She liked him because he had told her not to say "Achtung!" so often before her songs, and she dropped this device from her repertoire.

Neville-Willing says, "I found Marlene endlessly fascinating. She was never less than exquisitely dressed, she did everything immaculately. She pruned her own flowers in her suite at the Dorchester with scissors and gardening gloves, she measured them with her eye to the exact size of the vase, she kept them alive *forever* with correct handling.

"She used to go out very boldly to public places. One day, she said, 'Let's go to Selfridge's.' I said, 'You're mad. You'll never have a moment's peace.' I was right. She didn't. No sooner had we got into an elevator than a little woman said, 'Oh, Miss Dietrich, don't you remember me? I used to manicure your mother's nails!' Marlene fled."

Neville-Willing went with Marlene to the House of Commons to see her friend, the plump Member of Parliament Bessie Braddock, who was among the many celebrities introducing Marlene before her show. Two men came by. One of them said, "By Jove, do you know who that is?" The other man replied, "No. Who is it?" The first man continued, "It's Greta Garbo!"

One time, Marlene went to a function for blind children at the invitation of Mrs. Douglas Fairbanks. The gushing head nurse rushed up to her and said, "Miss Dietrich, the children are longing to see you!"

She went to see the children, and they knelt and hugged her and felt her face as she gave them chocolates. They told her they were going to the seaside and asked her if she would wave them off. She went to Victoria Station and kissed them as they climbed aboard the train, taking them by the hand one by one and singing to them softly.

She was very fond of one of the waiters at the Café de Paris, a Cypriot married to an English girl. She was horrified to read in the paper that the Cypriot's mother, Mrs. Cristofi, had murdered his wife, and had been arrested after burning the body. Marlene immediately told Neville-Willing to give the waiter all the money he needed to arrange for the children to be sent away to a country home.

About four months later, Neville-Willing told Marlene: "You remember that waiter you helped? He came to my office this morning." "What did he say?" Marlene asked him. "He said, 'They're hanging my mother in the morning. Could I have tomorrow off, please?' " Marlene sank into a chair.

Marlene received a letter from a man saying, "My friend and I booked tickets for your show tonight. But my friend is so ill from cancer he had to go to the hospital. We had to cancel. I know this is an impossible thing to ask, and you don't even know me. But could you possibly visit him?"

Marlene told Neville-Willing, "Don't say anything to the hospital. I'm going." Neville-Willing found the correct room number. They went up to the room, and Marlene said, "Wait outside!" Neville-Willing sat there listening to the faint sound of Marlene singing. She sang for half an hour to the dying man.

Sometimes, Marlene had to go to premières. She would push messages through a hole in her dressing room door to Neville-Willing when she didn't feel like talking, discussing the arrangements. Neville-Willing says, "Sometimes we'd go to the premiere and she'd appear to be talking to me, she'd open and shut her mouth but no words would come out—the public outside thought she was speaking. Actually, if I'd been able to lip-read, I'd probably have discovered she was saying, 'Why do we have to do this boring thing?' But to the crowd it must have looked like 'Oh, I'm so very pleased to be in London!' "

Neville-Willing continues, "A fantastic thing happened. Marlene had a dresser. She was *very* important. When she arrived at the Dorchester she was told there was a room where the ladies' maids ate their meals. She said, 'I'm not goin' to eat in no room where the ladies' maids are at. I'm goin' to eat in the goddam restaurant. And you see to it, Major Baby!'

"She used to sit in the restaurant in her glory, ordering the most expensive dishes on the menu, *pâté de fois gras*, smoked salmon, rich desserts. The handsome waiter who always served her was crazy about her. She was in the *clouds* over him.

"She used to take Marlene's precious dress home every night: Jean Louis did it and it cost *thousands*. One night very late I had a phone call. She was hysterical. She screamed, 'Dunno what I'm gonna do! I went home with that goddam waiter for the night and I took Mama's dress in a box. Well, I've gone and left the dress at his place, and I can't remember the *ad*-dress!

Where does that guy live? It's the only dress we have for the show. She'll kill me!'

"I told her, "How would I know where my waiters live?' 'It's in a place called Soho!' she said, very distressed. 'Well, I can't ring all the bells in Soho,' I told her. 'You'll have to wait till tomorrow.'"

There are several versions of what happened next. The most colorful has the dresser finally discovering the waiter's address from an employment agency. She rushed to his lodgings, located the box, threw it into a cab and got to the Café de Paris exactly five minutes before Marlene arrived to change for the evening's performance.

After the run at the Café de Paris, Marlene left with Neville-Willing for appearances in Paris and Amsterdam. Just before the performance in Amsterdam, Marlene said to Neville-Willing, "I want to go to the house of Anne Frank." Neville-Willing said, "A local museum has the key." Marlene—who else could do this?—got hold of the key, took all the flowers out of her dressing room, and went with him to the house. An official came up and said coldly, "What's she doing, going in there?" "She's Marlene Dietrich, and she's going in to pray," Neville-Willing replied. That silenced the man.

Marlene stayed in the house for half an hour, and came out, her eyes red with weeping. She never mentioned the episode again.

That same evening, two hours before the performance, the manager of the theater ran up to Neville-Willing and said, "The unions will be furious! There's an unauthorized person hammering the stage boards!" Neville-Willing ran up to the stage. He saw a woman, in a man's overall and cap, busily hammering every loose nail or other protuberance until not the smallest irregularity could be seen. It scarcely seems necessary to mention who the woman was.

Presenting her in a series of very successful performances at the Queen's Theatre years later, Major Neville-Willing introduced the idea of flowers in Marlene's finale, flowers brought up in massive bouquets to the stage by her admirers. The major dragged the flowers out of the dressing room and around the back of the auditorium, placing them in the cocktail bar when nobody was looking. In the interval, he went to all the young people he could see in the back rows and asked them to run up to the stage with the bouquets, as soon as he tapped them on the shoulder. One night, the necessary number of bouquets failed to arrive, so he took the only one available and arranged for it to be taken by a stagehand back into the theater after Marlene had accepted it, and then taken back again. It kept going around and around until the audience had the impression that fifteen bouquets had been sent.

From this device, everyone thought the audience was spontaneously heaping Marlene with flowers. Neville-Willing used to lie on the floor at the back of the orchestra, out of sight, and shout for particular songs which had already been included in the evening's repetoire. People looked around to see who had called out and then, sheeplike, would repeat the cry. "I told her to say," Neville-Willing recalls, " 'Now I'm going to sing the song that made me famous.' Everyone thought it was going to be 'Falling in Love Again.' Then I'd scream, 'Sing *"Lola!"* ' " And she'd say coyly, 'Oh, you remember! You all remember!' Of course, nobody did.

"She mentioned Richard Tauber and nobody knew who he was any more. So I used to yell and shout and clap at the mention of the name, and of course everyone followed suit. One night I was coming out of the toilet when a man rushed in and hit me so hard with the door he knocked me down. I lay in agony and forgot to call 'Lola,' clap at Tauber's name, and scream, 'Encore!' She was furious. I went around afterwards to apologize, and she said, ignoring my explanation, 'Oh, it doesn't matter. I'll get someone else to do it next time. I don't need you.'

"That was one side of Marlene. Here is the other side. Many people in London made fun of me because they said I really wasn't a Major. One day, Marlene gave me a small jewel case. I opened it, and it contained a gold bracelet. On one side of it was an inscription in an exact replica of her own handwriting

which read, 'Love, Marlene.' I turned the bracelet over to examine the inscription inside. It showed, very clearly, my own
army number. She had called the War Office, obtained my
particulars, and had the inscription made so that everyone
would know I wasn't lying. There's no one alive like this."

The two most dominating male presences in Marlene's life in
the 1950s were her arranger-conductor, Burt Bacharach, and
the theatrical genius Mike Todd. Marlene used to introduce
Bacharach as her *amitié amoureuse* and mentor at concert performances, giving rise to gossip all over the world.

Major Donald Neville-Willing, also very close to Bacharach,
says, "Marlene used to say in all her performances, terrifyingly,
'And now I want to give you the one person who is everything
to me, he does my music, he plays for me, I love him, he's my
friend, he's Burt Bacharach!' Burt used to stand there in front
of the orchestra, *squirming.* He used to say to me, over and over
again, 'How can I stop it?' And I told him, 'You can't. That's her
big moment.' And of course it was his, too. It made him famous.
But he hated it, every moment of it.

"She depended on him utterly. The entire show hung on a
hair of his head. Every note in the music. She would never have
dared say to him, 'That's the wrong note!' He could have given
her a look that would have destroyed her.

She was devastated when he composed hit songs and became
so big he could no longer perform for her. She was so upset she
wouldn't answer the phone from him when he called. He used
to ask me, 'What have I done?' And I told him, 'She feels you
deserted her.'

"After they had broken up, he met Angie Dickinson at
Trader Vic's in London. He and Angie clicked in two minutes.
Marlene said to me, when I asked her what she thought about
the romance, 'Ridiculous. *Angie Dickinson!* Nobody can smile
that much and for such long periods! It's not real!' When she
finally saw Burt again she said, 'Why not marry Julie Andrews?
It might be better!' "

Marlene spent a lot of time with Mike Todd in the 1950s, and
became fascinated by him. Forceful, with blue eyes and black

hair, he had a middleweight's physique. He smoked sixty-five-cent cigars at the rate of a dozen a day, and made an average of four hundred telephone calls in a twenty-four hour period. The actress Joan Blondell had divorced him in 1950. In 1952 and 1953, he had presented *A Night in Venice* at the Jones Beach Marine Stadium—a bizarre compendium of Johann Strauss music with a cast of three hundred, including Metropolitan Opera singers. The show was staged on a stage with a 104-foot proscenium and a revolving center. It cost $380,000 and was described by one critic as a cross between "Strauss and a hot dog."

Marlene told Mike Todd's biographer Art Cohn, "Wouldn't it be wonderful if everyone spent money like Mike? If people were so secure they wouldn't have to hoard money. And think of the money in circulation."

Marlene also told Cohn: "Mike said we had to stop going together. 'Why?' I asked. 'Did I say or do something wrong?' 'I'm afraid I'll fall in love with you,' he said.

" 'No man falls in love with me I don't want to have fall in love with me,' I told him."

Marlene appeared for Todd in his elaborate and fanciful movie version of Jules Verne's *Around the World in Eighty Days,* as a San Francisco dance hall queen who greets the traveler Phileas Fogg and his valet Passepartout on their journey. Frank Sinatra was the barroom pianist. She liked Sinatra immensely, calling him "The gentlest man I know;" and she was happy to renew an earlier friendship with David Niven, who played Phileas. When Niven had been a starving actor in Hollywood in the early 1930s, she had characteristically helped him with gifts of food.

On March 21, 1958, Mike Todd and Art Cohn left for New York to attend a Friar's Club tribute in Todd's honor at the Waldorf-Astoria. They took Todd's private plane, the *Lucky Liz,* named for his new wife, Elizabeth Taylor. The plane flew off in drenching rain from Burbank airport, Los Angeles, at 10:41 P.M., and a few hours later crashed and burst into flames in a valley in New Mexico. Marlene was shattered by the news.

On January 22, 1954, Marlene thought she had lost two more of her friends. She had been in touch with the Hemingways on and off since the immediate postwar period, when they had enjoyed drinks together at the Little Bar of the Ritz in Paris. She frequently called them on the telephone when she was in New York and they were in Cuba, and she always enjoyed their occasional meetings in various cities. She was horrified to learn that after leaving West Nairobi on a Cessna Aircraft they had crashed, colliding with live telegraph wires. They were lost for several days while they wandered about looking for firewood and signaling approaching planes. Finally they were picked up by a bush pilot and flown to Entebbe. Just as they were about to leave Entebbe, the plane burst into flames. Ernest and Mary managed to smash their way out, and in great pain, his head broken and her kneecap smashed, they made their way by Land Rover to Masindi.

Marlene followed the details on the shortwave radio, immensely relieved to learn that her friends were still alive. With her usual determination, she was able to reach them on what did service for a local telephone line, and sent them encouraging messages until they were fully recovered. No doubt, given the slightest encouragement she would at once have flown to Africa with healing nostrums for them. Their experience did nothing to lessen the tremendous number of hours she spent in airplane flights each year, through every kind of weather, which she bore with fortitude—even indifference. Hemingway's death years later was a great blow to her.

Marlene and Noel Coward had a love-hate relationship during those years. He found her sometimes tiresome, especially when she grumbled about everything and everybody around her. She could also be scintillating and witty. Their careers had both been at a low point before the war, and this gave them something in common: they were survivors who fought back. They had both rediscovered themselves through performing for the troops. It was of course normal (as Coward's lifelong friend and biographer Cole Lesley observes) for Marlene, as a beautiful woman, to succeed with this. A middle-aged man scarcely had an appeal of the same kind. But they were equally triumphant when their experiences at the front led them into the cabaret world.

"Marlene was an enormous help to Noel," Lesley says. "He had, of course, introduced her at her first night at the Café de Paris. In response, Marlene compelled Noel to go to the Desert Inn in Las Vegas. She said it was the only place for him to begin this new phase of his career. Noel had been offered almost any spot in the United States in which to play, and he discussed his decision with Marlene at great length. She found he had a major problem: he could not take his pianist with him because of union rules. He interviewed many people without success. Finally, Marlene called him from an airport in New York, reaching him at his hotel in that city, saying she was on her way to Europe. Dietrich said, 'You *must* get together immediately with the most amazing young man, Peter Matz. He's an outstanding arranger and a marvelous pianist.' Coward listened to her carefully and then said, 'Marlene dear, I've seen *everybody*. It's hopeless.' But he *did* see Peter Matz and the working relationship between them was most successful. Dietrich had helped a very great artist, and Noel was eternally grateful to her."

A sad event of the early 1950s was the end of a friendship: with the actor and painter, Martin Kosleck. Kosleck says: "I had known Marlene constantly from that first day when I came to Hollywood and she picked me up in the Rolls-Royce and took me to the screening of the day's rushes of *Shanghai Express*.

"Most of the time, my friend Hans von Twardowski and I were very close to her. She always took a warm interest in my painting.

"In the 1930s, I created a portrait of her which, I believe, is my finest work. She adored it. She sank to her knees before it, as it hung over my fireplace, and said, 'You have made me immortal.' I gave it to her.

"For many years, the picture hung in her Park Avenue apartment. In the meantime, she had shown great generosity to me over a painting I had done of Nijinsky. I had had an exhibition in New York in 1939, and she had just returned to the United States to make *Destry Rides Again*.

"I was very distressed because the one painting I didn't want to let go, the Nijinsky portrait, had been sold. I told her about this. She invited me to her suite at the Waldorf Towers and told me to go in the living room. I walked in there, and had the shock of my life. The Nijinsky was looking at me. She had managed to find the buyer, and had bought it back for me.

"Years went by. In 1952, I appeared in that wretched radio show, 'Café Istanbul,' with her. She was icy and removed, and I was shocked. I knew she had quarreled with Hans but I didn't think this would necessarily affect me.

"After the show was done, I trailed along after her and the producer, even though I had not been asked. She ignored me completely. Finally, we reached her apartment. She pointed to a blank space on the wall and said to the producer, 'That's where his painting of me used to be. You know why it isn't there? Because he stole it back!' I was paralyzed. I didn't know what to say. Her voice was shrill, accusing. I had never seen her like this before.

"I ran out. I immediately called Marlene's former secretary, Violla Rubber, who told me, 'But Marlene forgot. Erich Maria Remarque hated that painting and insisted it be stored in the basement of the Beverly Hills Hotel. Marlene forgot to pick it up! She never had it in Park Avenue!' I was much too devastated to say anything more to Marlene about this. I still have nightmares about it. I toss and turn. After all, Hans and I were closer to her than anyone. I remember when she left Hollywood in 1938, her career washed up. Hans, I, and her cook Rezi were the only ones at the train station to see her off."

Another friendship ended that year, in death. Gertrude Lawrence, the sparkling musical comedienne, had recently had a triumph in *The King and I*. Her costar Yul Brynner had dated Marlene frequently, giving rise to much discussion of a romance. Marlene heaped him with gifts. According to Mercedes McCambridge, she obtained the part of the king for him by shaving his head and taking him to the producer for a reading.

Marlene greatly admired Gertrude Lawrence, and was concerned about Lawrence's heavy drinking and neurotic breakdowns. She was horrified when Gertrude Lawrence's gradual psychosomatic disintegration, hidden behind the smiling facade of her performances, was followed by cancer. Marlene did everything she could to help the stricken star with various forms of medication, but it was useless. An extraordinary photograph of Marlene and her daughter at Gertrude Lawrence's funeral indicates the extent of her grief.

In 1957, Marlene finally achieved an ambition to appear as Christine Vole, the villainess of Agatha Christie's *Witness for the Prosecution.* According to the director, her old friend Billy Wilder, he undertook the job of handling the picture in order to make it easier for her to get the part. Marlene told me something different: "I was not sure I could do this role. But Billy told me I could. Noel Coward and Charles Laughton helped me."

Christine Vole was the wife of Leonard Vole (Tyrone Power) who has been charged with the murder of a rich widow. In attempting to save her husband from the gallows, Christine pretends to be his vindictive enemy, testifying against him in the witness box. She also disguises herself as a cockney in one scene, supplying letters to the defending counsel which in effect invalidate Christine's testimony. When she discovers that her husband is guilty, she stabs him to death.

Marlene had the major problem of disguising herself effectively as the cockney. She dressed up in an ugly brown wig, a cheap plastic mackintosh, and a checked dress; and used all her masterful knowledge of makeup in simulating the crude face of the blackmailer. Elsa Lanchester (Mrs. Charles Laughton) remembers: "Marlene was forever up at our house, trying on scarves, shawls, and various wigs, and taking lessons in cockney from Charles. She was obsessed with this impersonation. I never saw anyone work so hard."

Marlene told Cecil Smith of the *Los Angeles Times:* "I remembered the nasal working-girl tones from my youth in Berlin. So often I've imitated them to make the kids laugh, to make my daughter Maria laugh when she was a kid. The servant-girl tone, it is the same in all cities—in cockney or in Brooklynese or in Berlin. So I did it."

Marlene's performance was among her best, though the cockney impersonation stretched her resources to the limit. Her use of *w* for *r* in one word gave her away, unfortunately. She was at her best in the courtroom scene when she screamed, "Damn you! Damn you!" after Laughton's Sir Wilfrid Robarts exposed her.

She said in more than one interview that the part had attracted her because Christine Vole was a woman who risked her life for a man and who was completely committed to love. Here was the romantic talking, the woman who had flung herself before Remarque and Gabin, Michael Wilding and Mike Todd, with no restraint, with open generosity and an open heart. Her performance earned her excellent reviews.

For her friend Orson Welles, Marlene played a bizarre revamping of her gypsy in *Golden Earrings* in *Touch of Evil* (1958), one of his most powerful creations and the best movie she had appeared in since *The Blue Angel*. Wearing what appeared to be her original gypsy wig, discovered by her at Paramount, she was the long-time mistress of Hank Quinlan (Welles), a grossly overweight sheriff of a border town in Texas. She played the part with an extraordinary combination of sardonic wit and sympathetic warmth that was particularly her own and for which critics praised her. Looking at her monstrous companion, she says, as only she could, "Lay off the candy bars." And at the end, when Quinlan lies dead, she laconically sums up her own philosophy of life in the phrase, "What does it matter what you say about people?"

In the late 1950s, Marlene had the pleasant experience of seeing four handsome grandsons growing up. They were all striking in appearance, with fine features. She was very proud of them. One time, when they were stranded in a storm in a hut on Long Island, she sang to them and told them stories for hours. She was saddened when Maria decided to abandon her career and devote herself to being a mother, but she accepted the decision.

Also, she was pleased to see that Maria had undergone a physical change after the birth of her first child and became as slim as Marlene. With children of her own, Maria became a far happier and more balanced human being, losing many of the tensions she experienced when younger.

In 1957, Marlene went to the south of France to make a tedious film entitled *The Monte Carlo Story* for the playwright-director Samuel Taylor. The actor Helmut Berger remembered recently, "Marlene again met, while working on the picture, an old friend, Luchino Visconti. She fell madly in love with him. She longed to marry him. She sent him love letters, which he showed me, and roses every day. Nothing eventuated.

"Years later, Marlene saw Luchino's film *The Damned*, in which I played the son of a rich industrial family, like the Krupps, who imitates her. She loved the imitation. I 'did' her in *The Blue Angel*. She sent me a framed photograph of herself as Lola-Lola, and of me in drag, with the note, 'Which of us is the prettier?' "

Marlene frequently returned to Las Vegas to perform in the later 1950s. Except for the dry air, which affected her throat, she liked the city: the freedom, the gambling, the atmosphere of nightlife with all its sharp glitter. Her dresses grew more and more elaborate and more and more transparent with the years. She managed to make her quick change from feathers and spangles into white tie and tails in less than sixty seconds, delighting Joe Hyams by letting him witness the change.

At the outset of the sixties, Marlene set out on a series of international tours which were to make her even more famous in far-flung areas. In 1959, she had been exceptionally busy: she had appeared in a nine-week festival at the Museum of Modern Art, devoted to her work, saying as she introduced it, "I was not so much the Trilby to von Sternberg's Svengali as Eliza Doolittle to his Professor Higgins." She began as a Miss Lonelyhearts radio commentator on NBC's weekly "Monitor" program, "Dietrich Talks on Love and Life."

She flew to Rio de Janeiro via Varig Airlines, which immediately became her favorite because it supplied her with a bed she could lie down in (what the other passengers thought if they saw the world's leading sex star preparing to get between the sheets can only be conjectured). Her record, *Dietrich in Rio,* one of the early LPs, gives a vivid impression of the ecstasy of her enormous audience.

When Marlene arrived in Rio, the largest crowd she had ever seen greeted her: about twenty-five thousand people, sweeping all over the airfield, across the tarmac, and even into the path of the plane itself. It was surely one of the greatest moments of her life.

Her fan John Marven saw Marlene in the Rio show. He says, "It was unbelievable. I never saw anything like it. The audience went completely mad. When she came on, there was a tremendous scream as though from one voice. She started to sing a number, and the screaming went on and on so deafeningly that she had to stop and start again. When she finished the first half of the show, something happened which I don't believe has happened in any theater before or since. The audience ran up onto the stage. Those who could not get onto the stage stood on their tables. Right at the end of one number, people picked up their knives and forks and banged them on the crockery. It was incredible. At the very end, when she was in her man's outfit, when she did her high kicks, and sang, as a man, 'I've Grown Accustomed to Her Face,' everybody started to cry; you could hear these sobs of hundreds of people in the dark."

In Buenos Aires, she almost fainted in the crush of thousands of fans who blocked the entrance to the theater. She was carried on the shoulders of four policemen, kicking her legs high, and laughing as a thousand voices cried, "Marlene! Divina!"

In 1960, she made an unforgettable return to Germany for her first German tour. An immense pile of clippings in the files of the Deutsches Institut für Filmkunde in Germany covers an event that must have been, both for her and for Germans, at once joyous and traumatic.

There were many who attacked her for her criticism of Germany, many who blamed her for deserting her country: Nazism was not dead there yet. At some performances, tomatoes and eggs were thrown at the stage, and there were bomb threats and talk of murdering her.

But she survived everything to give perhaps the most remarkable performances of her career. Singing in German again gave her a freedom, an ecstatic release from language problems, which we can now appreciate on her German releases. Her Berlin songs, with their echoes of the Claire Waldoff era, were brilliantly rearranged and reworded by Max Colpet.

In June 1960, Marlene flew to Israel, only to find that she was forbidden to sing German there. Two weeks before, Sir John Barbirolli had conducted Gustav Mahler's Second Symphony in Jerusalem and Tel Aviv and had been told not to permit the vocal parts to be sung in German. He had agreed. But Marlene refused to accept the Israeli ruling. She said, "It's stupid. I always sing in English, French, and German. Why shouldn't I sing in German here, where it is the language of so many people?"

Furious, Marlene sang in English "Look Me Over Closely" and then immediately plunged into German with "Peter," "Johnny," and other songs. The audience ignored the attitude of officialdom. They gave Marlene the supreme accolade of her career, a thirty-five-minute standing ovation which had never before been equaled in Tel Aviv, and was repeated in Jerusalem. Undoubtedly, the Israelis remembered with every fiber of their being Marlene's refusal to work for Hitler, and her work with the refugees in Hollywood. It is easy to imagine the profound effect this tour had on her: the mysterious current which linked her Aryan spirit with Jewry had at last found its fullest release, as she poured out her pacifist and romantic spirit in the songs which were closest to her.

While she was in Israel, a most curious item appeared in the *Berliner Morgenpost*. It contained an interview with several people living at 54 Bundesallee, which had formerly been 54 Kaiseralle—her home in the 1920s. Astonishingly, many of the people she had known, including her landlady and her neighbors, were still there. They mentioned that they had watched her (through keyholes) running down the stairs to her various dates or theatrical performances, and observed her golden hair flying as she made her way into her husband's green automobile or the cars of her various friends.

Over the years, Marlene was offered a number of parts on the stage, which she declined to do. Garson Kanin wrote a play for her. Vernon Duke composed a musical version of *Rain* in which she was supposed to be Sadie Thompson. Cheryl Crawford offered *One Touch of Venus* and Moss Hart offered *Lady in the Dark*. And she came very close to being the narrator in a proposed musical stage version of *The Blue Angel* composed by Harold Arlen. The director was to be Ted Flicker.

"I'll tell you why that particular project came to an end," Ted Flicker says. "Marlene decided that she, Harold Arlen, and I should take a look at the original film. We went to the Museum of Modern Art and had it run for us. At the end of the screening, Marlene turned to us and said, 'That was made in 1929. What an incredible year that was! Germany was on the bread line. Hitler was just coming along. It was the beginning of the end of Germany!'

" 'That wasn't the beginning of the end for me,' I said, 'it was the beginning of the beginning. That's the year I was born.'

"I knew at once what I had done. Marlene went very pale. She got up, and left without a word. The project was canceled immediately."

Marlene also turned down the offer of playing Orlovsky in *Die Fledermaus* in Vienna. George Marek of RCA Victor begged her to do it, but her voice was probably unequal to the task. Billy Wilder wanted her to make a film, set in Europe, in which she would play a female bartender with a wooden leg. A man falls in love with her and makes a date with her; but once he sees the wooden leg, he is unable to make love to her. By this point, the woman has fallen in love with him. She sets out to destroy him. Both Marlene and Billy Wilder finally decided this was too depressing and outré a subject to be popular.

In the 1960s, Marlene grew even more free with money than she had been in times when taxes were lower and she was among the more highly paid women in America. Hans Kohn was horrified to discover that for thirty years she had continued to pay three hundred dollars a month for storage of a sixteen-cylinder Cadillac she had left in a garage in Hollywood in 1935.

He begged her to sell it, but she refused, evidently because of its nostalgic associations. Finally, it was sold as a movie prop for one hundred dollars. If she had only auctioned it as Marlene Dietrich's car she would have fetched fifty-thousand dollars at least, but she declined to do so.

She would send a friend from London to Paris to buy a particular kind of bandage, fly special bread from Paris to New York for her daughter, spend hours on the phone from Paris to New York talking to the stocking department at Saks trying to find a salesgirl who had served her months before, dispatch oysters or cakes or cheese to Rudi by plane and helicopter so they could be delivered to him in person at the ranch. He was embarrassed by these gifts, complaining that the oysters had been sent in the wrong month, the cheeses were smelly because it was July, or the cakes were stale on arrival. There was no pleasing him.

Her sister Elisabeth retired from her poorly paid teaching job in Berlin, and Marlene gave her financial support. She paid for the education of her four grandsons at the very expensive Le Rosay in Switzerland, and flew there often to bring them gifts.

Marlene's attitude towards Germany, she told me, was ambiguous in those postwar years. She regretted the loss of her fatherland, the land which had existed before Hitler had destroyed German culture; and she remained unflinching in her condemnation of those Germans who had covertly supported Hitler and were now pretending that they were barely aware of his existence. When she saw her aging sister (who died in 1974) on visits to Berlin, she was reminded of the horror of Belsen. Friends testify that it was a constant source of distress to her that several of Rudi's relatives in the Sudetenland had become Nazis. In interviews, she refused to exonerate Germany from its guilt.

Yet she said to me she loved Germany, the Germany of Goethe and Schiller and Heine; and she continued to quote from them and from Kant and Hegel. Although, as she told me, she found postwar German literature, art, and music a grievous disappointment, and the Kurfüstendamm a mere echo of the dazzling thoroughfare of her youth, she could not find it in her heart to hate the country. She was, despite her American citizenship, still profoundly German.

The German attitude towards her was equally ambivalent. When in the 1960s she returned home to sing, she was once more attacked in some quarters; and at some performances, members of the audience let off stink bombs. They had again not forgotten her criticism of Germany or her assertion that "good Germans" still must be blamed for tolerating or supporting the Nazis.

On the other hand, the majority of the audiences now welcomed her, because she had represented a Free Germany in exile as strongly as de Gaulle represented the Free French. Her opposition to fascism endeared her to Germans who had turned against Nazism, and to the new generation of Germans who had grown up in the starvation and misery of war.

Year after year, the press celebrated her birthday, writing glowing praise for her career as the greatest of all the German stars, while at the same time irritating her by constantly reminding readers of her age.

In 1960, the producer-director Stanley Kramer approached Marlene to appear as Madame Bertholt, the widow of a general, in *Judgment at Nuremberg*—a part that appealed to her strongly both because it gave her an opportunity to act as herself, a dignified Prussian, and because it gave her the chance to appear with Spencer Tracy.

Stanley Kramer says: "I wanted her badly for the part. I went to her apartment in New York, and discovered that she was immediately impressed. She was passionately convinced that neofascism still existed in Germany, that the message of *Judgment at Nuremberg*, which laid the guilt firmly at the feet of the German people as a whole, was still valid.

"She said she was convinced that many Nazis were still at large, and this was long before the Eichmann case. She was utterly simpatico with the ideals of Abby Mann's script. The film also attracted her because she felt Mrs. Bertholt accurately represented the viewpoint of the Junker class to which she

belonged—the upper class which said, 'We hated Hitler, hus-
bands and wives alike.' "

Once she agreed to do the film, Marlene picked out her own
clothes for the part. She had a brown-and-black suit with a long
skirt specially made for her by a Viennese seamstress in New
York; and a black hat and fur collar were carefully made for her
also.

In Germany, she obtained heavy silk stockings (since nylons
would not have been available to Mrs. Bertholt) and solid, box-
toed shoes, everything made in a heavy-handed, Germanic
style which was ideally appropriate and also quite unflattering.
Stanley Kramer continues: "Marlene accepted, without even
seeing a script. I simply told her what it was about and she said,
'Ja!' When we started working together, in Hollywood, she was
a revelation. She knew what was good for her almost beyond
anyone I have ever known. Tracy would often wait a long time
for her to be made up. Then we'd go into rehearsal, she would
finish the scene, and go and reset all the lights herself. She
would raise and lower them, she would check the chin line, she
would shift the key light. She knew exactly how a baby spotlight
would shine in her eyes. The cameraman took a back seat. He
would say to me, 'She's perfectly right! Much better than I am!'
She took direction with no arguments, no problems.

"The problems were with other actors. Montgomery Clift
was on the verge of a nervous breakdown and Judy Garland was
terribly overweight. Marlene was around her with medications
and nostrums. She used to bring strüdels on the set, which she
said she had prepared the night before. Actually, she had
bought them in a shop in Beverly Hills."

The movie, which came out in 1961, was a great personal
triumph for Marlene. The last of her major screen roles, it
earned her enthusiastic reviews. The *New York Herald Tribune*
said: "As a German aristocrat, she has just the proper air of
world-weariness, the veiled arrogance tempered with sensitiv-
ity."

Another actor in the film, Maximilian Schell, says, "I felt I had
immediate contact with her. She was what the French call *une*

copine, a chum. She never appeared to be a star. I was a very obscure actor at the time, and she made me feel comfortable; she treated me as an equal.

"We had never met before, but she came straight up to my suite at the Chateau Marmont in Hollywood and cooked a meal for me on the spot. She also sang a song for me from her new show, just like that. She discussed, very frankly, the relationships between men and men, and women and women. She was supremely worldy-wise and without illusions. She had that Berlin touch, a capacity to handle kings and beggars with equal skill.

"She was generous and witty, but still at heart a Prussian hausfrau. She managed the scenes in the film quite beautifully, even though she was aware of their sentimentality. To my austere taste, the idea of a judge having an affair with the widow of a high-placed Nazi at the time of the Nurenburg trials seemed far-fetched, to say the least.

"I think all the scenes with Marlene were put in for commercial reasons, to cash in on her name.

"I got the impression that when she met people she didn't want just to chat with them; she wanted to *challenge* them. There was a kind of confrontation rather than a consolation in knowing her and I found that refreshing."

In 1962, Louis Clyde Stoumen, a documentary filmmaker, approached Marlene to narrate an account of Hitler's career entitled *The Black Fox.* He obtained many thousands of feet of footage, and prepared three cut reels, which he showed her. Stoumen says, "I felt she was the only possible person to do it.

"A friend of hers, Viva Hellman, arranged it. Marlene saw the reels, and decided to go ahead at once. Just like that.

"There was no talk of money or contracts. I got the impression that she was deeply moved. I went to her apartment. I was surprised to find that it wasn't a typical star's apartment; it was more like an intellectual's with books everywhere and papers scattered on the floor.

"She was a dedicated editor, and she cut and rearranged the script with great flair. I was impressed by the sharpness of her mind. She made no attempt to *impose* herself on the material. Rather, she sought to tighten it and sharpen it, give it more point or subtlety where these were needed.

"I remember the extraordinary devotion with which she did the recording. Her voice broke into emotion only once, when, referring to the concentration camps, she read the line, 'And Hitler did not even spare the children.' I could tell the effect the scenes in the concentration camp were having on her. But I did not know her sister had been in Belsen."

Marlene's quiet, humble, and definitive reading of the script undoubtedly helped *The Black Fox* to earn an Oscar. Years later, Stoumen, now a teacher at UCLA, was helpful in arranging entrance to the university for her young grandson, John Michael Riva.

The death of friends was an anguish for her in that time. Hemingway's suicide by gunshot, Gary Cooper's lingering death, Gérard Philipe and Cocteau struck down—these tragedies hurt her grievously. She stopped going to funerals after about 1963. They obviously reminded her all too acutely of her own mortality.

Erich Maria Remarque suffered a stroke which laid him low. Even before that, Marlene was worried about him, unhappy that he was married to Paulette Goddard. She constantly telephoned and wrote Remarque's friends in Switzerland, George and Hilda Marton, for word of him. She begged them to invite him to a party they gave for Josef von Sternberg, when von Sternberg's films were shown at a nearby film festival at Locarno. She arrived with von Sternberg, showing him the utmost respect, kindness, and consideration; but she was severely disappointed that Remarque was not present, and told the Martons that she blamed Paulette for his absence. She suffered badly when Remarque died several years later.

Marlene in the nineteen sixties and seventies was more frequently in London than she had been before. She had always been fond of British people: Jo Carstairs, Noel Coward, 'Binkie' Beaumont and numerous other English people had played important parts in her life. The leading British fan of the stars,

John Marven, who is also a ship's steward, says: "I remember my first encounter with her. She was staying at Claridge's. It was when she was here to make *Stage Fright*. I waited around for hours to see her. She came out all in cream: cream cloche hat, cream costume—marvelous. She was in a hurry on her way to the Caprice to dine. There was such a crowd that taxis with fans in them were bumping into her car. She told us to wait for her outside the Caprice. She came out with Danny Kaye and Jane Wyman. Danny Kaye said, 'Don't sign them, Marlene, because they'll pester you all the more.' Marlene said, 'No, I promised to give them autographs, and I will.' She did every one in turn. It was twelve-thirty in the morning.

"No messages—she just wrote her name in this dreadful scrawl. It was just a squiggle, with an *M* that ran into a *D*, and a long line that went off the page.

"I remember when I was in Switzerland, and I asked Spencer Tracy for his autograph. When he saw hers, he said, 'Jeezus, what's *that?*' I told him. He said, 'What could you expect from such a silly old bag?'

"She doesn't really like signing autographs, but she does it just the same—she's much better than Hepburn in this respect. She preferred to hand out pictures with printed autographs on them. Marlene didn't mind getting up on top of a car and showing her legs. Things like that. I used to follow her at first nights. She was at Orson Welles's *Moby Dick* with her daughter; she went into the box, there was a tremendous reception, and then she left after the first act.

"One time, another fan and I went over to Marlene's apartment house on Park Avenue. I had three pictures of her I wanted to have signed. I noticed a woman scrubbing the front entrance. I didn't think anything of it. She had a bandanna round her head. No makeup, an ordinary loose blouse. A bucket beside her, full of gray slops, and a large brush in her hand. She was scrubbing away with furious energy, We did a double take. My God! It was Dietrich!

"I saw her empty the bucket into the street, and she disappeared. We wouldn't have *dared* talk to her, in the circumstances. We mentioned to a woman next door what we had seen and she said, 'Oh, that's nothing. She's *always* scrubbing!'

"Noel Coward's attitude to her was funny. One time, I took him a photograph of them together, rehearsing at the London Palladium for the Night of the Thousand Stars. Mr. Coward said, 'Oh, my God!'' signed his half of the picture and then said, 'Now I'll get the other old bag to sign it!'

"Marlene, like Katharine Hepburn, had to use the back entrance of Claridge's when she wore slacks. So she preferred the Dorchester. Later, she favored the Savoy. There was a girl called June who used to pursue Marlene. Marlene came in one night, and June saw her for the first time. Marlene got out of the car and June threw herself in her path. Marlene was in a filthy mood, and snapped, 'No! I will *not* do it! I will *not* sign an autograph! June was devastated. She started to cry, she looked as though she was on the verge of a nervous breakdown. Marlene realized she had distressed her terribly and she put her arm around her, she kissed her and said, 'Don't distress yourself, dear. Really, I'm not worth it. Come to my room.' She took the girl up, she made her tea, calmed her down, and gave her a beautiful autograph. For once, she wrote her name out in full. She only did that when she cared. "She wrote on the picture, 'With my very best wishes. I'm very sorry.'

"There was another fan called Thelma. You can stand opposite the entrance to Claridge's and see the stars coming in and out. Owen had the Rolls, he was revving up, and Marlene came out. With that, Thelma dashed across the road, and right in front of the car as it swung around to pick Marlene up. Marlene came out of the door. She grabbed Thelma, and pulled her from under the wheels of the car. She gave her the most terrible lecture: 'Silly girl! You could have been killed, just for me! You'd do this for me? You're crazy!' She was raging at her. In fact, she wouldn't even sign for her. Thelma didn't get her autograph until at least a couple of weeks later.

"Another fan, Derek, was in charge of some of her overhead lighting in Glasgow. When she was singing 'Where Have All the Flowers Gone?' he picked up hundreds of rose petals and showered them down on top of her. She was quite unprepared for this. She was alarmed at first, then delighted. She included it in her act after that.

"When she was playing the Mark Hellinger Theater in New York, there was a young man with binoculars in the front row. She saw this, and she stopped right in the middle of a song. She said sharply, 'You don't have to do that. Don't kill the illusion.' Everyone laughed uproariously and the poor man was hopelessly distressed, throwing the binoculars under the seat."

In May 1964, Marlene made a hugely successful visit to Russia. She had become enamored of the autobiography of the great Russian writer Konstantin Paustovsky, and when he appeared at one of her performances, being unable to speak adequate Russian and overcome by his presence, she sank to her knees before him. He began to cry. At one of her performances there were forty minutes of encores before an audience of 1,350. She told the audience when at last it quietened down, "I must tell you that I have loved you for a long time. The reason I love you is that you have no lukewarm emotions; you're either very sad or very happy. I am proud to say that I think I have a Russian soul myself."

Nineteen hundred sixty-five was her busiest year to date, with tours of South Africa, Sweden, and Norway, and the British provinces: Liverpool, Bristol, Brighton, and Manchester. She renewed an earlier love for the British people, and for the polite and considerate police, who always lifted her gently and put her on top of the van to talk to the crowd and sign autographs. It was a relief, she told me, to sing to so many young people, who had never heard of *The Blue Angel.*

In the mid-1960s, Marlene established her own group of musicians, led by William Blezard or by Stan Freeman, according to schedules. Joe Davis executed her Sternbergian ideas of lighting. The musicians were always English. Marlene liked the reliable, confident, and quiet atmosphere of a British ensemble. Occasionally, inferior musicians were used, both in England and on her overseas tours, and she was loud in her complaints; her perfectionism, more intense as she grew older, often grated on her colleagues. Burt Bacharach stopped working for her after the Edinburgh Festival in 1964, though she retained his outstanding arrangements: he had simply became too famous and important to continue to be her conductor.

She never discussed her personal affairs with her band. Her drummer since 1964, Andy White, says: "She was always good to us, but a little remote. She gave her lighting and sound men hell, but never us. She was a perfectionist always: she knew exactly what she wanted. Yet she allowed changes in tempo: her *own* tempo changed from performance to performance, according to her feelings about the interpretation. People always said she gave the same performance after 1954: it isn't true, the variances were subtle, but real.

"I've seen her lose her temper—when the microphones were not exactly in the position she asked for them to be, or when the spot hadn't fallen just the way she wanted it.

"She always gave us beautiful gifts, on birthdays—she never forgot one—or at Christmas, each present carefully thought out for the person. She'd never write a personal letter when between shows; she'd just write 'officially' discussing details of her next tour. She always typed the letters herself. She was incredibly considerate. We had a lighting man whose hands became ineffective; he had to go in a wheelchair. He told her he couldn't use his hands to write, so she bought him a special typewriter used by paraplegics."

During the 1960s and 1970s, Marlene made three visits to the famous Dr. Paul Niehans clinic at "La Prairie" in Clarens, near Vevey, Switzerland. The pressure of working constantly had worn her down, and she needed the rejuvenation the Niehans treatment could give her.

She did not arrive in Geneva by plane, since the astrologer Carroll Righter had instructed her not to, but by train. The last-minute decision was so hurried she even forgot to turn in her plane ticket for a refund.

She transferred from the train to a large black Cadillac limousine at the Lausanne station, and drove to the clinic. Max Ringli reported in the *Neue Post:* "Dr. Walter Michel of the clinic gave her a thorough examination, to determine whether there was any infection in her system. Meanwhile, only one hour before, a pregnant sheep from a farm in the Faubourg canton had been butchered. The unborn lamb foetus was smashed and ground down so that heart and placenta cells could be obtained. One instant's delay could mean that the cells would lose the vibrancy of new life. Packed in ice, the precious cells were rushed to the patient and inoculated in her buttocks—an excruciatingly painful procedure. The area could not be anesthetized as this would have reduced the rejuvenating effect of the drug."

Complete rest followed the treatment. Dietrich was forbidden to smoke or drink during that period. X rays, saunas, or direct exposure to the sun were not permitted. It was twelve weeks before she felt the rejuvenating effects, which would only last for a period before the treatment became necessary again. A portrait of her, signed for Dr. Michel, hangs in the lobby of the clinic—her token of gratitude.

In November 1963, Marlene appeared in the Royal Command Variety Performance at the Prince of Wales Theatre in the presence of Her Majesty the Queen Mother. The show was also the big breakthrough for the Beatles. She also gave special performances: at the Royal Albert Hall, for the Eighth Army Annual Reunion, in the presence of Field Marshal Bernard Montgomery; and at the Drury Lane, with Sophie Tucker. She also played a season for Binkie Beaumont at the Queen's, followed by an appearance in the Golders Green Hippodrome.

In those years, her most intimate friendships were with Marti Stevens, millionairess daughter of movie mogul Nicholas Schenck, a beautiful woman of great wit, style, and intelligence; and Iva Patcèvitch, publisher and *bon viveur*. She gained much from these remarkable sophisticates.

Eleven

Meeting
at World's End

It was 12:15 P.M. October 5, 1965, at the white stone, coldly impersonal entrance of the Southern Cross Hotel in Melbourne, Australia. A massive black Pontiac drove up to the glass doors; a pale hand at the window, a look of slightly bewildered surprise, and a woman got out. An opalescent, checked wool costume, the kind of thing a European aristocrat would wear to Longchamps, had a surprisingly sensible air. Low-heeled, tiny shoes, pale gray stockings, a band in her Garboesque, pageboy hair, and in her hands a spray of white orchids, held almost defensively against her body. She walked into the lobby, nervously tentative, frowning against the white light which almost made her delicately beautiful face dissolve against the white pillars, white stone floors. Her almost splayfooted, uneasy walk was that of a girl on her first date.

She vanished into an elevator; not long after that she re-emerged to go straight into a rehearsal with the band. And from the rehearsal theater, having changed into a dark blue blouse and a white satin Chanel costume, she went to a dining room at her hotel, which was oddly rigged up as a theater, with a dais, a seat for her, and a waiting microphone. Again, she sidled into the room, smiling coolly. She saw the stage and the chairs arranged in threatening half-moons, the reporters packed tight near the cocktail bar. "But it's so formal," she whispered. "I might be giving a concert." The photographers must finish first; she refused to be interviewed with lights flashing in her face. As the shots went on and on, she grew impatient. A finger beckoned the impresario, Kenn Brodziak. "Am I going to get tough with them, or are you?" Understandably, he hesitated, but then the shots were finished, and she settled down to talk.

A few words, half in German, half in English, with an excitable Jewish reporter who once saw her perform in Vienna. And, during the discussion, some memorably bizarre exchanges: "Miss Dietrich, Tasmania is an island off the coast of Australia." "Yes, I know. But I always used to think Ernst Lubitsch invented it." (The reference was to a film one thought everyone had forgotten, *The Princess of Tasmania*.) And: "Were you disturbed when they asked you to get into a monkey suit?" (The reference was to her ape dance in *Blonde Venus*.) "I was asked to do all kinds of crazy things in those days." And she was very quick to slap down the impertinent: "Do you wear a hairpiece?" some man asked. "Do you?" she replied, dissolving a nervously half-hostile room in laughter.

In the middle of all this, there was a curious little scene, staged expertly for the columnists. A foreign waiter stepped up to Marlene's chair, carrying a tray with a flourish. On it sat a huge, glistening ice cream in the shape of an apple. The waiter's schmaltzy little speech had been flawlessly rehearsed: the apple was the first fruit, with which the first lady tempted the first gentleman. "We have it here tonight; and we have given it the name, 'Madame Marlene.' "

The star put the "Madame Marlene" firmly on the floor and changed the subject. No, she had no interest in seeing countries; she would leave Australia the moment the tour was over. ("I'm not a tourist.") It was getting towards the end of the conference; she was really tired now, and her eyes grew restless. Then someone asked her a question, and the answer crystallized her whole personality, the whole tone of one's encounter with her. She had been saying that she carries on only in order to do her duty. "What is your duty?" She paused for a moment, thinking; then smiled with an expression of sharp intelligence, drawing herself up proudly. "To answer that I must go back to Goethe, with whom I was educated." She remembered a phrase from his 1816 *Maxims and Reflections:* "Was aber ist deine Pflicht? Die Förderung des Tages." ("What is your duty? Whatever the day demands.")

It was opening night, the Princess Theatre, the evening of October 7. A dazzle of diamonds and furs and white shirtfronts in the stalls, as the orchestra, sounding oddly "dead" (as though it was in rehearsal and the sound system was turned off), struck up a medley. Unfortunately, Burt Bacharach, Marlene's usual conductor, was absent and the band missed his panache. (The lighting, copied from Joe Davis's in London, worked well.) At first, the star emerged from behind the curtain hesitantly—still (after two days), uncertain of the country and the audience, perhaps trying to gauge its temper. At the moment it was looking very rich, stolid, and bored.

She had a remote, lunar quality on stage: drifting bubbles of white fur, a silver gown, her hair in the light a darker color than I had remembered it earlier. She belted straight into "I Can't Give You Anything But Love, Baby," and appeared genuinely shocked into relieved laughter at the applause. She appeared to deliver most of her numbers with far more skill and point than on her recent recordings—or was it just that one needed her real presence to give impact to a song? Her arms were held tightly against her body or behind her back, her fingers used sexually or accusingly or mockingly as she pointed at the audience or caressed the microphones. Her body was always stock-still except when she bowed, furs tumbling forward, hair in a shock over her face, to acknowledge the cheers.

Once again, one was impressed with the iron control of her every movement. Tears, laughter, mocking smiles were turned on and off at will, and the real agony of emotion seldom broke through; when it did, as in the superb song from Israel about hunger, "Shir Hatan," the effect was all the more powerful because of her cool self-discipline in the rest of the songs. Time had put an extra edge of refinement on her voice, and her range —switching from the brazen, harsh insolence of Frederick Hol-

lander's "Lola" to the delicate romanticism of "Warum" without a hint of strain—was as astonishing as ever. One's eyes
dazzled with tears in the harsh lights; the audience was on its
feet, cheering and cheering; it was no less than she deserved—
as the last of the great diseuses, natural heir to Hortense
Schneider and Claire Waldoff—and she knew it, darting in and
out of the curtain like a silver bird, dodging a rain of flowers.

Backstage after the show, she asked a handful of people—
John Casson, Sybil Thorndike's son, and his wife, the *Variety*
reporter, and me—to drop round for a chat. She clung to my
arm eagerly, like a young girl. "They [the audience] were so
quick!" She was delighted with them. "In England I have to say
each joke slowly, so they get the point. But here, when I referred to the way I sang an American song for my test in *The
Blue Angel* and that it was not the song that got me the part,
they laughed at once! And usually only Americans are as quick
as that!

"You know the studio test in which I sang that song is still in
existence, in East Germany. The Russians took all the UFA
studio material and they have it there. . . . Wouldn't it be fun
to see it again. . . ." She sang, with wit and charming self-
mockery, a few phrases of the number in her squeaky voice of
1929: "You're the Cream in My Coffee."

Then she looked more serious. "What did you"—this with a
more earnest clinging to my arm—"think of that press conference? You know something happened there which has never
happened to me in my life. A girl said to me, 'When are you
going to retire?' And I asked that back of her. And she said, 'But
I'm only twenty-two and I have such a long time ahead of me.'
You know, it's on occasions like that that I wish I were a bitch.
I would have said to her, 'Get down on your knees, my dear, and
pray that you don't die before you get any older.' " She laughed,
forgivingly: the disciplined conference victim and the brilliantly stylish professional of the stage have turned into a
charming, intimate woman, and one felt, at that late hour of the
night, that all masks were off.

Next afternoon I was in my hotel room when the telephone
rang. The voice on the other end was unmistakable. "Hello, this

is Marlene. I would have called you earlier, but people have never stopped calling me. They all seem to have deadlines at eleven o'clock tomorrow morning. I don't understand it at all. But let us meet privately. Why don't you come and have supper with me after the show?"

I arrived at the theatre at ten-thirty; half an hour later the performance was over and I was backstage. Cavernous darkness; looming, threatening props and struts; tiny knots of agonized people arguing about the best way to get the star out of the theater through the crowd, how many were going to be in the car, and who would be invited to supper. A dresser rushed to and fro, her face strained. Theater staff argued perfunctorily. Every few minutes someone came from the stage door: "The crowd is getting restless. Is she ready?"

She emerged, in a soft, blue-gray woolen costume. The tension increased. We were in the corridor leading to the stage door. Suddenly the door flew open: the crowd was wild with excitement, clusters of hands rushed out at us. She shrank back, anxiously, as pens were thrust into her hand for autographs. "This one doesn't work," she said, handing a pen back. "Where are my pictures? My pictures?" she said. The dresser had forgotten to give her the autographed portraits she would hand to the crowd; someone raced off and returned with fistfuls of photographs.

A boy crushed his hand in the car door, but still the crowd would not relent. I was in, but the door wouldn't shut. I pulled it to. Hands clutched through the window: "Close it halfway up, not completely," someone said, and I obeyed. But the hands were still clawing, only retreating when I had thrust bundles of pictures into them. The cries were fierce: "Make her sign this! I came all the way from Queenscliff and I won't go until she signs it!" "Leave your name and address at the theater!" someone snapped at the angry, male, foreign voice. Women screamed: "Ask her to look this way!" "Oh, she looked at me!" "Let me get a look at her!" It was horrifying, appalling; hands drummed relentlessly on the car roof; were we going to be tilted over?

As we moved, Dietrich kept calling out: "Watch out for the

children! That little boy there! He may go under the wheels! Oh, please be careful!" At last we were away, and around a sharp corner. We drove first to the Southern Cross Hotel to deliver the suitcases. It was incredible, but several of the crowd at the theater—by no means all of them young—had managed to spring hundreds of yards from Spring Street to the hotel ahead of the car. Dietrich wasn't surprised. "It's the same in England. And in Liverpool they have the most wonderful trick. They knock the policemen's helmets forward. The policemen are blinded, naturally, and let go, so the crowd can get through. Aren't they clever?"

Then we were really off, down dark, deserted, rainswept streets. It was like the car journey in Cocteau's *Orphée:* The driver in his cap motionless and silent, the two men with us from the theater also stock-still, and the star beside me, staring out into the black night. We drove up to a restaurant with a glass front deep in the backwaters of the rich suburb of Toorak. Inside, a pianist was tinkling away, a few couples at the end of the evening were polishing off liqueurs, and we slipped into a corner table. Marlene ordered escalope and a plain pancake with lemon. She had brought wine with her; the waiter put champagne in a bucket on the table. "No, we won't have that! Take it away!" Then he offered her her own red wine to taste. She gently ignored the faux pas, and asked him to pour.

Over dinner, after some strained discussion of problems in the theater, the star turned to reminiscence of the war years. She talked about the vast influx of Europeans in Hollywood—refugees from Hitler and frequently men of great talent, such as Mann, Brecht, Frank, Werfel—who fled there via Paris before and during World War II.

"The German Jews loved Germany so terribly, in spite of everything that was happening there. Even in Paris, they would say, 'This bread is so bad. It isn't like German bread.'" And these, she indicated, were people who had just escaped from the gas chambers.

"Even in Hollywood they would complain about everything. But I think it is a terribly difficult thing, living in another country. Billy, Lubitsch, and I got these people little jobs around the studios, just so they would be working. But they still longed to go back to Germany, they loved it so; and some did go back . . . to what?"

Then she looked up at the waiters; they were tired, waiting for us to go. It was half past one in the morning, but she still had energy left. She looked at the waiters with pity. "We must let them leave, go home." We drove off, couples in evening dress still wandering about everywhere, thrown up from the darkness by the headlamps. "So late at night!" she said. "This is some jumping town!" We were at the hotel. She squeezed my hand, trotted briefly through the rain, and was gone.

It was in Australia that Marlene met Hugh Curnow. I had gradually come to know her better after the tense but exciting early days of the beginning of her tour. She lived a routine as strict as a soldier's: she was still very much the daughter of a military officer turned policeman. But hers were not military hours; they were the hours of an owl. She was as pale as the moon; I knew her as a creature of the night. She rose at noon, attended to her business, tapped out letters on a typewriter using two fingers, and made long telephone calls to every part of the world. She liked to call close friends in distant places: Noel Coward, Paul Gallico, Mischa Spoliansky, Burt Bacharach. She read everything. In addition to Elizabeth Kata's *Be Ready with Bells and Drums,* she had just discovered Harper Lee's *To Kill A Mockingbird,* ideal (to her) in the purity and brevity of its style, and its theme of children and the horrors of racial prejudice.

She suffered, I remember clearly, from insomnia. She put this down to the change of time, and sent me a note reading, "The pills I take make me feel worse than not sleeping at all." Somebody explained to her at a party that since she was in Australia, she was walking upside down. She was delighted by the idea, and laughingly told everyone about it.

Her dietary habits were strange. She ate little during the day, and drank almost nothing, indulging herself only in a glass of champagne at three in the afternoon. Then, at midnight, she would eat a substantial meal; it was hard to imagine how she could sleep at all.

I gave a dinner party for Marlene in collaboration with the Australian novelist Elizabeth Kata. I can see her now. Arriving by car, she walked delicately down a steep hillside near the azure harbor of Sydney. It was a typically fresh, iridescent Sydney afternoon. She was wearing a pale-pink and brown Chanel costume with a ribbon in her fair hair. She looked incredibly youthful, and entirely out of place. Against the rough-hewn buildings, the raw red brick uncomfortably copied from an English suburb in this exotic setting, she was like a civilized ghost. She walked quickly past palm trees brown and brittle from a long drought. The new moon surprisingly accompanied the sun. It looked as fragile as a fingernail.

The apartment was large and handsome in an old-fashioned style, reminiscent (like so much in Australia), of the early 1930s. Marlene entered the living room, unerringly choosing the one chair where the daylight would fall comfortably on her face. She moved about subtly during the course of the conversation to make sure that the daylight still flattered her as it slowly faded.

When night fell, she suddenly climbed up on a window seat and knelt like a little girl of eight, peering out into the dark. A series of ferries twinkled by like glowworms in the profound blackness. It was a magical sight. She responded to it ecstatically, saying, "Now I am seeing the city for the first time!"

She was immense fun at dinner, digging into a baron of beef with the enthusiasm of a marine. She told funny jokes about the way she imagined a German expatriate critic who had attacked her show. His name was Uli Schmetzer, a name she found uproariously funny, and every time she toasted it ironically in champagne, she made it sound more absurd: "Uli Schmetzer! Uli Schmetzer! Uli Schlemieltzer! Uli Schlochser! Uli Schmaltzer!" Each time the variations improved.

Later I saw her on a special occasion—a trip to a bay for a fish dinner with Elizabeth Kata and the critic Joel Greenberg. She walked along the narrow sidewalk next to a tiny beach, watch-

ing the surf lapping the stones and breathing an air redolent of
tar, gull feathers, smoke, and spume. She signed deeply: "It's
like the North Sea in Heine's poems. I love it. I live again." She
walked into the Ozone Café, a romantic shack with dishes
chalked up on a distant blackboard, which she made a special
point of reading without glasses. "I feel I'm in Normandy now.
So wonderfully simple." She was happy that the place was almost empty—just a young couple with a baby, which she tenderly embraced and kissed. The European waiters were struck
dumb by her appearance, as she murmured happily over the
moules marinière and sent back the bouillabaisse because it
contained garlic. She talked entertainingly and often unquota-
bly about some of the biggest stars. It was the last time we dined
together before she met Hugh Curnow.

Hugh Curnow was about thirty at the time, broad-shouldered, with a large, ruddy face and with pale-blue eyes set in
prematurely fleshy sockets. He exuded ambition, sexual confidence, a lumberman's attack on obstacles. He was typically
Australian in his steely, chipper optimism and slightly ignorant
but audacious upward mobility. Working with him for most of
the year in a magazine office—I was literary editor, he a roving
reporter—we learned a kind of cautious cameraderie, like the
crew in a submarine. Some weeks, there were so few on the staff
that between the two of us and two others we virtually wrote
everything from the editorials to the crossword puzzle clues.
And the temperature was 110 degrees day after day, the office
like a dog kennel, the humidity making one feel that it was
raining indoors.

I was aware that Hugh, though kind and considerate, looked
at the world with cheerful greed. He was not an intellectual: his
highest interest in music was John Gary. He told me he was
desperate to interview Marlene. Our boss, the *farouche* Sir
Frank Packer, insisted he talk to her when he was transferred
from the weekly to a daily newspaper. She wouldn't see him.
Another reporter disguised himself as a waiter and made his
way into her suite with a notebook in his back pocket, only to
be detected at once and asked to leave.

One morning, Marlene called me at the office. She said that

Hugh had written to her, expressing great admiration for her, and saying that his children would suffer if he lost his job; he might lose it if he did not get to see her. Privately I thought, I didn't know he was so clever. He had reached her by piercing her Achilles heel—her love of children. It was masterly of him.

When she asked me should she give him an interview, I didn't have the heart to tell her not to. I told her, "Don't blame me if you don't like what he writes. On the other hand, you may like it very much indeed."

"It's six of one and half a dozen of the other, then?"

"Yes," I told her.

Within a week they were dating. Though scarcely on the same level, he was the same physical type as Jean Gabin: the massive head fixed on an almost neckless trunk, the spatulate hands, the heavy chest, and sudden, surprising narrowing of the hips. His extreme virility undoubtedly had its effect on her, and her friend Walter Reisch has described how profoundly attractive she found Curnow. But it is doubtful if she found him any more satisfying at a deeper level than she had found Gabin.

Sir Frank Packer gave a party for her, and soon after, she called him, and obtained special leave for Hugh to go to Paris. They were to work together on her memoirs of the two wars, *Tell Me, Oh, Tell Me Now*. Marlene's last call to me before she left was very strange indeed. She told me that Maria and William Riva were now living in Rome, and that she must obtain a "bush baby" to send to her youngest grandson.

I pointed out that bush babies were not Australian, but South African mammals. She asked me if I could get one from the local zoo.

I called the zoo's director, Sir Edward Hallstrom. He told me, "We only have two, and one of them is dying. Sorry."

Marlene called an agent in South Africa who had handled her in Johannesburg. No dice. Finally, I had a brain wave. I told her of a toy factory and suggested; "Why don't we have them make a copy of a bush baby?"

She was delighted by the idea. I called the factory, and sent over some photographs of bush babies from the magazine files.

The manager said, "*One toy!* She wants us to make *just one?*" I told her it would cost a fortune. So far as I know, she paid for it.

A series of articles by Hugh appeared in the local press. They covered a night-long drive with her around the city, including a visit to Harry's Café de Wheels, which looked exactly as it sounds and where she ran into some sailors on a late night pass, and ended at dawn at a beach, where she walked barefoot. They left for America, his wife and children staying at home.

Later reports came from Hollywood, where she and Hugh attended Charles Aznavour's opening and ran into Hedy Lamarr. She also went with Hugh to visit Alfred Hitchcock on the set, and he embraced her warmly, reminiscing happily about *Stage Fright.*

Delicate touches of detail in these articles suggested that perhaps Marlene had a hand in them: the angry tinkle of glasses at the Aznavour party; the figure of an unknown man, pale and propped upright, who might have been a corpse, sliding in a black Cadillac out of the hard shadow of the black administration tower at Universal City.

They continued together to Paris, and the articles began to dwindle. I gradually came to understand that the relationship had burned out. And the book didn't "work," either because Marlene felt that it was insufficiently important after the Kennedy assassination, which cut her to the heart, or because Hugh simply wasn't capable of writing it on the level she wanted. He came home. I saw him. He told me an odd little story, which may or may not have been true. "One night we went to the Duke and Duchess of Windsor's for dinner. Judy Garland was there, and Paul Gallico, an old friend of Marlene's. Just as we left the apartment, Marlene put a parcel under her arm. She wouldn't tell me what it contained.

"The guests were very intrigued by the parcel. Marlene kept hugging it all evening. Finally, she yielded to pressure—she *would* show it. She unwrapped it with great ceremony. It contained two specially made, unreleased phonograph records in blank white sleeves. 'Oh, Marlene, these must be your new discs!' Wallis Windsor said. Marlene smiled mysteriously and took them over to the phonograph.

"She played the first one. It was she—singing a German song in German. It was followed by applause. Half an hour later, we were still listening to that applause! Every now and again, Marlene would say, 'Zat was Paris. . . . Zat was London. . . . Zat was Rio.' You couldn't, of course, tell one mass of handclaps from another. Then she played the second record—it was all applause. She finished; she said, 'We'll go home now!'; and she swept me out to the car. The guests were astounded; and as for the Windsors, her host and hostess, they looked horrified. Marlene didn't care.

"We hardly ever went out. Another time we did was when she told me she had a very special treat in store. I got excited: what could it be? The journey to our destination seemed endless. Finally we reached a tall, narrow house. Everything was dark; the chauffeur had to show us through a back door with a flashlight. We climbed a tall, narrow stairway. I thought, 'My God, what is this?' At last we reached a small, small room, and we sat down. A pencil of light shot past us into the nearly total darkness. I was prepared for anything. She clutched my arm. 'Ah,' she said, and suddenly gave an almost sexual gasp. And you know what happened? *The Blue Angel* appeared on the screen.

"I never did find out who owned the house, nor why he neither greeted us, nor said farewell."

I asked Hugh about his life with Marlene. Hugh's sharp blue eyes smoked over. "At night, we'd look at her scrapbooks. The scrapbooks were jammed tight under the beds and she'd drag them out and show them to me. She had marked statements she liked in red ink. She'd say, suddenly, "Harold Hobson,* isn't he a dear!"

Time went by. In 1968, Marlene also returned to Australia for the Adelaide Festival of the Arts, and was due to open one night in Melbourne. That same afternoon Hugh, who had been put

---

*Then theater critic of the *London Sunday Times*.

on routine assignments by his boss, was sent to cover an oil discovery off the coast of Victoria. He and a team of journalists were accompanied by my friend Noel Buckley, public relations man for Esso Petroleum.

Hugh was evidently in good spirits, tanned, blue-eyed, laughing, just past thirty. The journalists jostled up and down on the swaying oil rig in a heavy swell.

The helicopter, with the Esso symbol, flew in to take photographs to release to the press. It was difficult to get the correct angle, and the pilot decided to hover directly over the oil rig, the seas now so heavy that a few of the journalists were seasick.

The top of an oil rig is a complicated steel structure. It swung over towards the helicopter, and struck one of the blades. The helicopter tilted sideways, and like a sick moth fell over onto the deck.

The blades continued whirling. Noel Buckley's legs were sliced off about the knee. The blades caught Hugh Curnow, and cut his head off instantly. He could not have known what happened. His head span out into the sea. His torso crashed down the steps that led to the lower deck, and lay bleeding at the foot.

Noel was unluckier. He lay all night in agony and bled to death shortly before dawn. It was probably just as well. He would not have wanted to live his life as a cripple.

Marlene opened in her show at the Princess Theatre Melbourne, only three hours later. Kenn Brodziak, her impresario, brought her the news. She paled, leaned against the door of her hotel suite, walked in, and closed the door. One could only speculate on her thoughts as she heard of the decapitation of the man who had lived with her as close friend and coauthor for so many months.

That night, she gave the public what it wanted. A flawless performance. To spare Hugh's widow and children, she did not attend the funeral. Clearly, she did not want to lend fuel to gossip, and, amazingly, the press played it cool.

She sent twelve white roses to Hugh as he lay in his coffin: the symbol of innocence.

Twelve

Her Seventies

In the late 1960s, Marlene was seen less frequently in public. She returned to Las Vegas and performed at the Hotel Tropicana's Blue Room. She made her Broadway debut on October 9, 1967, in the Nine O'Clock Theater at the Lunt-Fontanne. Jean Louis designed a new dress for her, valued at $30,000, with bugle beads all lined with fourteen-carat gold. She told reporters at a press conference at the Étoile, "I will sing twenty-two songs if the audience is responsive, and twenty if they are not." Her sharpness with silly questions was more noticeable than before. When one reporter asked her, "Would you describe your hat?" she replied, "You do it. That's your business." When another inquired, "What happens in your show?" she snapped back, "You come to see it and find out." A man asked her, was there anything in her professional career that she had wanted and not achieved? "I never wanted to play Joan of Arc, if that's what you mean," she said.

She appeared in a famous airline advertisement, stretched out in a seat. She discussed German food and fashion, and how to keep a figure, in a Pan American cassette recording played to passengers on a specific channel on their way to Germany.

In 1969, she suffered another grief: the death of her friend and "Professor Higgins," Joseph von Sternberg. Towards the end of his life, von Sternberg frequently visited the home of the movie collector David Bradley, watching the pictures he had made with Marlene over and over again, puffing quietly at a pipe, refusing to say anything afterward. For years, he had been an embittered relic of the industry, and I'll never forget interviewing him in a somber house in Los Angeles, a far cry from the fabulous Neutra steel house he had owned in the San Fernando Valley. He sat in the dimly lit room surrounded by Chinese screens, fingering a book of verses. Somnolent but watchful as a sly Persian cat, he padded down narrow stairs into his den in the basement, and surrounded by carvings, told me, teeth gritting over a pipestem, a pack of self-serving lies. Despite the fact that von Sternberg attacked Marlene in his memoirs, she remained loyal to him, and friendly with his widow, Meri, his second wife, who helped her grandson enter UCLA.

Walter Reisch recalls: "The funeral was held in midwinter. Many people said, 'Where's Marlene?' She wasn't present. I thought, 'It's the worst weather in the East. A blizzard held up the plane. Otherwise, surely she would have come.'

"Meri von Sternberg went back to the house after a small memorial gathering at the neighbors'. As Meri entered the living room, Marlene was there. Marlene had defied the blizzard to fly out to be with Meri! Marlene said to her, 'I didn't want to go to the funeral. I would have stolen the show from Jo!' "

An amusing event took place in the early 1970s. Impatient with the slow-moving London traffic, Marlene decided to travel by subway from the Savoy Hotel to the suburb of Wimbledon, many miles distant, where she was performing.

It was the first time she had set foot in a subway since the late forties, when she and Gabin used to be seen on the Métro in Paris together, braving its fetid depths to make their way from one place to another when taxis were difficult to obtain.

David Wigg of the *London Daily Express* says, "I was there. She made her entrance onto the train to Wimbledon in a white trouser suit, like a queen. She was recognized by almost nobody. As she hung on a strap—no man gave her a seat—some woman said, 'No! It can't be!'

"Then one woman accepted a dare and spoke to her. She

thanked the woman, royally. Finally the other passengers realized it was she. A man put down his newspaper and said, 'Good Lord, Marlene Dietrich on a train. What's wrong? Is she broke?' And a fan, a young female fan, when she realized she wasn't dreaming, actually fainted."

On December 29, 1971, the *New York Times* reported: "The East German and West German press are rarely in agreement, but their accord was notable on the occasion of the seventieth birthday of Marlene Dietrich. *Der Abend,* a West Berlin newspaper, said Miss Dietrich had never been more thoroughly German than she was during World War II, when she condemned everything German because of the Nazis. Another West Berlin newspaper, the *Berliner Zeitung,* called her "Marlene, the unwitherable." And joining these papers on the same side, for once, was *Neues Deutschland,* the official Communist party organ, which called the actress, "the most charming grandmother in the world!"

In 1972, Marlene taped her first television special, *I Wish You Love,* for Alexander Cohen at the New London Theater in England. She had always hated television, and apparently undertook the task only because of the money, reputed to be the largest amount ever paid to a television entertainer for one performance: $200,000. It was probably the worst nightmare of her career. The manager of the theatre, George Biggs, says: "It was quite an experience, in many ways. First of all, the building wasn't finished. It was supposed to have opened in August, but it wasn't until October 1972 that all the details were finalized.

"We had cement mixers and drills going when she came in to rehearse. I think that she was alarmed that the place wasn't completed, and couldn't understand it. She just appeared suddenly out front, in a jeans suit, a kind of student's cap, and sunglasses; and sat down. I didn't realize who she was! She just *materialized.*

"She was *furious* about the set. It wasn't what she wanted at all. It had to be taken out and redone overnight. The worst thing was to see her turn up at the times she was asked to turn up at rehearsal: she was ready to go, and the orchestra wasn't ready. I'll never forget her standing on the stage, helplessly angry, and calling out, 'Isn't there *anybody* out there?' "

Her sound man, Jim Douglas, says: "It was one of the few times she'd been confronted by television cameras, she'd not been in so big a TV studio in her life, and she was entirely at sea. She didn't know what to expect and nobody had told her what to expect, least of all Alex Cohen. He lost his temper with her, smashing a glass as he slammed it on a table. Alex cleared the theater and had a word with her. She almost gave up the whole thing.

"She was told to do her standard stage show. She expected a makeup artist to tell her what to do; there was a makeup girl there—but they were frightened to use the girl because they were afraid of Marlene's reaction. She expected to sit in front of a camera and see herself on a monitor. They had a weird design of petals behind her, which with her very good taste she objected to strongly. Then she had ten times as much lighting as she ever had in her life. We got around that one by Joe's lighting her from the front, so that she could see the lights she normally saw.

"The sound wasn't too bad. The snag was that we had the orchestra offstage right so that the only way she could hear it was through the speakers. She didn't kick too much over that. The whole bit was a bad trick. They gave her a totally new microphone, much more modern than she was used to. The stage set moved three or four times. She hated doing the show, although she gave a very passable performance twice over—but it wasn't magic at all. They couldn't do justice to her."

Jim Douglas adds: "When they finished the shooting of the show, they made Marlene do some extra shots. They had people throwing flowers at the stage. Nobody told her what they were going to do. During a break in the shooting, she got to a microphone and told the story about a time when she was making a film, probably with von Sternberg, and there was a final shot of her and the leading man walking off into the distance. She said, 'We started off—we started walking—and after we got about half a mile down the road, we wondered whether we ought to turn back. Nobody ever told us whether they had finished filming or not.' "

In the mid 1970s, a major lawsuit blew up. The following report was released to the press. It read as follows:

LIBEL DAMAGES FOR TV MAN.

TV producer Alexander Cohen and Bettwood Productions accepted a suitable sum in damages in the High Court yesterday from Associated Newspapers for an interview with Marlene Dietrich. The article, headed DIETRICH'S AMAZING INQUEST ON HER OWN TV SPECTACULAR, written by American journalist and critic Rex Reed, appeared in the *Daily Mail* January 4, 1973, three days after the show had been screened in Britain. Mr. Richard Hartley, Q.C. for Mr. Cohen, and Bettwood, said that in their view the article implied that they had produced and managed the show incompetently, inartistically, in unjustified haste, and without making adequate financial provision for it. It also implied that they were in financial difficulties and had deliberately disregarded Miss Dietrich's wishes in matters of artistic importance. Mr. Hartley said that Mr. Cohen and Bettwood, both of New York, accepted that Associated Newspapers, who bought the first British rights in the article, published it in good faith. There was a dispute over what had been said at the interview, but the court was not concerned with that yesterday. Mr. Richard Rampton for Associated Newspapers told Mr. Justice Griffiths that they did not admit that the article bore the meaning that Mr. Cohen and Bettwood claimed. But they did not seek to justify it and any allegations it may have contained.

Jim Douglas analyzes the reason Marlene was dissatisfied with the conditions of the show. "She's the only person I've ever worked with who can create total stage magic, but everything has to be *exactly* right. In a live performance, the audience is incredibly silent. They *daren't* move a muscle. There is a subtle balance. The main speakers feed out the sound to the audience —you have to have an exact balance between these and the house speakers. She could actually feel her voice leaving her like a spirit and going out into the house.

"I operated by feel. She controlled her own dynamics. All you had to do was bring her down occasionally when she went off key, or did odd little things she later accepted as false in her performance. You could hear the top of the mixer vibrating when she hit certain notes. If you didn't feel it vibrate, it was wrong, you had to push it up, or bring it down a bit. The adjustments were microscopic. You had to watch her every instant.

"When everything was perfect she was completely static: three to six inches from the microphone. Motionless, almost. When something was wrong you could see her start to twitch, move her head, in one direction or another. At last she'd find the perfect spot. She knew it to *half a hair.* When she began moving all over the stage you knew she was in trouble, and you were going to be, too. She was going to come off the stage and give you hell.

"She was the only star I've worked with whom the band would discuss after the show. She fascinated us more than any-one else. Some of the talk about her was horrible, some of it was good, but whatever it was, it was obsessive: it caught the imagi-nation."

Jim Douglas adds: "After finishing her special, Alexander Cohen wanted her to do an introduction for the Tony Awards. She couldn't memorize the script: it was quite a long piece. He had thirteen large cue cards prepared. He tried stacking them one over the other; but she couldn't concentrate sufficiently to remember what one contained before she had to go on to the next. He tried various positions: the cards were brought closer to her; it didn't work. He tried them in pairs. Still no luck. She was getting niggly, and Cohen ordered everyone out. They quarreled loudly. In the end, thirteen men stood side by side in the orchestra. As she finished reading each card a man would dive out of the way, another one would pop up, then *he* would dive out of the way, and so on. Fortunately, Cohen used a very low angle camera, and only one of the cards could be seen above the frame line."

No sooner had Marlene recovered from this unpleasant expe-rience—and she hated the TV special when it appeared—than she experienced a severe fall on the stage. She had had various mishaps during her career: when she broke her arm during the run of *Broadway,* on the stage; when she broke her ankle on *The Lady Is Willing;* and during her German tour in 1960, when she fell down and (as Max Colpet recorded in his memoirs) wandered about pale and miserable for days.

While onstage in her show at the Queen's Theatre in London, she tripped over backwards, the audience crying out in horror, and lay unable to move until Stan Freeman helped her to her feet.

Worse, while playing in theater-in-the-round near Washington, D.C., she literally tumbled off the stage itself. Her drummer Andy White records: "The orchestra pit was very deep: about six feet. She acknowledged Stan Freeman. He reached up from the pit to shake her hand. But it was a very long stretch. The following night, he decided to make it easier by standing on a piano stool. He clung to her hand, and the stool suddenly tilted and went over. He would have let go immediately, but she held on and finished up in the pit. She gashed her leg. She lay there, and said, in agony, 'Clear the theater' Just that, 'Clear the theater.' Her dress was covered in blood; and she didn't want anyone to see her."

Marlene went on to Houston, Texas, for skin grafts—from the left buttock cheek to the leg. They did not heal and she had to go about in a wheelchair.

Later, she returned for extensive surgery. She went back to England for a season at the Grosvenor House. Terry Miller, her agent, advised her not to do the show: prices were too high. She called her former impresario, Robert Patterson, telling him there were ghastly problems, and he must come over. He did. The open, protruding stage upset her—the kind of "cabaret" setting she disliked most, because it brought the audience too close.

She had to be rushed to the stage in her wheelchair by two security officers, Brian Dellon and Graham Morris; then make her way up a long ramp to the stage. Brian Dellon says: "We took her down in the service elevator. The first time, a crowd of waiters saw her, and she was furious. Another time, the heavy elevator doors caught her wheelchair on either side and we thought we were going to have a very slim variation on Marlene Dietrich, but we caught them just before they would have crushed her.

"She had to be held steady while we lowered her into the chair, and tucked her dress under her bad leg. We wore dinner suits so we wouldn't attract attention, and she wore a wig. We *rushed* her down the corridor. I don't think anybody noticed us —just two men with a nice old lady. She was hugely grateful. She gave us signed photographs and five pounds, and she wrote on the photographs, 'To the fastest wheels in the West.' "

There was an odd little English storm in a teacup over Princess Margaret. Marlene's impresario at Grosvenor House, Robin Courage, says: "I received a call from Kensington Palace, Margaret's royal residence, asking if Margaret could come with Kenneth Tynan to the first night. I said, 'Of course.' The princess expressed a desire to meet Marlene. She had known her before. I said, 'That's easily arranged,' Marlene said, 'OK.' But when it came to the night, Marlene wouldn't see her; she said, 'No, no, it's no good. I have nothing to wear. I've been trying to get through to Paris to see if Ginette Spanier can bring something over, but she can't get away. So it's off.'

"What could I do? I telephoned the palace and told them she was too tired and that she'd been rehearsing herself to death. Princess Margaret came anyway. Then Richard Burton, who had agreed to introduce Marlene, came up behind Dietrich as she was being helped up the ramp for a rehearsal. He said, 'Marlene, I'm behind you.' She turned around, saw him, and went bananas—she freaked; she *screamed*. She flew into a temper, saying, 'What is he doing here? Nobody's allowed behind me!' He was wonderful. He said, 'Marlene you look so beautiful, so young, you've got nothing to worry about.' She calmed down. He came over to me and whispered, 'I've never seen anybody so nervous in all my life.'

"Then Princess Margaret arrived and said, 'Mr. Courage, where am I meeting Miss Dietrich?' I said, 'Ma'am, she's tired. She can't see anyone.'

"The Princess told me, 'I don't care where it is—even in the lobby—I *will* see her!' It was a royal command! After the show I went up to the suite, Marlene had been rushed back in the wheelchair. She was in the bathroom. She yelled out, 'Oh, no, no!'

"I said, 'It's a royal command.'

"She screamed, 'Oh, God. Well, give me five minutes—I don't know what to do—give me five minutes,' and as I turned round, the princess was right behind me! Kenneth Tynan was there, and a BBC man, and then Burton and *his* party. I told Marlene loudly, 'Your guests have arrived!' I sweated through several minutes. Then Marlene suddenly emerged, smiling, in a shirt and jeans. She was marvelous, and everyone had a good time."

An unpleasant incident took place in Boston, when a former GI who had seen her at the Anzio beachhead rushed on to the stage behind her and tried to grab her. She was terrified and called for security officers, who pulled him from the stage. Soon after, she broke her right leg in her apartment in Paris.

But her worst mishap took place in Australia, in September 1975. The film historian Joel Greenberg describes it:

"Of all nights to attend her show, I would have to pick last Monday, September 29. The theater—Her Majesty's at Railway Square, built in 1973—was half-filled, with about five to six hundred people. After a reportedly rapturous reception from a full house for her Sydney opening the previous Monday, bookings for the remainder of the season were poor. That is why she'd agreed to break her no-press rule and hold a media conference, though barring cameras and television crews (as reported in *Time*). With one or two isolated exceptions, she'd had a uniformly bad press here because of her ban; they even failed to review her show until the season was half over.

"I arrived at the theater shortly before intermission deliberately to avoid her warm-up act, a singing duo called Bill and Boyd. Intermission over, the curtain rose to disclose the little orchestra, led by Dietrich's regular English conductor William Blezard, as it launched into a medley of her signature tunes—'Falling in Love Again,' 'Boys in the Back Room,' etc. After several false climaxes, each of which seemed geared to anticipate the star's entrance, there were signs of movement at the left of the stage, and everyone stared intently in that direction. Then suddenly a hank of hair fell into view from behind a curtain, followed by a glimpse of clutching hands, and sounds of scuffling, and Marlene stumbled backwards to the bare wooden floor. There was shocked silence for a moment, broken by a cruel round of sarcastic applause. Then the curtain descended and the show was over. I couldn't believe it: everything had happened so quickly, within seconds.

"I hung around for a while afterwards, to book for an alternative night if possible, and to try to find out exactly what had happened. Presently a doctor arrived carrying a little black bag, and then an ambulance, and soon after that I joined a somewhat ghoulish band of people, mostly middle-aged women, who clapped as they watched Dietrich being driven away in a car, her face muffled, languishing in the arms of Ginette Vachon, variously described as her secretary or traveling companion. Next day it was announced that doctors had examined her at her hotel and diagnosed a broken femur in her left leg, whereupon she was transferred to St. Vincent's Private Hospital to have the offending limb swathed in plaster from the waist down. It had been obvious from press reports of unsteadiness on her feet during performances that the right leg, broken some eighteen months before, and the steel pin in her right hip were troubling her, and on that awful night something evidently gave. Yesterday, she left by plane for New York 'to consult her medical advisers,' hoisted on to the aircraft by forklift."

Marlene told me on the telephone in 1975: "The Australians were wonderful. They took marvelous care of me in St. Vincent's Hospital. They wrapped me in a sheepskin, the most comfortable thing I've ever slept in. It completely protected me from any jarring movements of the plane.

"When I got to Los Angeles, I went straight to Rudi in an ambulance. He was in UCLA Hospital. Once I had heard he'd had a stroke, I had to get to his side. He couldn't speak to me; but at least he could see me.

"Maria insisted I come to New York for treatment. It was a terrible mistake. But I always take orders. I hated the hospital. I had a horrible view of a wall. I was so depressed. I hate television, but one night I watched 'Mary Hartman, Mary Hartman.' I couldn't believe it. An old, old man came on and said, 'I have gonorrhea.' Could I have heard this? Could this possibly be on television? Was I hallucinating after drugs? And then he said, 'And I got it from a man.'!'"

As if all this were not enough, Marlene had not recovered from the complicated surgery performed in Texas the year before. Hugh Curnow had told me she was suffering from hardening of the arteries in Paris as early as 1965; and she had suffered from increasingly poor circulation, especially in her famous legs. Indeed, it now emerges according to her friend, the actor Murray Matheson, that her falls were due not only to this but to the tight, fine rubbery sheath which she wore under her stage gown in order to improve her figure and give her a look of firmness.

Her financial position was not good by the mid 1970s. She had earned millions in her lifetime, and had spent almost everything. Even though she could still command high fees, these were decimated by her generosity to her family and the expenses of her dresser, her band members, and her conductor, all of whom she had to transport and put up in hotels as well as keep on high salaries. Hans Kohn says she could afford to give her husband only a pittance of one hundred dollars a week. Rudi lived in constant terror she would fail to meet the mortgage payments on the ranch, and he would be left homeless.

She was forced to rent out her apartment on Park Avenue. A go-between even asked Maria's near neighbors on East Ninety-fifth Street, the great caricaturist Al Hirschfeld and his wife Dolly Haas, for twenty-five thousand dollars, the Hirschfelds say, for Marlene to meet some bills. The three hundred dollars a day charged her by the hospital she recuperated in after her fracture in New York, and the cost of her serious illness and leg operations, reduced her resources still further. She also hoped to obtain reparation money from Germany, because Rudi, she believed, had been deprived of his property by Hitler. But, Hans Kohn says, after a most desperate ransacking of the records, she discovered something she had forgotten: Rudi had left Berlin in January 1932, before Hitler had come to power.

Marlene, after telling me on the telephone from New York that she was going to make a tour of either Scandinavia or South America in the summer of 1976, came instead to Hollywood in May of that year. Friends had installed nurses at the ranch and air conditioners to allay the summer heat. She wanted to disperse the animals from the ranch and put Rudi in the Motion Picture Country Home and Hospital, where he would be better taken care of, but his friends refused to permit this, insisting that if he were to wake up in a hospital without his beloved Tamara's things around him, her little knickknacks, he would die at once.

Marlene was overruled. She flew back to Paris in late May. Ironically, Rudi died after she arrived there.

Rudi's rosary and service were attended by only a tiny handful of intimate friends: Hans and Varya Kohn, the antique dealer Peter Gorian, Walter Reisch, and Rudi's housekeeper, the devoted Eva Wiere. Marlene was anxious to obtain Rudi's diaries, which he kept religiously since the early 1920s, and giving an indispensable account of their lives at 54 Kaiseralle, as well as descriptions of his life with Tamara in Paris at two apartments, and at the Hotel Lancaster, where they had lived with Marlene. She did not attend the funeral.

She wanted Rudi's diaries for her planned autobiography. In January 1976, German *Esquire* had approached her for an interview or contribution in connection with a planned issue on Berlin in the 1920s. She had declined the interview, but her friend Max Colpet had suggested she dig up the material about her life as a soldier's child in World War I, originally worked on by Hugh Curnow and prepared by her for her abandoned book for Macmillan, *Tell Me, Oh, Tell Me Now.*

She acceded to Colpet's request to supply the material, and it appeared in the fall. Impassioned, romantic, it is the essence of Dietrich. It is puzzling in that it omits all dates, all but one name (that of her French teacher, Marguerite Bréguand), addresses, and officers' ranks, and confusingly combines her stepfather and father into one person.

This material became the basis for a fourth attempt at her memoirs. She had begun the effort of re-examining her past in the 1950s, asking her friend Leo Lerman to help her; he had declined. Doubleday had contracted for a book by her through the William Morris Agency, but after much discussion the deal collapsed and Doubleday published fragments of the projected work in *Marlene Dietrich's ABC* instead. She tried again, for Holt, Rinehart, and Winston, but decided to return the money. She finally paid back the *Tell Me, Oh, Tell Me Now* money to Macmillan in the year of Hugh Curnow's death—1968.

Marlene recommenced plans after an eight-year interval. Simon and Schuster persuaded her; and her agent, Robert Lantz obtained a $150,000 offer. A German deal involving the famous magazine *Die Sterne* and the publisher Bertelsman assured her about a quarter of a million more.

Suddenly, Putnam announced that they were going to publish the book. Simon and Schuster sued Lantz for two and a half million dollars, claiming he had sold a book to Putnam which they had already been promised.

Fenced about by this new problem, Marlene stayed on in Paris in the severe winter of 1976, determinedly working on her book. It was painful, she wrote to a friend, to have to go back over the past, especially since she had rejected any suggestion of a ghostwriter. Max Colpet, who dropped by from Munich to help her with some errands, would have been the perfect choice. She was alone much of the time, attended only by a maid or cleaning woman, although at times she was with her close friend Ginette Vachon, heiress and warm admirer. Bank officers and grocers who came to the door barely recognized her.

Even in those days of being old and sick, Marlene enjoyed little jokes. When her friend Arnold Weissberger, the well-known attorney, called her, she said, "Paris is so dumb on Sundays. Why don't you come here to lunch?" But just before he left his hotel room, the phone chirruped and a tiny, high-pitched voice came on the line. The voice said, "Miss Dietrich asked me to call you! She had to go to Switzerland at once to see her doctor! She is so sorry! She hopes to see you later!"

Weissberger was baffled. He called Marlene's close friend in Paris, the couturière Ginette Spanier, who laughed and said, "But that wasn't the maid! That *was* Marlene! She does that all the time!"

Jean Gabin died suddenly in November 1976. Marlene was miserable, called their mutual friend Marcel Dalio, and said, "Now I'm a widow for the second time."

On November 19, 1976, in the presence of his family and friends, an urn containing Gabin's ashes was placed in a box weighted with lead and flung from the stern of the naval vessel *Le Détroyat* off the coast of Normandy, together with a bunch of violets from his wife and children, which floated for a while on the surface of the waves.

Marlene was rushed to a hospital a day or two later. Evidently the thought of his death, a year of constant pain, and the loss of Rudi as the only solid anchor of her life had combined to shatter even her powerful spirit. Not even the usual innumerable telephone calls abroad and locally, nor writing letters in green ink in her famous scrawl, could ease her suffering. And there was always the harrowing knowledge that her famous trademark, her legs, had been the first part of her to go, and that even she must eventually die.

In the spring of 1977, a long-standing feud between Marlene and Alexander Cohen over *I Wish You Love*—her TV special for him—blew up again. The *New York Post* reported on April 3: "Marlene Dietrich is entitled to full pay for her one woman TV show even though she bad-mouthed it, the (NY) State Appellate Division has ruled."

The article went on to state that Alexander Cohen, by a decision of the higher court, would be compelled to pay the unpaid balance of $100,000 due to Marlene.

Meantime, Cohen pursued a suit for libel against her, claiming that in an interview with Rex Reed, she had maligned him in attacking his conduct of the show. It was reported in the *New York Post* of May 9, 1977, that "the lawyers huddled in New York, and both sides agreed to drop all litigation." Cohen's payment was reduced to "in excess of $50,000," which would be "payable in installments," in consideration of his dropping the libel suit in New York, the *Post* reported. This also settled the London end of the case.

Marlene felt compelled to turn down, in 1976, the important role of an actress who seems to be eternally young, in her old friend Billy Wilder's film of Tom Tryon's story "Fedora," from the best-seller *Crowned Heads*. "Fedora" had been based on her: she would have been perfectly cast. But, her health and her doubts about the material ruled her out.

Marlene deserved the world's compassion in those days.

But then her fortunes suddenly improved. The enormous sums advanced for her memoirs paid many bills. She won an injunction against a filmmaker who portrayed her inexcusably as Hitler's mistress in a work entitled *Hitler and Marlene*.

She was even photographed by *Paris-Match* in her favorite going-out clothes of jeans, cap, and jacket, elegantly dining with Jean-Pierre Aumont in the French capital. She looked superb. She also went out with another old friend, Sir John Gielgud.

She said she would be buried in a certain French village selected for her by Charles de Gaulle. "Why?" somebody asked her. "Because it has a three-star restaurant," she replied. "When the tourists stop by, they can enjoy a superb meal, and, after that, feeling very well, they can come and visit me."

Film
Performances
(Co-stars listed in parentheses)

(GERMANY)

1922: *The Little Napoleon* (Egon von Hagen)
1923: *Tragedy of Love* (Emil Jannings)
1923: *Man by the Roadside* (Alexander Granach)
1924: *The Leap into Life* (Walter Rilla)
1925: *My Wife's Dancing Partner* (Willy Fritsch)
1926: *The Joyless Street* (Asta Nielsen)
1926: *Manon Lescaut* (Lya de Putti)
1926: *The Imaginary Baron* (Reinhold Schunzel)
1927: *A Modern Du Barry* (Maria Corda)
1927: *Madame Doesn't Want Children* (Maria Corda)
1927: *Heads Up, Charly!* (Anton Pointner)
1927: *His Greatest Bluff* (Harry Piel)
1927: *Café Electric*—first starring role (Willi Forst)
1928: *Princess Olala* (Hermann Bochner)
1929: *I Kiss Your Hand, Madame* (Harry Liedtke)
1929: *The Woman One Longs For* (Fritz Kortner)
1929: *The Ship of Lost Men* (Fritz Kortner)
1929: *Nights of Love* (Willi Forst)
1929: *The Blue Angel* (Emil Jannings)

(UNITED STATES)

1930: *Morocco* (Gary Cooper)
1931: *Dishonored*—made in 1930 (Victor McLaglen)

1932: *Shanghai Express* (Clive Brook)
1932: *Blonde Venus* (Herbert Marshall)
1933: *Song of Songs* (Brian Aherne)
1934: *The Scarlet Empress* (John Lodge)
1935: *The Devil Is a Woman* (Cesar Romero)
1936: *Desire* (Gary Cooper)
1936: *I Loved a Soldier*—uncompleted (Charles Boyer)
1936: *The Garden of Allah* (Charles Boyer)
1936: *Knight Without Armor* (Robert Donat)
1937: *Angel* (Herbert Marshall)
1939: *Destry Rides Again* (James Stewart)
1940: *Seven Sinners* (John Wayne)
1941: *The Flame of New Orleans* (Bruce Cabot)
1941: *Manpower* (Edward G. Robinson)
1942: *The Lady Is Willing* (Fred MacMurray)
1942: *The Spoilers* (Randolph Scott)
1942: *Pittsburgh* (Randolph Scott)
1944: *Follow the Boys* (All-star cast)
1944: *Kismet* (Ronald Colman)
1946: *Martin Roumagnac* (Jean Gabin)
1947: *Golden Earrings* (Ray Milland)
1948: *A Foreign Affair* (Jean Arthur)
1949: *Jigsaw* (Franchot Tone). Marlene did a walk-on.
1950: *Stage Fright* (Jane Wyman)
1951: *No Highway* (James Stewart)
1952: *Rancho Notorious* (Arthur Kennedy)
1956: *Around the World in Eighty Days* (All-star cast)
1957: *The Monte Carlo Story* (Vittorio de Sica)
1957: *Witness for the Prosecution* (Charles Laughton)
1958: *Touch of Evil* (Charlton Heston)
1961: *Judgment at Nuremberg* (Spencer Tracy)
1962: *Black Fox*—narration
1964: *Paris When It Sizzles* (William Holden). Marlene did a walk-on.

Theater Performances

1921: Miscellaneous appearances with Rudolf Nelson's Girls and in Guido Thielscher revue.

1922: *The Circle*, by Maugham. Kammerspiele.
A Midsummer Night's Dream, by Shakespeare. Theater in the Königgrätzerstrasse.
The Taming of the Shrew, by Shakespeare. Grosses Schauspielhaus (also on tour).

1923: *When the New Vine Blossoms*, by Björnson. Theater in the Königgrätzerstrasse.

1924: *The Imaginary Invalid*, by Molière. Theatre in the Königgrätzerstrasse.
Spring's Awakening. by Wedekind. Deutsches Theater.

1926: *From Mouth to Mouth*, by Charell/Offenbach. Grosses Schauspielhaus.

1927: *Broadway*, by Abbott/Dunning. Komödienhaus (Also in Vienna).
Duel on the Lido, by Rehfisch. Staatstheater.

1928: *Die Schule von Uznach*, by Sternheim. Staatstheater.
It's in the Air, by Schiffer/Spoliansky. Komödie Theater.
Misalliance, by Shaw. Komödie Theater.
Back to Methuselah, by Shaw. Komödie Theater.

1929: *Two Bow Ties*, by Kaiser/Spoliansky. Berliner Theater.

OTHER CITIES

1943–45   War tours
1954–75   Miscellaneous solo appearances in the United States, Scandinavia, France, Germany, Russia, South America, South Africa, Australia, Holland, Japan, etc.

Index